S0-AEY-356

ADMISSION MATTERS

ADMISSION MATTERS

What Students and Parents Need to Know

About Getting Into College

Sally P. Springer
Marion R. Franck

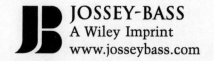
JOSSEY-BASS
A Wiley Imprint
www.josseybass.com

Copyright © 2005 by Sally P. Springer and Marion R. Franck

Published by Jossey-Bass

A Wiley Imprint

989 Market Street, San Francisco, CA 94103-1741   www.josseybass.com

No part of this publication may be reproduced, stored in a retrieval system, or transmitted in any form or by any means, electronic, mechanical, photocopying, recording, scanning, or otherwise, except as permitted under Section 107 or 108 of the 1976 United States Copyright Act, without either the prior written permission of the Publisher, or authorization through payment of the appropriate per-copy fee to the Copyright Clearance Center, Inc., 222 Rosewood Drive, Danvers, MA 01923, 978-750-8400, fax 978-646-8600, or on the Web at www.copyright.com. Requests to the Publisher for permission should be addressed to the Permissions Department, John Wiley & Sons, Inc., 111 River Street, Hoboken, NJ 07030, 201-748-6011, fax 201-748-6008, or online at http://www.wiley.com/go/permissions.

Limit of Liability/Disclaimer of Warranty: While the publisher and author have used their best efforts in preparing this book, they make no representations or warranties with respect to the accuracy or completeness of the contents of this book and specifically disclaim any implied warranties of merchantability or fitness for a particular purpose. No warranty may be created or extended by sales representatives or written sales materials. The advice and strategies contained herein may not be suitable for your situation. You should consult with a professional where appropriate. Neither the publisher nor author shall be liable for any loss of profit or any other commercial damages, including but not limited to special, incidental, consequential, or other damages.

Readers should be aware that Internet Web sites offered as citations and/or sources for further information may have changed or disappeared between the time this was written and when it is read.

Jossey-Bass books and products are available through most bookstores. To contact Jossey-Bass directly call our Customer Care Department within the U.S. at 800-956-7739, outside the U.S. at 317-572-3986, or fax 317-572-4002.

Jossey-Bass also publishes its books in a variety of electronic formats. Some content that appears in print may not be available in electronic books.

Library of Congress Cataloging-in-Publication Data

Springer, Sally P., date.
  Admission matters : what students and parents need to know about getting into college / Sally P. Springer, Marion R. Franck.— 1st ed.
    p. cm. — (The Jossey-Bass education series)
  Includes bibliographical references and index.
  ISBN-13: 978-0-7879-7967-6 (alk. paper)
  ISBN-10: 0-7879-7967-8 (alk. paper)
  1. Universities and colleges—United States—Admission. 2. College choice—United States. I. Franck, Marion R., date. II. Title. III. Series.
  LB2351.2.S67 2005
  378.1'61'0973—dc22
                              2005012458

Printed in the United States of America

FIRST EDITION

PB Printing   10 9 8 7 6 5 4 3 2

The Jossey-Bass Education Series

To Our Children

CONTENTS

It Used to Be Simple . . . But Not Anymore • The Echo Boom • Social Changes • The Role of the Internet • Where the Real Crunch Lies • Which Colleges Are the Most Selective? • Why Is There So Much Interest in Such a Small Group of Colleges? • The Importance of Fit • The Rankings Game • Concerns About Rankings • Why Are Rankings So Popular? • "I'll Make More Money If I Graduate from an Elite College": Another Myth • Getting into Graduate School • Looking Ahead

How College Admissions Has Changed • What Matters Now • The Academic Record • Standardized Tests • Engagement Beyond the Classroom: The Extracurricular Record • Personal Qualities: The Person Behind the Paper • Hooks • Fitting It All Together

Who Works in Admissions? • Ambassadors *and* Gatekeepers • What Happens to Your File? • Reading and Rating • Tentative Decisions • Making the Final Decision • Building the Freshman Class • The Role of Your High School Counselor • A Word About Private Counselors • The Parents' Role • Taking Responsibility

ACKNOWLEDGMENTS

This book was born out of our desire to make the college application process a better experience for both parents and students. Many people share that goal—from high school students and their counselors, to college faculty and administrators, to parents and grandparents—and they helped us in the writing of this book.

We particularly thank all the students and parents who generously allowed themselves to be interviewed, knowing that their names would never appear in the text. We also thank everyone who read and commented on all or part of our manuscript: Bill Caskey, Cindy Clark, Marilyn Geiger, Fred Hargadon, Arlene Jones, Bruce Madewell, Gail Martinez, Dorothy Missler, George Rooks, Mary Ryan, Courtenay Tessler, Jill Theg, Leon Washington, and Fred Wood, as well as three anonymous reviewers. Greg Critser and Deanne Urmy offered much-needed encouragement at a critical point in our efforts. Special thanks go to our talented editor, Lesley Iura, her wonderful assistant, Kate Gagnon, and our top-notch production editor, Michele Quiroga, for supporting our enterprise with enthusiasm and expertise.

From Sally . . .

I would like to thank my friends and colleagues in the Offices of the Chancellor and Provost at the University of California, Davis, especially Chancellor Larry Vanderhoef, Provost Virginia Hinshaw, and Assistant Chancellor Maril Stratton, for their support and encouragement from the very beginning of this project. I am also grateful to Marion, my coauthor, for contributing her talents to a project that became much larger than either of us ever envisioned.

I am indebted to my husband, Håkon, and my children, Mollie and Erik, for providing unwavering love, patience, and encouragement over the two and one half years it took to bring the book from concept to completion. In a very real sense they have written it along with me as they lived with a woman on a mission tackling a project that consumed almost every waking moment outside of normal working hours for months on end. There would be no book without them.

From Marion . . .

I would like to thank my coauthor, Sally, who started on her own but invited me to share the adventure of writing this book. I am particularly grateful to Sally for the many tasks she picked up so that I could respond to the illness and death of my stepmother, which occurred during the preparation of the manuscript. I would also like to thank my husband, Bob, my children, Beth and Daniel, my future son-in-law, Casey, my women's group, and my friends, Evelyn Lewis and Ann Marie Wagstaff, all of whom were never too busy with their own lives to listen and advise during the creation of this book.

August 2005

Sally P. Springer
Marion R. Franck
Davis, California

INTRODUCTION

This is the book that we wish our teenage children had read when they began to think about applying to college. Unfortunately, it was yet to be written. There was, to be sure, no shortage of books that described different colleges or offered advice on how to submit a "winning" college application. These books were often written by former college admissions officers, journalists who specialized in higher education, and even recent graduates of elite colleges eager to tell the secrets of "getting in." Each book provided its own limited window into the college planning and admission process, and sometimes the advice in one book contradicted what was said in another. But most frustrating, none provided the "big picture" of current college admissions that would help make sense of it all.

Admission Matters: What Students and Parents Need to Know About Getting into College provides important insider insights into the ways college admissions has changed and continues to change. At the same time, it offers practical, hands-on advice about how to use these insights to your advantage. Our focus is on admission to selective colleges and universities—those that accept less than half of their applicants—although much of what we discuss is relevant to *all* colleges.

Admission Matters will give you, our student readers, the tools you need to take charge of the college admissions process and submit strong applications to colleges that are a good fit for you. *Admissions Matters* will guide you, our parent readers, in appropriately supporting your child at all points along the way. Although other books about college admissions are written primarily for just one audience—students or parents—*Admission Matters* is designed for both. Sometimes "you" will refer to the student. Sometimes it will be "you," the parent. The context will make it clear which is which, but there are no separate chapters for students and parents. We want both of you to read it all. We believe that students and parents need to have a common understanding of what is involved and what their different but complementary roles should be in the college admissions process.

Students and parents today find themselves barraged by evidence of "college mania." Newspapers and magazines regularly regale readers with horror tales about the competition involved in gaining admission to selective colleges as application numbers rise and admissions rates fall. Classmates, relatives, neighbors, and even virtual strangers are all too eager to share war stories about terrific kids with great stats and extracurricular activities who were rejected by the colleges of their choice.

Businesses that offer costly SAT prep courses bombard students and parents with advertising that promises dramatic increases in scores for those who sign up. Ironically, at the same time the test prep industry is burgeoning, some influential educators are making the case for eliminating the SAT altogether, claiming that students waste valuable time preparing for a test that adds little to the ability to predict future success in college. And once a student does take the SAT or other standardized tests, he or she is likely to receive a disturbingly large number of glossy brochures from colleges all over the country actively encouraging him or her to apply. Selective liberal arts colleges commonly send out mailers like this to well over 50,000 students as they seek to fill a freshman class of less than 500 students. And these are just a few examples of college mania. You can probably make a list of your own.

When you put all of this together, it is not surprising that college admissions has taken on elements of a crisis for many students and their families. Each year more and more students end up vying for a limited number of freshman spots at many of the best-known colleges. They find themselves and their families caught up in a high-stakes competition in which they are uncertain about the rules and even more uncertain about the outcome. Parents can find themselves in the uncomfortable position of trying to support their children in a process they do not completely understand. Even those who consider themselves knowledgeable may quickly find that much of what they know is out-of-date or based on rumor that bears little resemblance to today's realities.

Complicating matters is the fact parents can be emotionally invested in the college admissions process, right along with their children, in ways that are understandable but not always helpful. Finally, the college admissions process is often about more than admission to college—it is also about leaving home and making the transition to adulthood. This simple fact can add considerably to the uncertainty and anxiety that many families experience.

But college admissions does not have to be, and should not be, a crisis. Having a clear understanding of the college admissions process can empower students and their families to make good choices for themselves and allow them to retain their balance and sanity at the same time. That is the goal of *Admission Matters*.

Admission Matters explains

- How rankings motivated by magazine profits contribute to the application frenzy
- How the admissions process at selective colleges really works and what can, and cannot, be controlled
- What you can do to submit strong and competitive applications to colleges that are a good fit for you
- How standardized testing has changed and what those changes mean for you
- When an "early" application makes sense, when it can be a mistake, and how to tell the difference at a time when early options are rapidly changing
- What you can expect from financial aid and how you may be able to increase the chances of receiving more
- What you—student *and* parent—can do to work together in appropriate and respectful ways at all points in the admissions process to achieve a happy outcome

And much more.

This book has been written to demystify the college admissions process by explaining how it works and to level the playing field for those without access to extensive assistance from knowledgeable high school counselors. It is also written for those who have access to good counseling but who would still like some extra help. It is designed to provide you with important insights to put college admissions into perspective, both as a process and as part of life, and keep the "if only I had known earlier" regret to a minimum. *Admission Matters* shows what parents and students can do to have the college admissions process end happily with their relationship intact, or even strengthened, and with an array of fine college choices.

Although *Admission Matters* is a comprehensive guide to college admissions, you may want more information on certain topics than space allows us to include. We provide a list of resources, many of them on the Web, that give detailed information on topics such as financial aid and athletic recruiting to supplement our own coverage. To keep *Admission Matters* as up-to-date as possible, we are maintaining a Web site with updates keyed to the pages in this book throughout the lifetime of this edition. You can access it for free at www.admissionmatters.com. We welcome your feedback.

We'd like now to introduce ourselves. Sally Springer has over thirty years of experience as a psychology professor and senior university administrator on both the east and west coasts. She has devoted her entire career to higher education and has essentially not left school since she entered college at age sixteen. Currently associate chancellor at the University of California, Davis, she received her B.S. degree from Brooklyn College, where she was a commuter student before venturing cross-country to Stanford University for her doctoral and postdoctoral work. She is an admissions reader for the Office of Undergraduate Admissions at UC Davis and a member of the National Association for College Admission Counseling.

Marion Franck is a freelance writer who received her B.A. from Brown University and did graduate work in comparative literature at the University of Wisconsin. Most of her previous career was spent in university settings as an advisor to new college teachers, as a lecturer in English and rhetoric, and as a student counselor. Her recent assignments include development of the award-winning Aggie Family Pack, an on-line resource for parents of UC Davis students, as well as a quarterly feature for parents in the UC Davis alumni magazine and a weekly column, "Between Friends," in the Davis daily newspaper. She has served as an alumna interviewer for Brown University for more than ten years.

We have tried, in several ways, to personalize the text. We have liberally sprinkled short boxes throughout the book to share the thoughts of students and parents we met through personal interviews or anonymous postings on Internet bulletin boards, as well as the views of distinguished academic leaders and experts in the field of college admissions. Marion, the columnist, has penned a few minicolumns that tell stories from her experience and offer her personal perspective on key issues. We hope *Admission Matters* will become a trusted road map to help you navigate the college admissions journey.

ADMISSION MATTERS

Why Has College Admissions Become So Competitive?

Applying to college was a pretty simple process for members of the Baby Boom generation born between 1946 and 1964. Those bound for a four-year college usually planned to go to a school in their home state or one fairly close by; a college 300 miles from home was considered by many to be far away. Few students felt the need to apply to more than two or three colleges, and many applied to just one. College choices were most often based on location, program offerings, cost, and difficulty of admission, with a parental alma mater sometimes thrown in for good measure. For the most part, the whole process was fairly low-key. If students did their homework carefully before deciding where to apply, the outcome was usually predictable. Of course there were surprises—some pleasant and some disappointing—but nothing that would raise the issue of college admissions to the level of a national obsession.

It Used to Be Simple . . . But Not Anymore

Fast forward to the early years of the twenty-first century. Newspapers headlines tell a story that is very different for students applying to college now. "Competition grows intense in college admissions game—More qualified students being rejected as applications soar,"[1] "Colleges reject top applicants, accepting only the students likely to enroll,"[2] "The college admissions game: Fear, uncertainty plague students and parents,"[3] "College parents 'out of control'—aggressive tactics may hurt students' shot at admission,"[4] "Fluent in French, 3.9 GPA, and UCLA still said no—Even top grades no longer enough for choice UC schools,"[5] "More parents are hiring pros to coach kids for admission."[6]

Colleges themselves make announcements that are equally jarring. In spring 2003, Harvard announced that for the first time it had accepted just under 10 percent of the students who applied for freshman admission for the class of 2007, or about 2,000 out of 21,000 applicants. Princeton made a similar announcement. Offers of admission were sent to about 1,600 students out of a pool of over 15,700. On the other coast, UCLA, a public university, reported that it had extended offers of admissions to just over 24 percent of the 45,000 students who applied for freshman admission, the lowest admit rate in its history. UCLA's northern California neighbor, Stanford University, also reported an admissions rate lower than ever before—12.1 percent. These were just a few of the many colleges reporting record-breaking numbers of applications and record low rates of admission, continuing a trend that began several years earlier. What happened to change the college admissions picture in such a dramatic way?

The Echo Boom

The simple explanation for the claim that it is harder to get into four-year colleges now than ever before seems to be supply and demand: there are more high school graduates than ever competing for seats in the freshman class. After declining somewhat in the late 1980s and early 1990s, the number of students graduating from high school in the United States has risen steadily each year since. In 1994 there were 2.5 million graduates; in 2003, there were 2.9 million. Projections call for steady growth through 2009, when the number of high school graduates will reach almost 3.2 million.

Part of the increase is the result of immigration, especially from Asia and Latin America, but most of the growth is attributable to the children of the Baby Boom generation that created the great demand for higher education in the decades after World War II. Known as the "echo boomers" or the Millennials, these children will be part of the largest group of high school graduates ever. And although there will be a slight decline from the 2009 peak in subsequent years, the number of high school graduates will remain above 3 million through at least 2018.[7]

Social Changes

But it turns out that the problem is not just numbers. Important social changes have taken place as well. Not only are there more students graduating from high school each year, but a greater percentage of them are interested in going to college. A college education is increasingly seen as key to economic success in our society in the same way that a high school diploma was once the minimum requirement. Studies confirm the value of a college diploma in terms of life-long earnings, and many desirable careers require education beyond the bachelor's degree. As a result, more students are seeking to attend four-

> *"I don't think anyone is complacent about getting a high-quality applicant pool."*
>
> **Harvard University admissions officer**

year colleges, including students from underrepresented minority groups whose college participation rate was previously low.

At the same time that more students are seriously considering going to college, colleges themselves have increased their efforts to attract large, diverse pools of applicants. Many have mounted aggressive programs to spread the word about their offerings nationally and internationally. Colorful "viewbooks" mailed directly to students, visits to high schools by admissions officers, college nights at local hotels, and information booths at college fairs are among the ways colleges are reaching out to prospective freshmen.

Started in earnest in the 1980s when the number of college-age students began to drop temporarily, these marketing efforts have continued and expanded even as student numbers have grown. They are used not only by colleges that may have problems filling their freshman class but also by colleges with an overabundance of qualified applicants. Colleges want to attract the most academically qualified, talented, and diverse applicants from which to select their freshman class, and they often go to great lengths to do it. One result of all these efforts is that more and more college-bound students have become aware of, and are willing to seriously consider, colleges in other parts of the country.

The Role of the Internet

The Internet has also played a major role in how students approach college admissions. Although printed material and in-person presentations are important ways for students to learn about different colleges, the Web is the #1 source of information for students who have grown up online. Students can "visit" campuses through sophisticated online tours and Web-cams and can get many of their questions answered by "frequently asked questions" posted on the Web. Colleges have invested heavily in the development of attractive, easy-to-use Web sites to showcase themselves.

Finally, the Internet has made it easier than ever to apply to college. Students no longer have to send for applications, wait for them to arrive in the mail, and then fill them out by hand. Forms can be downloaded from many college sites or, better yet, completed and submitted directly online, saving some of the time and effort that a traditional paper application requires. Some colleges even waive their application fee (usually in the $40 to $70 range) for those who submit their forms over the Internet. Simplifying things even more, over 250 colleges now accept the Common Application, a standardized form that can be filled out once (often along with a school-specific supplement) and submitted electronically or by mail to as many of the participating colleges as a student wishes. With admission less certain, students are now submitting more applications than ever. Eight to ten applications are now the norm at many private schools and high-performing public high schools—twelve to fifteen or more applications are not uncommon.

> *"As word spreads about the competition for college admission, students respond by applying to even more colleges to increase their chances of acceptance. In so doing, they end up unwittingly contributing to the very problem they are trying to solve for themselves."*
>
> *High school counselor concerned about the trend*

These factors taken together—growth in the population of eighteen-year-olds, greater interest in college, sophisticated marketing efforts, and ease of access to information and the ability to apply made possible by the Internet—help explain why it seems to be harder to get into college now than ever before.

But this is not the whole answer.

Where the Real Crunch Lies

Most people are surprised to learn that with relatively few exceptions, four-year colleges in the United States still accept most, if not all, of their applicants. In fact, each year many fully accredited four-year colleges have vacancies well into the summer for their freshman class that begins in the fall. Despite all the social and demographic changes we have just considered, there are still ample spots for prospective freshmen in four-year colleges. How can this fact be reconciled with the newspaper headlines (not to mention first-hand reports from students and parents) that there is a crisis in college admissions?

It turns out that the real crunch in admissions—the crunch that drives the newspaper headlines and the anxiety that afflicts many families at college application time—is limited to about 100 colleges that attract applicants from all over the country and the world and that are the most selective in their admissions process. Bill Mayher, a private college counselor and author of *The College Admissions Mystique*, summarizes the problem succinctly: "It's hard for kids to get into colleges because they only want to get into colleges that are hard to get into."[8]

Which Colleges Are the Most Selective?

The percentage of students offered admission to a college is a major factor in determining its selectivity. The other factor affecting selectivity at a given college is the academic strength of the applicant pool. Both play a role, since applicants tend to "self-select" when applying to certain colleges known for their academic rigor. To simplify things for our discussion here, however, we will define selectivity in terms of admissions rate only, and focus on colleges that admit fewer than half of those who apply. We'll further divide the group into three categories—superselective colleges (those admitting less than 20 percent of applicants), highly selective colleges (those admitting less than 35 percent of applicants), and very selective colleges (those that admit less than 50 percent of applicants). These are artificial boundaries, but they give a sense of the relative difficulty of gaining admission.

Even though over 2,000 four-year institutions of higher education in the United States admit 50 percent or more of those who apply (and most admit more than 80 percent), many students focus their attention on these 100 selective colleges that fall into one of the three groups we have just defined. A rough estimate is that about 250,000 students applied to one or more of these "elite" colleges to be part of the class of 2007.[9] That number is likely to rise for the next several years as the population of high school graduates continues to grow.

The students applying to selective colleges are the ones experiencing the "crisis" in college admissions. The crisis does not affect those applying to community

Colleges by Admission Rate for the Class of 2007

Super-Selective (less than 20 percent of applicants admitted)

Amherst College

Brown University

Cal Tech

Columbia University

Dartmouth College

Harvard University

MIT

Princeton University

Stanford University

Yale University

Highly Selective (less than 35 percent of applicants admitted)

Barnard College

UC Berkeley

Boston College

Bowdoin College

Carleton College

Claremont McKenna College

Colby College

Colgate University

Cornell University

Davidson College

Duke University

Georgetown University

Hamilton College

Haverford College

Johns Hopkins University

UCLA

Middlebury College

New York University

Northwestern University

University of Notre Dame

University of Pennsylvania

Pepperdine University

Pomona College

Rice University

University of Southern California

Swarthmore College

Tufts University

Vassar College

Washington University

Washington and Lee University

Wesleyan University

College of William and Mary

Williams College

Very Selective Colleges (less than 50 percent of applicants admitted)

Bard College

Binghamton University

Brandeis University

Bucknell University

Carnegie Mellon University

University of Chicago

Connecticut College

University of Delaware

Emory University

Gettysburg College

George Washington University

Harvey Mudd College

College of the Holy Cross

Illinois Wesleyan University

Kenyon College

Lafayette College

Lehigh University

Macalester College

University of Maryland

University of Miami

Muhlenberg College

Northeastern University

University of North Carolina

Oberlin College

Occidental College

University of Pittsburgh

Reed College

University of Rochester

UC San Diego

Sarah Lawrence College

Skidmore College

Spelman College

University of Texas

Trinity College (CT)

Union College

Vanderbilt University

University of Virginia

Wake Forest University

Washington and Jefferson College

Wellesley College

Wheaton College (MA)

colleges or those seeking admission to one or more of the many colleges that accept most or all of their applicants. It is a crisis of limited scope that affects only a small percentage of high school seniors overall. Nevertheless, it is very real to those who are applying to these selective colleges now or expect to apply in the next few years. If you are reading this book, you (or your child) may be one of them. Keep reading. Our book is designed to help you. If you'll be applying to less selective schools, keep reading as well. Most of what we have to share in this book will help you, too.

Why Is There So Much Interest in Such a Small Group of Colleges?

What is behind such intense interest in a small group of colleges and universities? Why, in particular, is there a mystique surrounding the colleges included in the "Ivy League," as well as a few others accorded similar status? What benefits do these elite colleges bestow (or do people believe they bestow) on their graduates?

> "I was happy and proud when my son was accepted at Stanford. I quickly became embarrassed, though, by the gushing responses I received when friends asked where he was going. He had just been accepted to college, after all—he had not won the Nobel Prize. Things have gotten rather warped."
>
> *Parent of Stanford freshman*

Prestige, of course, is one obvious answer. By definition, the more selective a college, the more difficult it is to get into and the greater the prestige associated with being admitted. The student enjoys the prestige directly (after all, the student is the one who was admitted!), but parents enjoy prestige by association. In a society that is becoming increasingly status conscious, surely going to a college ranked #5 is better than going to one ranked #10 or #80 or one that your friends never heard of. Or is it? Prestige is often important to parents who equate brand name with quality or who may find themselves, often unconsciously, attracted to the pleasure of being a "winner."

> "Lots of times it's kids, I think, trying to define themselves by their school choice, not so much choosing the school that's right for them, but trying to look good through it. I'm not sure if they get it from parents or from other kids or from teachers. But they get it from somewhere."
>
> *Volunteer in counseling office at private high school*

> *"Harvard is perhaps the most overrated institution of higher learning in America. This is not to imply that Harvard isn't a good school — on the contrary, Harvard is an excellent school. But its reputation creates an unattainable standard; no school could ever be as good as most people think Harvard is."*
>
> **Comment by Harvard student**

Parents can be the primary driver of the push toward prestige but, especially interesting, students often report similar pressures from peers in high school.

Although some people openly acknowledge considering prestige in college choice, many more will cite the quality of the educational experience as the basis for their interest in an elite college. But this rationale is often based on the unstated, and often unexamined, assumption that a good indicator of the quality of something is how much others seek it. In the case of colleges, this means that selective institutions are presumed to offer a better education; the more selective, the higher the quality. But is this true?

Take the eight colleges that comprise the Ivy League, for example—Harvard University, Yale University, Princeton University, Brown University, Dartmouth College, University of Pennsylvania, Cornell University, and Columbia University. The Ivy League originally referred only to a group of colleges that comprised a football league. (Only seven colleges were included in the group at first. Brown University was eventually selected as the eighth member, although several other colleges were considered possibilities at the time.) Over time, though, Ivy League colleges have become known among the general public primarily for academics rather than athletics and are accorded high prestige. Each Ivy has an admissions rate that places it in the super-selective or highly selective category, and each has renowned faculty as well as an accomplished student body. Everyone agrees that they are fine institutions, but do the Ivies automatically offer undergraduates an educational experience that is superior to that at many other institutions? The answer, well known in academic circles but surprising to many others, is assuredly no.

> *"Some kids want that acceptance letter to Harvard, Yale, or Princeton so desperately, but they really do not know why except to impress family, friends, whomever. It is one thing to include prestige as a factor in your list of schools. It is a problem when it becomes the only factor, and I am seeing this more and more."*
>
> **Private counselor concerned about the emphasis on prestige**

Marion's Confession

What I have long viewed as my toughest job as a parent came into play, perhaps more powerfully than ever, during the college application process.

I had to fight the part of me that wants to use my children to feel good about myself. Put more baldly, I had to fight the part of me that wants to show off.

Let me explain.

Many years ago, when my children were toddlers, I confessed to a counselor that I looked forward to the day when their pictures would appear in the newspaper. Our newspaper is small and local, and it runs frequent photographs of students holding artwork, playing soccer, or receiving awards. I wanted to see my children's smiling faces on those pages. I knew it would feel good somehow, and I couldn't wait.

When I finished telling this to my counselor, she responded very seriously. "What I am about to say is really important. Don't live through your children's accomplishments. If you want to be in the newspaper, do it yourself."

I took that advice home and followed it, to the best of my ability. All through my children's primary school years, I worked hard not to bask in their accomplishments. When their pictures did appear in the newspaper, usually for musical events, I smiled but I didn't go ape.

When other people's children appeared in the newspaper holding huge shiny trophies, when I felt a shimmer of jealousy in spite of myself, I remembered the words of my counselor. "If you want to be in the newspaper, do it yourself." I actually contacted the paper and submitted a few things.

Then it came time for my children to apply to college and my internal struggle bubbled up again. I fought it. I did not pressure my children to apply to big name schools. I talked about the value of finding a place that felt good, fancy name or not.

It helped that in between the newspaper had called and hired me as a columnist.

They run my photo every week.

M. F.

The Importance of Fit

This book will not attempt to dissuade you if prestige is important to you in selecting a college—you have a lot of company. What we will do, however, is talk about many other dimensions that are important to consider in selecting colleges. We believe that the college admissions process should be about fit—the fit between a student and a college. Many factors besides prestige go into determining fit, and we will talk about them at length in Chapter Four and encourage you to think carefully about them. You may find, in the end, that you are making the same choices as you would have before, but we believe your choices will be more informed. You may even find yourself seriously considering other options of which you had been unaware. Either outcome is fine—our goal is simply to help you understand as much as possible about the college admissions process so that you can make the best choices for you.

The Rankings Game

A major contributor to the mystique of selective colleges has been the annual rankings of colleges published by *U.S. News and World Report*. Their first rankings, published in 1983, were based on surveys of college administrators. Over time, the rankings proved to be so popular that they outgrew the magazine itself. *U.S. News and World Report* now publishes a separate guidebook, "America's Best Colleges," each August that includes information and advice about applying to college in addition to college rankings based on a mix of reputation and statistical data about the colleges. The yearly rankings, though, remain at the heart of "America's Best Colleges," generating great attention among readers and great controversy among those who believe the ranking process is fundamentally flawed.

> **"** I am extremely skeptical that the quality of a university — any more than the quality of a magazine — can be measured statistically. However, even if it can, the producers of the *U.S. News* rankings remain far from discovering the method.**"** [10]
>
> *Gerhard Casper, former president of Stanford University*

Gerhard Casper, while president of Stanford University, expressed his concern about the rankings to the editor of *U.S. News and World Report* as follows: "As the president of a university that is among the top-ranked universities, I hope I have the standing to persuade you that much about these rankings—particularly their specious formulas and spurious precision—is utterly misleading. I wish I could forgo this letter since, after all, the rankings are only another newspaper story. Alas, alumni, foreign newspapers, and many others do not bring a sense of perspective to the matter."[11]

What Goes into the Rankings

Twenty-five percent of a college's ranking in the *U.S. News* survey is based on reputational ratings it receives in the poll of college presidents, provosts, and admissions deans that the magazine conducts each year. These administrators are simply asked to rate the academic quality of undergraduate programs at schools with the same mission as their own (for example, liberal arts colleges or research universities) on a 1–5 scale from "marginal" to "distinguished," with the option to respond "don't know." Many of those who receive the questionnaire acknowledge that they don't have the kind of detailed information about other colleges that would be needed to respond meaningfully.

The remaining 75 percent of a college's ranking in the *U.S. News* survey is based on data collected in five different categories, each weighted in the final calculation as follows: retention and graduation rate (20 percent), faculty resources (20 percent), student selectivity (15 percent), financial resources (10 percent), alumni giving (5 percent), and graduation rate performance (5 percent).[12]

Each of these five categories, in turn, contains several submeasures. For example, *U.S. News* has defined student selectivity as being composed of several factors for the freshman class—admission rate, the twenty-fifth and seventy-fifth percentile of SAT or ACT scores, the percentage of students in the top 10 percent of their high school class and, until it was dropped from the formula in 2003, something called "yield." The yield at a given college is simply the percentage of students offered admission who actually accept

> "I am delighted to announce that, for the third year in a row, [our college] has been placed in the top tier of its category by *U.S. News and World Report*. While we continue to be suspect of the rankings, this is still a very promising position for the College." [13]
>
> *Letter posted by college president on campus Web site following release of the U.S. News rankings*

admission and subsequently enroll. A high yield is seen as better than a low yield, since it implies that those who are accepted by a college are eager to attend, presumably because it is a great place to be.

The *U.S. News* Formula

All of this information is collected annually and put into a formula that assigns weightings to the different kinds of data and then computes an overall "ranking." To avoid comparing apples with oranges, *U.S. News* ranks campuses in relation to those with the same mission, so that research universities and liberal arts colleges, for example, are ranked separately. (We'll talk about the differences between these two kinds of institutions in Chapter Four when we look at factors to consider in choosing colleges.) The staff of *U.S. News* determines what factors are included in the formula and how much each one is weighted in the final outcome. Each year the magazine slightly modifies the formula it uses, ostensibly to improve its usefulness as a tool to assess educational quality but also to sell the rankings as "new and improved."

One consequence of these changes is that a college's ranking can shift fairly significantly from one year to the next simply as a result of changes in the formula used to compute the ratings. In 1998, for example, the California Institute of Technology (Cal Tech) ranked #9 among research universities. Following changes in the formula, Cal Tech moved to #1 in 1999. The next year the formula changed again, returning Cal Tech to a less prominent position. A few years earlier, the Johns Hopkins University moved, over the course of three years, from #22 to #10 to #15. Over the same time period, Columbia University moved from #9 to #15 to #11. Did the quality of these universities relative to their peers really change over these short periods? Of course not. Critics of the rankings argue that meaningful changes in college quality are not possible over a period as short as one year, and that formula changes are primarily designed to keep interest in the rankings high and sell more magazines.

Concerns About Rankings

The *U.S. News* rankings are very popular with the general public, particularly parents, and are a source of joy or frustration for colleges themselves, depending on a college's ranking in a given year. The most important criticism of the rankings is that they are not based on any direct measures of educational quality or student satisfaction. Educators readily acknowledge that educational quality and student satisfaction per se can be hard to assess and tricky to put into numbers, but there *are* ways to measure them directly.

For the last several years, the National Survey of Student Engagement (NSSE) based at Indiana University has attempted to measure quality and satisfaction by asking students direct questions about their educational experiences and how they spend their time. *U.S. News* has started to report some data from the NSSE in its "America's Best Colleges" issue, although the results are not counted in the calculation of the rankings. Unfortunately, many highly regarded colleges have chosen not to participate in NSSE, including most selective ones as we have defined them. And some colleges that do participate do not make the results public. Even though NSSE is not used or reported as broadly as it might be, we think it is important for you to know about it, since it gives you an idea of the kinds of dimensions that are

Representative Questions from the National Survey on Student Engagement

1. To what extent has your experience at this institution contributed to your knowledge, skills, and personal development in the following areas:

   a. Acquiring a broad general education

   b. Writing clearly and effectively

   c. Thinking critically and analytically

   d. Learning effectively on your own

   e. Understanding people of other racial and ethnic backgrounds

2. Overall, how would you evaluate the quality of academic advising you have received at your institution?

3. In your experience at your institution during the current school year, about how often have you done each of the following (rated from "very often" to "never" along a four-point scale)

   a. Asked questions in class or contributed to class discussion

   b. Worked on a paper or project that required integrating ideas or information from various sources

   c. Discussed ideas about your readings or classes with faculty members outside of class

4. If you could start over again, would you go to the same institution you are now attending? (rated from "definitely yes" to "definitely no" along a four-point scale)

Used with permission from Indiana University.

important in assessing educational quality. You can learn more about NSSE and see the colleges that have chosen to participate at www.indiana.edu/~nsse/.

Critics have pointed out that while the variables used by *U.S. News* can be contributors to educational quality (perhaps higher salaries lead to better faculty and smaller classes mean more personal attention), educators have not reached agreement about how those variables can be used to measure the quality of a college.

And to make things worse, some of the factors that are used in the *U.S. News* formula can be manipulated. As much as colleges disparage the ranking process and see its flaws, the *U.S. News* rankings are too high profile and too influential among the general public for colleges to ignore them. Alumni, boards of trustees, and even bond-rating agencies on Wall Street are also very much aware of the rankings and expect to see "improvement." Under pressure, some colleges take active steps to do better.

One common but harmless approach is the production of elegant, full-color booklets that typically highlight a college's new programs and facilities, as well as its ambitious plans for the future. In addition to distributing them for fundraising and recruitment purposes, some college presidents send them to their colleagues at other campuses in the hope that the booklets will raise awareness of their college. And greater awareness may lead the reader to offer a more favorable rating when the *U.S. News* questionnaire arrives the following year.

> "Now more than ever, people believe that the ranking — or the presumed hierarchy of 'quality' or 'prestige' — of the college or university one attends matters, and matters enormously. More than ever before, education is being viewed as a commodity. . . . The large and fundamental problem is that we are at risk of it all seeming and becoming increasingly a game. What matters is less the education and more the brand." [14]
>
> *Lee Bollinger, president of Columbia University*

Another tactic deals with how data are reported. Colleges have always had some leeway in how they report their statistics, and they sometimes choose to present themselves in the most favorable light for the ratings. In the past, for example, some colleges chose to exclude the scores of recruited athletes in the SAT scores they reported for freshmen. Recruited athletes as a group usually have lower SAT scores than other new freshmen and would bring the average score, and hence the college's ranking, down if they were included.

The Common Data Set

Efforts have recently been made to make the reporting of data more systematic. The Common Data Set initiative is a collaboration between colleges and publishers in which the colleges agree to provide basic statistical data each year, including detailed information about the composition of the freshman class along with admission and wait-list numbers. These data are then made available for use by the participating publishers, including *U.S. News,* as well as the general public if the college chooses to post them. (You can usually find the report by checking the college's "institutional research office" Web page or by entering "Common Data Set" as a search term on the campus Web site.) This attempt at standardization has made it easier for different groups to access the same information. It has not, however, eliminated the flexibility that colleges have to report some numbers in a fashion they deem advantageous. As long as the public views rankings as an indicator of educational quality, it is not surprising that some colleges will respond to what the marketplace demands.

Admission Rate and Yield

Admission rate and yield are also under the control of colleges to a considerable extent. As we noted earlier in this chapter, *U.S. News* dropped yield from its ranking formula in 2003, acknowledging that it really wasn't very useful as a measure of college quality. But a college's yield—the percentage of students offered admission who actually accept—can indirectly affect its admissions rate. If a college has a high yield, it can admit fewer students and still fill its classes. If it has a low yield, it has to admit more. And regardless of how it is achieved, a lower admission rate translates into a higher *U.S. News* ranking for a college.

> "A college that rises in the annual rankings often receives more applications the next year because of the increase, which, in turn, raises their ranking even more."
>
> *High school counselor reflecting on how rankings reinforce themselves*

Increasing the size of the applicant pool is the most direct way to lower the percentage of those admitted. Aggressive outreach to students to encourage them to apply, although only a fraction of those applying will be admitted, is the easiest way for a college to become more selective. Although some colleges engage in outreach with an eye on improving ratings, others may have more noble goals—but the result is the same. Rachel Toor, a former admissions officer at Duke University, describes her own experience vividly as follows: "I travel around the country whipping kids (and their parents) into a frenzy so that they will apply. I tell them how great a school Duke is academically and how much fun they will have socially. Then, come April, we reject most of them."[15]

In addition, admission percentages can be kept low by limiting admission offers to those students who are most likely to enroll. Taken to an extreme, this means admitting as large a percentage of the incoming class by "early decision" as possible.

Early decision is an admissions option available at many colleges in which students submit a completed application by November 1 or November 15, rather than the traditional January 1, in exchange for an admission decision by mid-December rather than early April. The catch is that early decision applications are binding on the student, meaning that the student is obligated to attend if admitted, subject to the availability of adequate financial aid. A student admitted by early decision is a sure thing for a college, since there is no guesswork about whether that student will attend. We'll talk more about early decision and its cousin, early action, in Chapter Seven, but we mention it now because it is an important way that colleges can increase their yield and thereby reduce their admit rate. Some elite colleges admit close to half of their incoming freshman class via early decision, leaving far fewer seats available for the much larger number of students applying in the regular time frame. For the class of 2007, for example, Wesleyan University, the University of Pennsylvania, and Princeton University each admitted 40 percent or more of their freshman classes early decision.

> "I overheard a conversation at a reception for the parents of newly admitted students at Elite U. A mom was chatting with a young admissions officer who was mingling with parents on the lawn of the president's house. 'I have a question I'd like to ask you,' she said. 'Since Elite U takes less than 15 percent of those who apply, why does the university work so hard to encourage more applications?' The admissions officer was silent for a moment. 'I'm afraid you'll have to ask the dean of admissions that question,' she said."
>
> *Parent of prospective freshman*

A college may also choose to increase its yield and lower its admit rate by rejecting, or more likely wait-listing, students they consider "overqualified" because the college believes the student won't accept the offer of admission and will go elsewhere. The dean of admission at one such college defended the practice at his institution. "We know our place in the food chain of higher education," he said. "We're not a community college. And we're not Harvard."[16] This practice is not common, but it is not rare, either.

Showing That You Are Interested

Some colleges try to identify who is seriously interested in them by tracking how much contact a student has had with the college—such as requesting an interview, chatting with a representative at a college fair, e-mailing a question to an admissions officer, visiting campus—and using that information when making the final decision. A student who has initiated a good deal of contact with a college is seen as more likely to enroll than a student who has not, and hence is a better bet for admission. Given hard choices among candidates with similar credentials, "demonstrated interest" can make the difference between an offer of acceptance and placement on the wait-list at some colleges.

Emory University is an example of a college that tracks contact and lets students know that it is important. Their application form states, "We carefully note demonstrated interest during the admissions process and expect candidates to have done their homework on us. Have you met us at a college fair, ordered the Emory video visit, attended an information session, or perhaps visited campus?" Not all colleges, however, consider demonstrated interest in the admissions process. One campus that does not is Stanford University. "While we meet and build relationships with

> "To think that when my older son applied we refrained from contacting colleges because we thought we were doing admissions offices a favor by not cluttering up their e-mail or phone lines. We won't pester them, but we won't have the same worry when our younger son applies."
>
> *Parent of college sophomore with another child in the admissions pipeline*

thousands of prospective students each year, we give no preference in the admissions process to such students," said Robin Mamlet, former dean of Admissions and Financial Aid.[17]

Even More Rankings

In all fairness, we should note that *U.S. News* is not the only publication that reports rankings of college quality—there are several others, just not as well known or influential. There are also lists of the top ten party schools, the most wired colleges, the "hottest" schools, and many others. Rankings, in fact, are taken so seriously by so many that even a ranking system devised solely to show how meaningless such rankings can be commanded a lot of attention.

> "I don't buy this whole college ranking thing. It's kind of like ranking ice cream flavors. Everyone has their favorite, depending on what they like. You can't tell me one is better than the other."
>
> *Parent skeptical about the value of rankings*

In the fall of 2003, the *Atlantic Monthly* published its first annual college issue. The editors of the venerable magazine known for its in-depth coverage of important social issues said they wanted to help calm the waters and bring rationality to the college admissions process for high-achieving students and their parents. As part of that effort, one of the articles made the case that a simple-minded ranking system based solely on selectivity measures would make about as much sense as the rankings in *U.S. News and World Report*.[18] A full-page chart showing this "new" ranking approach accompanied the article. Despite the clearly worded text pointing out that the chart was close to meaningless as an indicator of college quality, lots of readers thought the chart was a serious attempt at producing yet another way to rank colleges.

Why Are Rankings So Popular?

It is not surprising that students and parents will turn to rankings like those in *U.S. News* when they are thinking about colleges. Deciding where to apply isn't easy, and having someone else do the evaluating is an attractive alternative to figuring things out on your own, especially if you have no experience. As a society we tend to believe that everything can be rated in the quest for the best, and it is only natural to include colleges as well. We have become used to having ratings assess the value of things—from washing machines to restaurants to athletes to hospitals.

There is a major difference, though, when it comes to college rankings. The rankings simply don't measure what they are supposed to assess—the educational experience for an individual student. Doing that requires a personalized look at a college through the eyes of the student who might potentially enroll. Although you no doubt have much in common with your friends and classmates, you also differ in important ways. There is simply no easy substitute for investing the time and effort to determine which colleges will be a good fit for you. Merely knowing which ones are the most selective or enjoy the highest reputations among college presidents (which, in large measure, is what the *U.S. News* rankings are telling you) doesn't get you very far toward finding a good match for you, a place where you will be happy and learn what you want to know.

"I'll Make More Money If I Graduate from an Elite College": Another Myth

But let's return now to the basic question of why there is so much interest in the group of about 100 colleges that are most selective. OK, you say, you now see that name recognition and rankings are not necessarily good indicators of educational quality. But maybe that is irrelevant. Isn't the real value of an elite college education the contacts you make while there? Everyone knows that the rich, the famous, and the well-connected attend these colleges. Wouldn't attending one of them increase your chances of making the right contacts, getting into a prestigious graduate school, or getting an important career-enhancing break—all eventually leading to fortune if not fame?

Several studies have actually been interpreted as supporting this conclusion. Years after graduation, graduates of elite institutions have a higher income than that of graduates of less well-known colleges, just as the income of college graduates is higher than that of those with a high school education. The simple interpretation is that the experience of going to a selective college is responsible for the income difference. But researchers Stacy Dale and Alan Krueger considered another possibility.[19] Perhaps, they hypothesized, the students who applied to and were accepted by elite colleges had personal qualities to begin with that were in some way responsible for the differences in income later in life. Maybe the kind of college where students received their undergraduate education wasn't an important factor at all.

To test their hypothesis, Dale and Krueger compared income figures for individuals who were accepted by elite colleges and actually attended those colleges with the income of people who were accepted by elite colleges but who chose to attend a less selective college.

> "Students may have a better sense of their potential ability than college admissions committees. To cite one prominent example, Steven Spielberg was rejected by the University of Southern California and UCLA film schools."[20]
>
> *Stacey Dale and Alan Krueger, researchers who studied the long-term effects of attending different types of colleges*

The results showed no difference in income between the two groups! (The only exception was low-income students for whom attending an elite college *was* related to higher income later in life.) The data even suggested that simply having applied to an elite college, regardless of whether a student was accepted, was the critical factor in predicting later income. Students who had the self-confidence and motivation to envision themselves competitive at an elite college showed the enhanced economic benefit normally associated with having actually attended such a college.

Getting into Graduate School

What about admission to graduate school? Does attending a selective college affect your chances of getting into a highly regarded law, business, or medical school or other graduate program? Anecdotal evidence and a small amount of published data would indicate yes, a disproportional number of graduates of selective colleges attend prestigious graduate and professional schools. But here, too, it may be that students admitted to selective colleges bring qualities with them that are responsible for their subsequent success in gaining admission to these schools after graduation. Perhaps those same students would have done just as well if they had gone to a less selective college.

Unfortunately, Dale and Krueger did not have enough data in their study to rigorously test this hypothesis—they were able to draw firm conclusions only about income. They did, however, have sufficient data to show that people who went to a selective college were no more likely to obtain an advanced degree than those who were admitted to a selective college but chose to attend a less selective school. In addition, preliminary analysis of their admittedly limited data supported the interpretation that it was the qualities of the students themselves, and not anything associated with the college they attended, that were related to *where* they went for graduate study. Students admitted to a selective college but who chose to attend a less selective one seemed to fare just as well when it came to graduate or professional school admission as those who actually attended the more selective college.

> " We didn't find any evidence that suggested that the selectivity of a student's undergraduate college was related to the quality of the graduate school they attended." [21]
>
> Stacy Dale, coauthor of Dale and Krueger study

Looking Ahead

We believe that the college selection process should be about fit—finding colleges that are a good fit for you. A number of factors contribute to fit—academic, extracurricular, social, and geographic, among others—and the determination of fit will be different for different people. Assessing fit takes time and effort and is much harder to do than simply choosing colleges by looking at a list of rankings. Stephen Lewis, former president of Carleton College, stated it well: "The question should not be, what are the best colleges? The real question should be, best for whom?"[23]

> " Do not choose a college by the numbers. Most of those numbers are about resources and reputation and not actual quality or performance. Base your choice on your own needs and aspirations and which colleges can best meet them. As Albert Einstein reminded us, 'Not everything that counts can be counted, and not everything that can be counted counts.'" [22]
>
> David Davenport, former president of Pepperdine University

What Do Selective Colleges Look for in an Applicant?

A comment often heard about college admissions is that the outcome is just not predictable. Everyone knows that it is harder to get into selective colleges than ever before, but in addition the criteria for admission seem to be getting murkier and murkier.

Take the student who is admitted to a super-selective college who finds herself placed on the wait-list at several less selective ones. Or the student admitted to three colleges but denied by three others, all equally selective. Why aren't decisions more consistent? Even more puzzling are cases that often occur when students from the same high school apply to the same college. One student may have a significantly stronger academic record than his classmate, yet be denied by a selective college while the classmate receives a fat admissions packet at notification time. Why wasn't the student with the stronger record accepted also? And although many colleges claim they use exactly the same criteria in the admissions process for early decision applications as they use for regular decision applications, anecdotal as well as documented evidence strongly argues that early applicants have an edge in the admissions process. Why should *when* you apply make a difference at all?

This chapter will help you understand the many factors selective colleges take into account in their review of applications. Knowing what colleges look for as they sort through thousands of applications can help you make sense out of the admissions process and provide you with what you need to approach it with confidence. We have no magic bullet or formula that will guarantee you or anyone else acceptance to a selective college—there is no such thing. But the more you know about how colleges go about selecting their freshman class, the wiser you will be in approaching the tasks before you—from choosing colleges to preparing your applications to dealing with the successes and even the disappointments that may occur at the end of it all.

How College Admissions Has Changed

Before we begin, we'd like to share a little history that dramatically illustrates how college admissions has changed over the years. Seventy years ago, colleges that are now considered among the most selective filled their classes in ways that reflected the time. Yale University, for example, filled its class of 1936 from a total of 1,330 applicants. Nine hundred and fifty nine men, or 72 percent, were accepted and 884 of them subsequently enrolled. Almost 30 percent were the sons of Yale University alumni, known as "legacies." Many of those admitted were students from "feeder schools"—elite prep schools with headmasters whose close relationships with college admissions officers virtually assured the admission of their graduates to the school of their choice. Less than 20 percent of the freshman class graduated from a public high school.[1] Women were not eligible to apply to Yale University; there were separate elite colleges for them, known as the Seven Sisters, which had similar admissions standards. Also excluded were young men who, no matter how bright and accomplished, did not fit the mold of privilege and wealth. But few of the latter even considered applying; the criteria for admission, social class included, were well understood by everyone.

Another example, this one from just fifty years ago, makes a similar point. The following description comes from a book on the history of college admissions:

> Until the 1950s admissions staffs typically consisted of one professional and possibly a secretary to take care of clerical work. Often, a dean would split responsibilities between admissions and some other aspect of administration or teaching. Colleges could function effectively with such a simple admissions structure because students tended to apply only to their first choice college, and they were usually accepted. A close collaboration between admissions officers and guidance counselors also facilitated such modest staffing. Admissions officers visited selected high schools, interviewed candidates for admission, and then usually offered admission to students on the spot. Philip Smith, [former] dean of

Changing Times at Yale University		
	Class of 1936	Class of 2007
Number of applicants	1,330	17,735
Accepted (%)	72%	11.4%
Size of freshman class	884	1,354
From public high schools (%)	< 20%	57%
Legacies (%)	30%	14%

admissions at Williams College, recounted a visit as an admissions officer in the late 1950s. After he interviewed students, Smith sat down with eight teachers; he was given a pat on the back and a Scotch, and was expected to offer admission to all the candidates right then.[2]

Today, of course, institutions like Yale University and Williams College pride themselves on the diversity of their student body and actively recruit high-achieving men and women from all backgrounds. The 2,014 men and women invited to join the Yale University class of 2007 were selected from an applicant pool of over 17,700; of the 1,354 enrolling, just 14 percent were legacies. Fifty-seven percent of the class came from public high schools. This example is typical of the current admissions picture at other elite colleges. Those who in a prior era would have easily been assured of admission by virtue of birth or circumstance no longer are. Some of the rules have changed.

What Matters Now

The Web pages of most selective colleges provide information about the characteristics they are seeking in their prospective freshmen. The posted information may even include details about how the college weights grades, test scores, or extracurricular activities in the final admissions decision. But information on the Web page is the public version of the admissions story. The private version is what actually goes on behind closed doors as admissions officers read through many thousands of applications to select the freshman class that often has just a few hundred places. The information on the Web page is not fabricated or intended to mislead. However, it is just part of the story. In this chapter, we will talk about the criteria that selective colleges generally take into account in their evaluation. In Chapter Three, we will turn our attention to the review process itself.

Students and parents are often surprised when they learn about the full range of criteria that are taken into account by admissions officers at selective colleges. Although some criteria are well known and predictable, others are not. The level of competition for admission to the most selective colleges can also come as a surprise to those who have not had recent first-hand experience with college admissions.

The Academic Record

The heart of a college application is the student's academic record—the courses taken and the grades achieved in those courses. Selective colleges uniformly state that they are looking for students who show convincing evidence of being able to do well in a demanding academic program and that they place the greatest weight in admissions decisions on that record.

What Do Admissions Committees Look At?

Academic Record	Standardized Test Scores
Grades	SAT
Class rank	ACT
Rigor of curriculum	SAT Subject Tests

Engagement Outside the Classroom	Personal Qualities
Extracurricular activities	Letters of recommendation
Community service	Essays
Work experience	Interview report

Hooks and Institutional Priorities

Legacy connection	Donation potential
Underrepresented race or ethnicity	Recruited athlete status
Socioeconomic and geographic background	Exceptional talent

How Challenging Is Your Academic Program?

Many colleges provide students with guidelines about the kinds of preparation they expect successful applicants to have in high school—the number of years of English, mathematics, foreign language, and so forth. Williams College, for example, provides the following guidelines to prospective students: "Applicants should pursue the strongest program of study offered by their schools. Wherever possible, you should take honors or advanced level courses, especially in fields of great interest to you. A challenging and well-balanced program of study ideally should include: a full four-year sequence in English and mathematics; study of one foreign language for three or, preferably, four years; and three years of study each in the social sciences and laboratory sciences. *These are not absolute requirements for admission,* rather they are recommendations for developing a strong high school record."

> *"Students and parents sometimes ask if it is better to get an A in a regular course or a B in an AP course. My answer is that it is best to get an A in the AP course."*
>
> Comment by Harvard admissions officer at group information session, followed by nervous laughter from the audience

Usually, these are minimum recommendations; additional years of a single foreign language or mathematics, for example, are viewed favorably. Colleges also expect students to take advantage of opportunities their school may offer to challenge themselves academically through honors or Advanced Placement (AP) courses, or by participating in the International Baccalaureate (IB) program. If opportunities for challenging classes are open to you, a selective college will expect you to have taken advantage of them.

Advanced Placement courses are designed to allow students in high school to take individual college level classes in subjects of their choosing. The IB is a rigorous two-year curriculum covering a range of subjects, also at the college level. Both are prized among college admissions officers at selective colleges, since they each culminate in rigorous subject matter tests scored by independent graders using calibrated standards. Strong performance in these courses (and, particularly, on the AP and IB tests themselves) is a good indication that a student is very capable of college level work. It has also become fairly common for students, particularly juniors and seniors, to take classes at a local community college or nearby four-year college in subjects where the students have exhausted their high school's offerings. College admissions officers also favorably note these classes.

The bottom line is that a straight A record will not make up for a weak course load if your school offers the option of more advanced coursework. Good grades are important, but the rigor of your course load is even more important. Many high schools reward a student who has taken a challenging course with a weighted grade at the end of the semester. If an A in a regular course is worth four points, for example, an A in an AP class may be worth five points. Grade weighting sometimes extends to the pluses and minuses that a student may receive as well, so that an A+ in an AP course might be assigned a total of 5.25 points, while an A– in such a course might be worth 4.75 points. The weighting of honors, IB, and AP classes can result in some astronomical grade point averages (GPA) for students who take heavy loads of such courses and do exceptionally well in them.

> "If your school offers AP classes, you look bad not taking them. You shouldn't take so many that you get bad grades, but you need to challenge yourself."
>
> *College freshman reflecting on her high school experience*

It is sometimes disheartening for students to learn that some colleges recompute each applicant's GPA in unweighted form, including only the years (usually tenth, eleventh, and twelfth) and classes (usually academic "solids" such as English, foreign language, math, science, and social studies) they wish to consider. Admissions offices do this to have a common standard for discussion. But rest assured that despite any recalculation, due consideration will be given to the nature of the courses you are taking, within the context of the opportunities you have had. A straight A average in a weak curriculum will definitely be less well received by a selective college than a somewhat more mixed record in a challenging one.

Putting the GPA in Context

While colleges place great emphasis on grades and courses, they recognize that grades can be hard to evaluate in isolation. Everyone, including college admissions officers, knows that some high schools (and some teachers) are generous with top marks, while others have more rigorous standards. Grade inflation has become a serious problem at many high schools, both public and private. According to the College Board, 42 percent of students taking the SAT in 2003 reported GPAs of at least A–. A decade earlier the figure was just 32 percent.

Grade inflation is a major reason selective colleges like to see students do well on AP tests in addition to doing well in the courses themselves. The AP tests you take at the end of the academic year are scored by the College Board according to national norms, so a student who gets a 4 or 5 on an AP exam (scored 1 to 5 with 5 as the highest possible)

"There is simply too much variance between schools, their grading policies, and individual grading by teachers for GPAs to have much meaning *by themselves.*"

High school counselor commenting on variability in the GPA

has demonstrated excellent mastery of the material, independent of his or her local teacher's grading standards. Selective colleges invite, but do not require, students to self-report AP test scores, and you are certainly under no obligation to report disappointing scores. But admissions offices will expect to see AP test results from most of the AP courses you have taken through your junior year, or they may question the rigor of the courses themselves.

Some high schools assign a class rank to students on the basis of GPA. Class rank provides information about a student's grades relative to his or her classmates, and colleges have found it makes the task of evaluating grades easier. But fewer and fewer high schools are now computing class rank. Private schools in particular have been reluctant to rank their students, since they believe it promotes a more competitive environment and magnifies what are truly small or insignificant differences in achievement. Class rank also does not take into account the strength of the student body overall. A student ranked in the lower half of the class at one school might rank in the top 10 percent at another. Increasingly, public high schools are recognizing these same drawbacks and have stopped ranking their students as well.

The School Profile

High schools generally include a "school profile" with each transcript sent as part of a college application. The profile provides summary information about the school's curriculum and grading policies so that a college can get a general idea of how a student has performed relative to his or her peers. A profile may show the grade range for each decile of the senior class, as well as the percentage of students who go on to four-year colleges directly from that high school, along with other statistics about the student body such as the SAT distribution, number of students taking and passing AP tests, and so forth. Colleges use this information to supplement data on class rank, or to provide much-needed context when class rank is not provided. Colleges also require students to have a school official, usually a counselor, complete a recommendation form that includes an evaluation of the rigor of a student's academic program relative to the offerings at the high school. This is another way for colleges to calibrate a student's grades while trying to ensure that students from poorer schools that do not offer many advanced classes are not penalized for not having taken a program chock full of them.

Part of the "college mania" noted in the Introduction is the frequently quoted tidbit that Harvard denies over 75 percent of the high school valedictorians who apply each year. Several other super-selective and highly selective colleges also deny a majority of the valedictorian applicants. But if you reflect on this for a minute, it is not really surprising. There are over 27,000 high schools, both public and private, in the United States. Each one of them has someone (or often several people) who achieved the highest grades. Clearly, grades can't be the whole story in college admissions—there are too many students with very high grades, and too much variation in what those grades really mean—for grades alone to determine who is admitted to an elite college.

Standardized Tests

Most selective colleges require standardized tests such as the SAT or the ACT. The question students ask most often is how much the tests "count" in admissions decisions. David Erdmann, dean of admissions at Rollins College, has perhaps given the most candid answer of all—"At most institutions, standardized test scores count less than students think and more than colleges are willing to admit."[3]

How Do Colleges Use the SAT?

Standardized tests are a way for colleges to gauge student performance that is independent of the grading standards of a particular school, thus making the measure seem more "objective." This is potentially very important, since high schools vary so widely in their grading standards. But the tests are not without their critics (we'll talk much more about the SAT, in particular, in Chapter Six) and most colleges are wary of relying too heavily on them because of doubts about what they really measure and lingering concerns that they may be biased in some way. Of special concern is the growth of the test prep industry that "guarantees" significant score improvements for students who take special courses that can cost $1 thousand or more. Clearly, such courses are open only to those who can afford to pay for them.

In response to all of these concerns, some selective colleges have made standardized tests optional—the decision whether to submit scores is left to the student. Sarah Lawrence College, Middlebury College, and Bowdoin College are examples of colleges that do not require them. A list of such colleges can be found at www.fairtest.org. Be sure to check individual college Web sites to confirm the specific details.

Although there have been calls to eliminate the SAT entirely from the college admissions process, it is likely that the test will continue to be used by most highly selective colleges for the foreseeable future. With grades difficult to interpret, most colleges are unwilling to lose the additional information, however imperfect, that a test like the SAT provides.

The College Board, the nonprofit organization that owns the SAT, encourages colleges to report the SAT scores of the middle 50 percent of their freshman class rather than average SAT scores when providing information to prospective students. It is much more useful to know the 25 to 75 percent midrange of scores (each part of the test is graded on a scale from 200 to 800) than a single average score, since the range gives you some information about how scores are actually distributed. Knowing that the midrange for the freshman class was 570 to 730 on the math section, for example, gives you much more information than simply knowing that the average score was 650. It tells you that 50 percent of the freshman class scored between 570 and 730 and that 25 percent of the class scored above 730 while 25 percent scored below 570. With just the average, you can't tell whether almost all students had scores right around 650 or whether scores were distributed more broadly.

> "I don't think the SATs are a fair indication of someone's potential for college. The math is insanely tricky. And they're so long. Four hours. By the end, you just can't think. You start making silly mistakes."
>
> *High school senior who wonders what the SAT really measures*

Evaluating Your Score

In general, if your test scores fall roughly in the middle 50 percent range of a selective college's freshman class SAT distribution, they won't hurt your chances for admission, while scores in the top 25 percent of a college's distribution may help your case. In the example just discussed, a math score of 740 or greater would fall in the top 25 percent of the freshman class and be likely to help make your case for admission. Just how much a higher score will help depends on the actual score, the weight the college places on it, and the rest of your record. Scores falling in the lowest 25 percent of the freshman class for a selective college (560 or less in this example) would usually need to be offset by one or more compelling factors (for example, an outstanding academic record or, as we will see later in this chapter, a special "hook") for you to be a viable candidate at that college, especially if the college has many more applicants than places in the freshman class.

Why Students Tend to Have Higher Scores Than Their Parents

SAT scores are another area that has experienced inflation. When the SAT first became widely used, the average score on each part of the two-part test (the current version now has three parts) was set by the test makers at about 500. Scores on each of the two parts—verbal and math—could range from a low of 200 to maximum of 800; a score of 500, right in the middle of the range, corresponded to performance in the 50th percentile of test takers. By the mid-1990s, however, it was clear that 500 was no longer the average score. In fact, the 50th percentile score for the verbal test had drifted down to 420; the 50th percentile math score was 470.

To compensate for this change that reflected a larger pool of test takers from a greater variety of high schools, the College Board "recentered" the test. Beginning in 1995, the average score for each part was adjusted and returned to 500. Thus, a verbal score of 420 before recentering was equal to a score of 500 after recentering, while an old math score of 470 was equivalent to a new, recentered score of 500. Overall, individual verbal scores increased as much as 80 points after recentering, while changes in math scores increased as much as 40 points, depending on where in the range prior to recentering a student's score happened to fall. The immediate result of recentering was an apparent dramatic improvement in SAT scores when, in fact, numbers and not actual performance had changed. SAT recentering is the main reason why Baby Boomer parents who took the SAT themselves as teenagers often find that their children's scores are more impressive than their own.

Recentering dramatically increased the number of students earning a perfect score of 1,600. (In Chapter Six, we will discuss changes in the SAT effective March 2005 that now result in a maximum possible score of 2,400.) Only thirty-two students earned a perfect 1,600 score the year before recentering, while 545 scored

1,600 right after recentering. In 2003, about 1,000 students attained a score of 1,600. Overall, 11 percent of high school seniors graduating in 2003 had SAT verbal scores of 650 or above on their most recent test administration, and 14 percent had SAT math scores at or above 650.[4] Given the large number of seniors taking the SAT, these percentages translate into big numbers: 155,000 students in the first case, and 207,000 students in the second.

Engagement Beyond the Classroom: The Extracurricular Record

Selective colleges not only expect students to be strong academically but also to be interesting, contributing members of the campus community and the community at large. People used to talk about the importance of being well-rounded and showing evidence of leadership in extracurricular activities. Now admissions officers talk about having a well-rounded class composed of students who each have exceptional talent or passion in one or two areas. The shift reflects the reality that there are just so many hours in the day and that achieving excellence in a given area can take up most of those hours. Or as David Gould, dean of admissions at Brandeis, has said, "The embodiment at age seventeen of a Renaissance person is difficult to find. We realized we could accomplish the same thing (for our freshman class) with lots of different people."[5] Colleges look to see whether a student has made a sustained commitment to an activity over a number of years; involvement in one long-term activity can be more helpful than involvement in several short-term ones.

Extracurricular Activities

But just what does exceptional talent or passion mean? In general, the more selective the college, the higher the bar with regard to evaluating extracurricular activities and leadership. Participation in debate, for example, can range from being a participating member of a team to winning occasional local tournaments to having a winning record at the regional, state, or national level. The more selective the college, the higher the level of achievement that will be needed to impress admissions officers. Being a dedicated member of the school orchestra is good, but being first violinist and student concertmaster is better. Better still is winning regional, state, national, or even international competitions as a soloist. We'll address the special case of athletic talent later in this chapter under the topic of "hooks."

Colleges like to see evidence of leadership in an applicant as well. Being president of an active high school club, serving as a student body officer, or editing the high school newspaper or yearbook are all examples of high school leadership activities that are commonly seen on applications to selective colleges. In general, the more selective the college, the greater the expectation that applicants will hold leadership positions and that they will be at the highest levels, possibly extending beyond the high school to local, regional, and state organizations. Colleges will differ, however, in the emphasis they place on leadership. Fred Hargadon, long-time dean of admissions at Princeton, was well known for preferring to see evidence of perseverance in applicants rather than leadership per se. Complicating matters is that leadership can be difficult to assess meaningfully, since the same position can vary greatly in importance and responsibility from high school to high school.

Community Service

Many colleges also like to see that a student has been willing to contribute his or her time and effort to help others through community service. There are lots of ways to do this, and in fact some high schools require a certain number of hours of community service for graduation. Just as in extracurricular activities, sustained involvement over

> *"*Have you seen 'Gilmore Girls,' the TV show? There's a character on there who really wants to go to Harvard. She is frantically calling soup kitchens right before Thanksgiving because she won't get into Harvard if she doesn't work at a soup kitchen over Thanksgiving and she's going crazy because she *has* to work at a soup kitchen. I think that's insane.*"*
>
> *High school senior with focused interests*

time is a plus, and a major time commitment will have more impact on your application than one that is less extensive. Generally, a leadership role in a community service activity, in addition to a major time commitment to it, will have the most impact of all.

Work Experience

Most college applications give students an opportunity to list their work experience. Depending on its nature, paid work can nicely complement a student's special interests (for example, designing Web pages or working with developmentally disabled children). Work can also demonstrate leadership ability, as in the case of a job where the student supervises others. Finally, an extensive work commitment can reflect the student's socioeconomic background and indicate that the student's income is important to her support and that of her family. Admissions officers are well aware that work responsibilities of this type can limit the amount of time a student can devote to other activities.

Follow Your Passions

In Chapter Eight, we will discuss how you can share information about your extracurricular, community service, and work experiences as part of your application. Students interested in applying to selective colleges sometimes try to get involved in activities they think will look good to college admissions officers. In reality, admissions officers are interested in seeing a student who has had sustained involvement in one or more activities and grown from them—it doesn't much matter what those activities are.

> "Students who do activities out of their own interests and passions and who create activities for themselves stand out—even if the activities were done down the street and not in an exotic locale. Students who do activities because their parents pay for them and they need résumé dressing are a dime a dozen and blend into the overall pool."
>
> *Parent with experience in the admissions process*

Second-guessing what colleges want is usually futile—and not much fun. Do what you love. It makes much more sense to get involved in what really interests you than to try to fit your interests to some preconceived (and probably inaccurate) idea about what colleges want to see.

Personal Qualities: The Person Behind the Paper

You know that your written record—test scores, GPA, and even a list of extracurricular activities—doesn't tell the whole story of what kind of person you are right now and what kind of person you might become. For that reason, colleges request subjective information as well: letters from people who know you, essays, and in some cases, an interview.

Letters

As you'll see in Chapter Eight, almost all selective colleges require a letter of recommendation from a student's high school counselor and two letters from teachers. (The campuses of the University of California are a notable exception.) Admissions officers look at letters for evidence that a student has, for want of a better word, "sparkle." They are looking for someone who is smart, intellectually curious, good hearted, talented, and energetic.

Letters of recommendation can vary widely, however, in their usefulness. Sheila McMillen taught English at the University of Virginia and was drafted one year to serve as a reader in the undergraduate admissions office. This is how she described her experience reading letters: "I had to take into account that the harried guidance counselors at the large urban school, writing hundreds of recommendations, often did not know the applicant well—this letter would be short and vague. The applicants attending private schools, where the rate of college acceptances is an important recruiting tool, received four-page tomes from their counselors. . . .Fairness demanded that I factor in the inequity, but invariably I was told more—though in hyperbolic terms—about the private school student than I ever learned about the public school one."[6]

Although four-page letters are very rare from any counselor, private or public, the lesson here is clear. Regardless of where you go to high school, try to get to know your counselor, even if your opportunities are limited. Some students go to schools with low student-to-counselor ratios and can get to know a counselor easily. Others have to work harder at it. It's not always easy, and it isn't fair, but it can be done.

It is also to your advantage to get to know several teachers well since you will have to ask two of them to write on your behalf. Being memorable (in a positive way) and being an active participant in your classes are the best ways to ensure that your teachers will be willing to write and will have something helpful to say. Hold onto your best papers and projects from your classes. At letter-writing time you may want to remind a teacher about the work you did in his or her class. A few colleges even ask applicants to submit a graded school paper, so you may have additional uses for work that you have saved.

The Essay

Perhaps no other part of the application process besides the SAT is as dreaded as the essay. The essay is an opportunity for a student to show how she writes, but more important, how she thinks and how she has been able to learn from her experiences. Some colleges require one long essay of about 500 words, some require two. Short paragraph-length answers to specific questions are also often required.

College admissions officers see the essay as one more way to gain insight into who the student is. With so many applicants who look similar in terms of grades,

GPAs, and activities, the essay becomes a way for the student to convey his or her own individuality. An effective essay is one that leaves the reader feeling that he has gotten to know the student, and that he likes what he sees.

How much do essays count in admissions decisions? A recent survey attempting to answer this question found that students and parents rated the essay as more important than admissions officers said it was. But the results confirmed that the essay can still make a difference in the admissions decision.[7]

A good essay can strengthen an application to an elite school, particularly if your qualifications are already strong. Not surprising, a boring, poorly written, arrogant, or silly essay can hurt your chances, especially if your qualifications are borderline. But even if your record is very strong, a weak essay can spoil your chances at a college that has many strong candidates to choose from. An essay that falls in the middle—neither strong nor weak but simply undistinguished—does little to reduce the reader's uncertainty about whether you should be accepted based on the rest of your file. A wise student tries to have as many factors in the "plus" column as possible—including the essay, which need not be dreaded if you start early. We'll talk more about writing your essays in Chapter Eight.

> " Save for the few instances in which candidates write essays so completely lacking in taste as to make us marvel at the fact that they even bothered to apply, in my experience no one is ever admitted *solely* on the basis of a great essay and no one was ever denied admission *solely* on the basis of a poor essay. " [8]
>
> *Fred Hargadon, former dean of admission at Princeton University*

Interviews

Interviews are perhaps the most misunderstood part of the college admissions process. Some colleges find them to be helpful in the overall evaluation of candidates, while others see them as a way for students to get more information about a college. Still others feel they add little value to the admissions process for either the student or the college and don't offer any interviews at all.

In a small percentage of cases, new information becomes available through an interview—either exceptionally positive or exceptionally negative. A potential student who is boorish or very immature could have an application jeopardized by an interview, but short of such exceptionally negative behavior, an interview is unlikely to affect the outcome of an admissions decision negatively. Most of the time, an interview confirms, more or less, what is already clear from the application. A great interview, however, may serve as a small tip factor in favor of admission.

Since it is hard to predict whether, and by how much, an interview will count, it is best to approach it as a serious yet friendly conversation that will give you a chance to personalize your candidacy, especially if you are applying to smaller colleges. If nothing else, participating in an interview indicates your interest in a college. As we saw in Chapter One, "demonstrated interest" may be part of the decision-making process at some colleges, especially in close cases. Chapter Eight will talk more about the different kinds of interviews, what you can expect, and how you can make a good impression.

> "Most applicants compete not with the whole applicant pool but within specific categories, where the applicant-to-available space ratio may be more, or less, favorable than in the pool at large. . . . Students in the selected categories, which vary from institution to institution, have a 'hook' because they help meet institutional needs." [9]
>
> Paul Marthers, dean of admission at Reed College, reflecting on admissions practices at selective institutions

Hooks

In admissions parlance, a *hook* is a special characteristic a college deems desirable, over and above the qualities it is seeking in its students in general. Hooks are institutional priorities that don't appear explicitly on any of the admissions forms but that can be powerful factors, tipping the outcome in favor of the applicant. A good understanding of the different kinds of hooks and the role they play in admissions decisions can help you appreciate the many factors beyond the traditional academic and extracurricular record that can lead to admission to a selective college.

Legacy Status

A *legacy* is a child of an alumnus who received an undergraduate degree (and the alum doesn't even have to be famous). Some colleges, like MIT and the University of Pennsylvania, also count grandchildren of alumni as legacies, and a few, like Stanford University, consider children to be legacies if a parent received an undergraduate *or* graduate degree there. Colleges are usually eager to recruit legacy children, since they believe that legacies are likely to have a strong commitment to their parent's college and will likely accept an offer of admission and become enthusiastic, contributing students. Parents, in turn, like the idea of having a child follow in their footsteps and are more likely to support their alma mater financially and in other ways if their child enrolls there. At colleges and universities throughout the country, alumni are regularly solicited for donations.

Giving special admissions preference to legacies can be a wise financial decision for colleges that depend heavily on contributions to support their programs. Tuition pays only part of the cost of educating a student at private institutions, and fundraising and other forms of external support are needed to operate colleges successfully. Many public research universities also receive considerably less than half of their funding from state sources and tuition. Legacy status may be a factor in admissions at some public institutions, but it plays an important role in admissions at most private ones. Some colleges, in fact, have special information sessions for legacy applicants, special legacy-only interviews, and staff assigned to deal specifically with legacy concerns.

> "We take a look at the level of loyalty— contributions, alumni interviewing, etc. that graduates have maintained over the years. If alumni have been engaged in the community since they left, supporting them in return just makes sense." [10]
>
> *Charles Deacon, dean of undergraduate admission at Georgetown University*

> "If it weren't for the generosity of alumni, we would not be able to provide the education we do. So yes, we do give preference." [11]
>
> *Thomas Parker, dean of admissions and financial aid at Amherst College*

How Big Is the Legacy Advantage?

At many selective private colleges, legacies tend to be admitted at up to twice the overall rate of admission or more. At the Johns Hopkins University, for example, 48 percent of legacy applicants were offered admission to the class of 2007, while 30 percent of applicants overall were admitted. At Amherst College, about 50 percent of legacy applicants for the class of 2007 were accepted compared to the general acceptance rate of 17 percent. Part of the difference in admissions rate is no doubt explained by the fact that the legacy pool overall is usually somewhat stronger than the general applicant pool, and that many legacies choose to apply "early," which, by itself, can boost the chances of admission. But clearly there is a separate, distinct boost associated with legacy status at many institutions. Being a legacy by no means ensures admission, however, since these colleges generally have low admission rates to begin with.

The Legacy of Being a Legacy

My daughter was a legacy candidate at the Ivy League college I attended back in the 1960s. She liked the school, too, and applied early action, which guaranteed a response on December 15th.

She jumped for joy when the coveted big envelope arrived. We hugged and danced around the house. She grabbed the telephone.

After a few calls, however, she returned to the living room looking suddenly weary. More than weary, she looked distressed.

"How do I know they really want me?" she asked. "Maybe I just got in because of you."

I reassured her that her SAT scores and her GPA were all mid-range for the college. I got ready to pull out the Fiske Guide to prove it. But this wasn't about numbers. Like me, my daughter knew that the tiniest tweak can sometimes make the difference between acceptance and denial. It was perfectly natural for her to worry that being a "legacy," rather than her own accomplishments, had given her an edge.

Meanwhile, I — the proud mother — thought about all the factors that legitimately make her special. Any one of them could have led to her success: playing oboe, reading every book Jane Austen ever wrote, publishing a humorous essay in the local newspaper. Maybe she hadn't slid in on a "legacy" but marched in on diligence and skill.

We would never know, of course, although years later, when I started working on this book, my husband said, "Maybe you could have access to her file now. Find out why she got in."

I shrugged him off because it doesn't matter any more.

My daughter tells me that the feeling of not being worthy did persist well into her time at college. It hurt whenever she heard the word "legacy." Then her grades started accumulating, and she realized that she was not only up to the rigors of an Ivy League school, she excelled.

Finally, she felt that she deserved to be there.

M. F.

The practice of legacy admissions has recently come under fire as inconsistent with the values of equal opportunity. Critics claim that because most alumni of selective colleges are well-off Caucasians, the use of legacy status as an admissions factor amounts to affirmative action for well-to-do white students. The 2004 presidential campaign included legacy admissions as a minor issue; both John Kerry and George Bush took positions in favor of eliminating the legacy preference. John Edwards, who competed for the 2004 Democratic presidential nomination before becoming a vice presidential candidate, included a proposal for an outright ban on the practice of legacy admissions in his presidential campaign platform. He called legacy admissions "a birthright out of the eighteenth-century British aristocracy, not twenty-first-century American democracy."[12]

Colleges, however, make the case that the legacy preference is small while the benefit to the institution is great. Colleges look to alumni as a major source of donations, some of which support need-based financial aid programs that help diversify the student body. Alumni whose children are admitted, the colleges argue, are more likely to make contributions that make institutionally based financial aid possible for those who need it. For now, legacy status continues to be a hook, and an important one, at most selective colleges.

Development Admits

The nonlegacy children of wealthy donors who have or will contribute significant sums of money to a college are also hooked. Many elite colleges have a small number of so-called "development admits" each year—students who would be unlikely to be admitted were it not for their potential to bring money to the college. How big a donation does it have to be? It varies from college to college, and not surprising, colleges are not advertising what those amounts might be. Colleges justify development admits because of the institution's need for additional funding to support new academic initiatives, new facilities, and scholarship programs.

The development office may or may not be actively involved in recruiting such students. But once they enter the applicant pool, development admits are usually flagged for special admissions consideration. In

> "There are typically ten or fewer major development cases each year. There is a rigorous standard to be treated as a development case. Significant donations over a period of years such as donating a building or something. Schools with big endowments don't really give that much advantage because their applicant pools are so large and well qualified and because they have so much money." [13]
>
> *Karl Furstenberg, dean of admissions and financial aid at Dartmouth College*

these cases, admissions staff determine whether the student can work at a level that will allow him or her to graduate from the institution. The ability to graduate from the college is usually what is meant when an institution says that a student is "qualified" to attend. Development admits are typically few in number and don't significantly affect the admission of other students. Nevertheless, the practice is kept low profile to avoid publicity that would call attention to it.

Underrepresented Students

Being a member of a traditionally underrepresented group (African American, Native American, or Hispanic) can also be a hook at elite colleges eager to diversify their student bodies. Asian Americans are occasionally included in this group but most often are not. Most colleges believe that a diverse student body is an essential part of a high-quality educational experience for all students, and many applicants agree.

The diversity hook in college admissions is formally known as race-sensitive admissions or, more commonly, as affirmative action. Race-sensitive admissions policies were challenged on the constitutional level in a case heard by the Supreme Court in 2003. *Gratz* v. *Bollinger* involved a white student denied admission to the University of Michigan's College of Literature and Science, although she had higher GPA and standardized test scores than some African American, Hispanic, and Native American applicants who were admitted. (Lee Bollinger, now president of Columbia University, was president of the University of Michigan when the lawsuit was first filed; hence the case bears his name.)

The Court ruled 6-3 against Michigan's policy of awarding an additional twenty points, out of a possible 150, to students who fell into one of these three racial categories (100 points were sufficient to earn admission to the university). The majority of the Court believed that a system that automatically awarded a substantial bonus to those belonging to particular groups placed too much emphasis on race. At the same time, however, a majority of the Court upheld racial and ethnic diversity as a compelling state interest and reaffirmed the importance of giving colleges and universities some leeway in how they approach admissions. Although a simple point system can't be used to achieve diversity, the Court's ruling allows colleges to use race as part of the decision mix in more subtle ways.

Most colleges that practice race-sensitive admissions have been unaffected by the ruling, since they did not use a point system to begin with. They can continue to consider race in the admissions process as they have in the past to ensure a diverse student body. Campuses using a point system have had to revise their processes, however, in order to continue to consider race in admissions. The ruling does not affect campuses that do not practice race-sensitive admissions. *Gratz* v. *Bollinger* does not apply to public universities in California and Florida, for example, since those states have laws that prohibit public universities from using race-sensitive admissions in any form. Ensuring diversity without directly considering race has been a major challenge for those campuses.

Recruited Athletes

Yet another important institutional priority or hook is outstanding athletic ability. Many highly selective colleges have active athletics programs (Harvard, for example, has forty-one varsity teams) that they see as an integral part of the college experience. The student body wants their teams to win. So does the development office, whose fundraising success may rise and fall along with teams' win-loss record. Most selective colleges allow coaches to identify a limited number of athletes they strongly support for admission. We will define a recruited athlete as one who earns a spot on the coach's final list for admissions purposes. The more important the sport at a college, the greater the weight of a coach's recommendations for admission. Basketball and football are two high-profile sports where the coach's recommendation counts for a lot. Although some recruited athletes have fine academic records that would have earned them admission independent of their special talent, some do not.

In *Reclaiming the Game,* William Bowen, former president of Princeton University, and his associate, Sarah Levin, examined the role that athletic recruiting plays in the admissions process at Ivy League universities and selective liberal arts colleges.[14] The book presents convincing data showing that some recruited athletes are only marginally qualified to attend the college that recruited them and that as a group, recruited athletes tend to "underperform" in college. Underperforming means that students do less well academically than would be predicted by their precollege academic record.

What Is the Admissions Advantage for Athletes?

Bowen and Levin present data from 1999 showing what they call the "admissions advantage" for athletes at Ivy League colleges—the difference between the average admissions probability for a recruited athlete and the average admission probability for any other applicant after controlling for differences in their academic records. The percentage point difference for male and female athletes was 51 percent and 56 percent, respectively. Since the average probability of admission in the Ivy League is around 15 percent, a boost of 51 percentage points means that a typical male athletic

> "The kids who get in on sports, they're good enough students to go there and hang in there, but they're not always students who were good enough to have gotten there on academics alone."
>
> *High school senior who understands the athletic hook*

recruit had an admissions probability of 66 percent (the 15 percent base rate for everyone added to the 51 percent athletic advantage). The average male recruited athlete, then, had four times the chance of being admitted to an Ivy League college than a male student with a comparable academic record who was not a recruited athlete.

The admissions advantage for underrepresented minorities and legacies, calculated in the same manner, turns out to be much smaller. Using the same Ivy League data set, Bowen and Levin report that the admissions advantage for underrepresented men and women was 26 percent and 31 percent, respectively. For male and female legacies, the respective admissions advantages were 26 percent and 28 percent.

These data suggest that exceptional athletic ability may be the strongest hook of all at most elite colleges. We'll talk at greater length about athletes and college admissions in Chapter Eight.

Socioeconomic and Geographic Diversity

Most selective colleges are eager to assemble a freshman class from a wide variety of backgrounds. Colleges are particularly interested in identifying students who are the first in their families to attend college and have succeeded against the odds. High school students from disadvantaged backgrounds who succeed despite the challenges of low income or poor schools, or both, are likely to be highly motivated, successful college students. Such students are often the first in their families to attend college.

Colleges are becoming increasingly aware of the need to actively seek out and support such students, since they can easily slip between the cracks and not even apply to selective colleges. In 2004, Harvard University made national headlines by announcing a change in its financial aid policy so that families with annual incomes of $40,000 or less would no longer be expected to contribute to the cost of attendance. "We want to send the strongest possible message that Harvard is open to talented students from all economic backgrounds," said President Lawrence Summers.[15]

Geographical diversity is another variable that many colleges consider in selecting their freshman class, since geographical diversity is often correlated with diversity of life experience. Students who come from "underrepresented" parts of the country can find themselves at an advantage when it comes to admission to a selective college. But the definition of "underrepresented region" is relative; it depends in part on the college in question. Although few students from Nevada may apply to Colby College in Maine, Claremont McKenna College in California is likely to have an ample supply from which to choose. Talented students from underpopulated Wyoming or rural Mississippi are in short supply everywhere. Major exceptions to the geographic diversity advantage are very selective public institutions such as the University of North Carolina at Chapel Hill and the University of California, Berkeley. In these cases, students from every other state are usually at a disadvantage because they are held to higher standards for admission.

It is interesting that while many private colleges seek geographic diversity in their student body, they also give a small preference to students from their own local area in an effort to build good will with the community. Tufts University, Williams College, Duke University, Northeastern University, and Harvard University are among those that acknowledge this kind of preference.

Special Talents

Still other hooks include exceptional talent—as a musician, dancer, actress, or ice skater; as a visual artist or published writer; or as a scientist, among others—that a college would like to have represented in its student body. An Olympic ice skater, an actress who has appeared in commercial films, the author of a published novel, and the winner of a major Intel science award—all of these applicants have hooks based on exceptional talent that will catch the attention of admissions committees. A diverse class with a wide range of exceptional talents is an interesting class. Although the majority of students admitted even to the most selective colleges do not have a special talent at this level, a large number do. If you are fortunate enough to fall into this category, it will be a definite plus when it comes to an admissions decision. In Chapter Eight, we'll talk about how a student with special talents can bring these to the attention of admissions officers.

Fitting It All Together

We hope this chapter has given you a good sense of the many factors that play a role in selective college admissions. Another important consideration—the timing of a student's application—will be covered in Chapter Seven, which deals with early acceptance programs. There is no single answer to how college admissions offices weight these factors and what process they use to make their decisions. Each college is free to shape its own admissions policies and practices based on college priorities, tradition, and sometimes the previous experience of a newly hired admissions dean. In the next chapter, we will consider how selective colleges generally go about the actual process of reviewing applications to reach their decision about who will receive an invitation to join the freshman class.

How Do Colleges Make Their Decisions?

For most students and their parents, the college admissions process is shrouded in mystery. Hundreds of thousands of applications are submitted every year to selective colleges. Each one is the distillation of the academic and personal accomplishments of a teenager hoping for admission. In return, after a period ranging from a few weeks to several months, the college's verdict arrives: the student is accepted, denied, wait-listed, or in the case of some early applicants, deferred until a later round of decision making. This chapter will focus on what goes on behind the scenes between the time a student submits an application and the time the mail carrier (or, increasingly common, the computer) delivers the college's response.

Personal glimpses into the confidential process of college admissions can be found in books written by former admissions officers, as well as in the first-hand reports of journalists who have had the opportunity to observe college admissions deliberations as a "fly on the wall." Although specific details vary from college to college and change with time, most selective colleges go about choosing students in much the same way. This makes it fairly easy to construct a composite picture that captures the essence of the process for all of them.

Who Works in Admissions?

The people who work in college admissions have varied backgrounds. Some make college admissions their careers and have many years of related experience, whereas others come to admissions after working outside of higher education entirely. Or they can be younger people, spending a few years in admissions before starting graduate school or embarking on other careers. Often the latter are recent graduates of the college for which they work who display the energy, maturity, and dedication to do a good job in a very demanding position.

Admissions staff tend to be an ethnically diverse group with varied personal interests and backgrounds. By design, each brings a different set of life perspectives to the table at decision time. Those who play a role in the actual decision-making process are referred to as admissions officers. Others, called readers, are hired by larger schools to help read and summarize applicant files. Readers do not usually participate in making the final decisions.

Evaluating applications is only part of an admissions officer's job, however. Admissions officers typically do much more than read applications and make decisions. The most senior officers work with the dean of admissions, who heads the office to develop the strategy for spreading the word about the college. This includes planning all the brochures, letters, and other mailings that come from the admissions office, as well as the Web site that increasingly has become the major way students and parents get easy access to information about a college. They decide who will get which mailings and when they will get them. Applications and viewbooks, of course, are sent to all students who request them, but special unsolicited mailings from some colleges target selected students as early as the sophomore year. We'll talk more about these mailings in Chapter Five.

Ambassadors *and* Gatekeepers

Because outreach to prospective students involves much more than mailings, admissions officers play a role as ambassadors, personally spreading the word about their college. Each fall, they spend as many as six to eight weeks on the road visiting high schools to meet with students and counselors. Some colleges assign their officers to different regions of the country (and even to foreign countries), so these visits help officers learn more about the high schools in those areas. Officers also participate in college nights at hotels in their assigned region. These events, sometimes hosted by a single college but increasingly by several together, are a way to familiarize parents and students with a college. More of them are being held in the spring to reach juniors before the following year's application cycle begins.

Admissions officers also conduct group information sessions on their campus for visitors to the college. Each fall brings a steady, continuing stream of high school seniors (and, increasingly, juniors and even sophomores) and their parents to visit colleges. These one-hour information sessions, along with a student-led campus tour, attempt to communicate to visitors what makes the college special.

Once the fruits of the admissions officers' outreach efforts arrive—the large pool of applications from eager, well-prepared high school seniors—the primary focus of their work shifts. Formerly ambassadors, admissions officers now take on the role of gatekeepers, determining who is admitted and who is denied.

What Happens to Your File?

Thousands upon thousands of pieces of correspondence descend upon college admissions offices right around application deadlines—the applications themselves, letters of recommendation from teachers, and transcripts and counselor recommendations. All of it has to be opened, date stamped, and sorted into applicants' files. The physical task of doing this is staggering and very time-consuming. Although the trend is definitely toward online applications and even online review, the process is still paper-in-

> "This morning the U.S. mail delivered thirty tubs full of applications, counselor statements, and teacher recommendations. Two staff members spent all day just opening the envelopes, another fifteen concentrated on logging everything in, and yet our mail room still looks as though a paper bomb went off in it."
>
> *Admissions staffer at a large public university*

tensive. Many of the colleges that accept online applications still print them out before they are read, so that adds to the deluge of paper as well. But once a file is complete, with all parts accounted for, it is ready for review.

At a typical selective college (we'll call it Elite U), an application file may be read by two people in the admissions office, and sometimes more, depending on the file itself. Of the two people who review a file, one is frequently the admissions officer assigned to the part of the country where an applicant attends school. This same officer may have visited an applicant's high school early in the fall to answer questions, and conducted a formal regional presentation for parents and students at a hotel in a nearby city. The other evaluator is often randomly selected from among the remaining group of admissions officers or readers. Sometimes both evaluators are randomly selected. Many colleges also have an admissions officer assigned the task of recruiting applicants from one or more minority groups. The appropriate officer may read the file of students of color as a third reader. A small number of colleges actively involve faculty members in the routine review of files, but many more use faculty as occasional evaluators of special talents—mathematical, musical, and so forth—where a professional assessment is needed.

Reading and Rating

Each of the two people assigned to a given file reads it thoroughly. The first person to read a file is usually responsible for extracting key information and entering it into an electronic file or on a summary card. Grades, class rank, SAT scores, notations about curriculum, codes for extracurricular activities—all get entered for an "at a glance" view of the file in objective terms. Other factors are noted as well—any special interest in the applicant by coaches or the development office, minority background, exceptional talents, and so forth.

Both readers then prepare written summary comments about the candidate's essay(s), letters of recommendation, and personal qualities that convey a sense of who the student is beyond a list of grades and activities. The first person to read a file, whether he or she is an admissions officer or not, will usually make more detailed notes than the second person to review it. Those are the notes that are generally read out loud if the file finds its way to committee discussion. A simple application might take only ten to fifteen minutes to read and work up. A complex file could take thirty minutes to digest fully. Admissions staff typically try to read twenty-five to thirty files a day during peak reading season, which normally runs from early January through mid-March. Long days and weeks are the norm for admissions staff once reading begins. On many campuses an admissions officer may read a thousand files or more over the application cycle.

Rating Academic and Personal Qualities

It is common for each evaluator to assign a rating along at least two dimensions—academic qualifications and personal qualifications—as well as an overall rating that combines the two in some way. The scale used by colleges can vary—from 1 to 5 at one, from 1 to 9 at another. But the idea is the same—to rate applicants along those dimensions as a rough basis for further consideration. Evaluators may have a list of specific qualities to rate as a key to guide them in assigning ratings on the broader dimensions. At Wesleyan University, for example, the academic rating is a rough average of the ratings, from 1 to 9 with 9 the highest possible, in three academic categories: academic achievement, intellectual curiosity, and commitment.[1] SAT or ACT scores get factored into the overall academic rating as well.

At Wesleyan, a rating of 4 in academic achievement is used for those with "fair to good recommendations" with "some weaknesses apparent in application." A rating of 5 is reserved for students with a "solid academic" load, while a rating of 6 or 7 is used for "an excellent academic record in a demanding curriculum." The top ratings of 8 or 9 go to those with a "flawless academic record in most demanding curriculum." A rating of 5 in intellectual curiosity would go to a student described as "conscientious," while "strong interest and activity" in "research, independent projects, competitions, etc." would receive a rating of 6 or 7. A student with a "sophisticated grasp of world events and technical information" and "passionate interest in numerous disciplines" would be rated 8 or 9 on the intellectual curiosity dimension. Other colleges use similar rating systems but don't try to average the ratings; instead, they simply total the ratings to get an overall score. Personal qualities are rated in a similar manner, with each reader assigning an overall "personal" rating or score based on different aspects of the record.

What Is the Academic Index?

The Academic Index, or AI for short, is a formula that has been used since the early 1980s by Ivy League colleges to ensure that the academic credentials of recruited athletes do not deviate too much from the credentials of their classmates. Other schools may use the term *academic index* in a different way; our discussion here is limited to the way the Ivy League defines and uses it. The components of the formula are the average of the student's SAT or ACT scores, the average of the SAT Subject Test scores, and a class rank score or equivalent. Each component can range from 20 to 80, with the resulting index ranging from a minimum of 60 to a maximum of 240.

The AI is used to compare recruited athletes, both individually and as a group, against the students who make up the prior year's freshman class. It is computed for all students so the appropriate athletic to nonathletic comparisons can be made, although it is rarely used directly in the admissions process for nonathletes. A free online AI calculator can be found at www.collegeconfidential.com/academic_index.htm. We'll talk more about the Academic Index in Chapter Eight when we discuss the application process for athletes.

Tentative Decisions

Once a reader or an admissions officer completes the ratings and notes for a given applicant, it is the moment of decision—his or her call on the applicant's status: *admit, deny, wait-list,* or perhaps something less definitive such as *admit-minus or deny-plus.* On some campuses, the decision can be the equivalent of *admit, deny,* or *further review.* This call can be a very difficult, subjective one. In reality, most applicants to elite colleges can succeed if the criterion of success is doing well enough to be able to graduate within four years. Who should be given that opportunity?

At this point the full range of a college's priorities play out, along with the personal preferences and inclinations of an application's readers. Colleges are complex academic communities that seek to create a rich, stimulating environment academically, culturally, athletically, and socially. This means crafting a class that includes not only academic superstars, but winning athletes, talented performers and musicians, students from all parts of the country and a diverse array of ethnic and socioeconomic backgrounds, the children of alums, as well as some whose parents are willing and able to make exceptionally generous donations. These categories are not necessarily mutually exclusive, but realistically few, if any, students can excel in everything. Thus decisions are made about individual students so that the class as a whole embodies the priorities of the campus. This is where the hooks we described in Chapter Two come into play. When there are lots of applicants to choose from with similar grades and test scores, there is a lot of leeway in exactly who the accepted students will be. Institutional priorities can play a big role in the outcome.

Clear-Cut?

Sometimes, though, the decision is clear-cut. Some applicants are so outstanding in dimensions important to the college that the decision is obvious to both reviewers of a file: *admit.* Sometimes the file will go to the dean for a formal, quick review; at other campuses, no further review at the dean's level is needed. In other cases, a file may be so outstanding that it is sent right to the dean with a recommendation to admit after being read by only one experienced admissions officer. Colleges that compute a rating total may automatically admit students who score at or above a very high threshold without further review.

Similar actions can take place at the other end of the continuum. Often files are prescreened to identify applicants who fall far short of a college's standards. Identifying these before they are thoroughly read can help readers save their time for the files that require careful consideration.

Sometimes a file is forwarded for review, and after careful consideration both readers independently recommend denial. At highly competitive colleges with many more applicants than spots in the freshman class, this is often the fate of applicants who do not distinguish themselves in some way. Here, too, this can be the end of the decision process or, depending on the college, the dean may review the file briefly to confirm the decision made by others. Colleges using ratings totals may also establish a threshold at the low end—students who score below the threshold will be denied without further review.

> *" The New York Times* ran an article yesterday about a Web site that provides kids with the probability of being accepted at eighty elite colleges for a $79.95 fee. I want the admissions staffs at those eighty elite colleges to be aware that there are computer programs out there that know just how and what you think. Before you start your discussions, you may want to make sure the room is not bugged in a clandestine effort to further enhance the prediction software.*"*
>
> **Skeptical high school counselor**

The Gray Zone

The most difficult decisions, of course, have to be made for those in the middle of the pack—the *deny-plus* or *admit-minus* applicants, those whose ratings total falls between the *deny* and *admit* thresholds, or the ones referred for additional review. A surprising number of applicants fall into this "gray" zone. These applicants have a lot that makes them attractive to the two reviewers, but so do many other applicants. This is where the decisions get tougher—more personal and more human—and, as a consequence, more unpredictable and to some extent arbitrary.

> *"* Years ago, Dartmouth College let me sit in on its process. I was struck by some of the vagaries. For example, the time—if your application came up at nine-thirty in the morning when everybody was full of energy, that made a difference, as opposed to coming up at five o'clock in the afternoon when people are thinking, 'I'd rather be somewhere else.'*"* [2]
>
> **John Merrow, The Merrow Report**

Making the Final Decision

At Elite U, the final round is usually review by committee. Consisting of all or a subset of the admissions officers at a college, and occasionally including a small number of faculty and students, the committee is typically presented with an overview of each applicant who is referred to it. That overview is usually provided by the admissions officer from the applicant's geographic region who serves as the applicant's advocate in arguing for admission. Questions go back and forth, thoughts are exchanged and debated, and then a final, usually decisive, vote is taken: *admit, deny,* or *wait-list* (or *defer,* in the case of early action or early decision). At some colleges, the committee may review and act on all decisions, even the easiest ones, while other colleges do not use committees at all, even in difficult cases.

Regardless of how the process unfolds, clearly many of the final decisions are difficult ones that, on another day and with another set of reviewers, might have turned out differently. The subjective nature of admissions reviews, along with all the dimensions that a college may consider in crafting its class, creates a lot of uncertainty. Two equally wonderful students apply to Elite U, and one is admitted but one is not. Why? Unfortunately, there may or may not be a clear answer, or the answer may be one that makes you uncomfortable. As Shawn Abbott, associate director of undergraduate admissions at Columbia University, has stated, "Most of the highly selective institutions in the country could easily fill their classes twice over with candidates possessing similar academic credentials."[3] The decisions are not always easy to explain or defend.

> "I don't know what colleges want. My daughter has the GPA and the curriculum (full International Baccalaureate with two extra certificates), extracurriculars (two state championships), high class rank and SATs, and still got deferred from Elite U. She is one of those amazing kids who parents and teachers think is so unique that of course they would want her. I guess we should have had her practice walking on water at birth."
>
> *Frustrated parent*

Building the Freshman Class

It should be clear by now that admissions officers consider many factors—not just academic record and extra-curricular activities—in their final decisions. Nan Keohane, former president of Duke University, offered the following candid

"I applied early to Yale and was rejected. I had great grades, high SATs, lots of ECs, blah, blah, blah. Everyone thought I was a shoo in—my parents, my teachers, my relatives, my friends. Then I was rejected. Just plain rejected. I was bummed out for a few days but got over it. But my mom couldn't understand how this could happen. She sent a nice e-mail to the admissions office asking for reasons. This is what they wrote back:

'Realize the personalities on Yale's committee are distinctive to Yale, as are the personalities on admission committees at other schools. And even within a given school, there are sometimes multiple committees that have different constellations of personalities presiding and voting as they see fit. Also within a single committee, three people may like an essay, recommendation, extracurricular activity, etc., but four or even three others on the committee may feel very differently. Such a divided sensibility would result in an unfavorable outcome. Frequently committee members do not agree which leads to some tough arguments and split votes. This does not mean that the applicant is not extraordinary, it just means that not enough people voted favorably.'

I'm not sure this made her feel any better."

High school senior

explanation of the role that alumni and development concerns play in admissions decisions. Responding to a *Wall Street Journal* reporter on this topic, she wrote, "Every year, highly selective institutions like Duke admit many students who are less 'qualified' than some of those we do not admit. Hundreds of high school valedictorians and students with perfect SAT scores have to be disappointed, in order for us to take other factors besides academic talent in the narrow sense into account. This may seem unfair to those who are turned down, but unfortunately a place like Duke has room only to accept a small fraction of the wonderfully talented students who would like to be here. . . . Every student must be able to succeed at Duke, in the judgment of the Admissions Office, but above that threshold—a demanding threshold, to be sure—many different factors come into play. We are committed to ethnic, racial, cultural, socioeconomic, and geographic diversity, to becoming more international, giving particular support to students from North and South Carolina (by reason of our founding indenture and our commitment to our region), admitting students with a range of probable academic commitments, succeeding in athletics, making sure that our drama and music and arts programs have students who will continue and enjoy their traditions, and more. Alumni and development concerns are just one part of this mix. . . ."[4]

The Outcome Can Be Unpredictable

We believe it is important for parents and students to realize how complex and fundamentally messy college admissions decisions at selective colleges can be. The purpose of sharing this information is not to discourage you, but to help you approach college admissions with the right mindset and to encourage you to develop a list of good-fit colleges that includes some where your admission is assured.

It is true that almost no one has a record that will guarantee him or her admission to the most selective colleges in the country—there are too many variables that enter the admissions equation to predict the outcome with absolute certainty. Institutional priorities that are not under your control can play a major role in the outcome. Knowing this may initially be disillusioning, but it can also be liberating. It can help you understand, in both your head and heart, that the *admit* or *deny* decision made in the admissions office of a selective college is not an evaluation of your worth as a student and as a person. And equally true, the decision is not a measure of the success of a parent's childrearing efforts.

Having an appreciation for what goes on behind the scenes in the college admissions process can help explain some of the puzzling situations with which we began this chapter. A student with a terrific record may be given very serious consideration at several highly selective schools. Because of the judgments involved, the differing needs of each college, and the subjective nature of the process of review,

> "Having my older sister go ahead of me helped me understand how random college admissions can be. She didn't get into Yale or Princeton. So I'm kind of ready to accept whatever happens."
>
> *College applicant whose sister attends Harvard*

> "I went to a college reunion. Some guy got up and said, 'You all need to know that 65 percent of you sitting here would not get into this college if you applied today.' Parents don't understand that. In our day if you were a really bright kid, got good grades, did well on your SAT, and could afford it, you could go. Today kids are playing, not just on a different field, but on a different planet. Kids feel that to please their parents they need to get in [to a highly selective college] and it just may not be do-able."
>
> *Mom who volunteers in the guidance office at a private high school*

> "It looks to the family that this is a perfect student, but most of the students look like that. We're making hairline decisions."[5]
>
> *Ann Wright, vice president for enrollment, Rice University*

some of the schools may admit her, while others end up wait-listing or denying her instead—same application, similar schools, different outcomes.

But It Is Not Random

Although the result of an admissions review may be unpredictable, it is not random. A super-selective college may have a 10 percent admissions rate, but that does not mean that all applicants to that college have the same 10 percent chance of admission. The overall admissions rate for a college is just that—an *overall* rate that does not take into account the factors that make an individual applicant more (or less) likely to be accepted.

If a college collected and shared more information about its admissions process, in principle you could know the probability of acceptance for a male legacy with a mid-range SAT score and 3.9 unweighted GPA in a demanding curriculum. Maybe the chances of acceptance for a student with that profile are 80 percent, not the 10 percent figure for the overall applicant pool.

But even then there would still be a fair amount of uncertainty about the outcome. An 80 percent chance of admission means that on average, eight out of ten applicants with that profile will be admitted, but two will not. What may seem like a fair and appropriate outcome to one of the chosen eight may seem capricious and random to the unlucky two. Although the same chance of admission applies to all ten, the outcome for a given individual can be strikingly different.

> "I have seen some kids get into selective schools with unlikely stats and some with very high stats get turned down. As a rule, though, the better the kid's stats, the better the chances. Every applicant does not have the same odds."
>
> *Experienced independent counselor*

> "There were about 130,000 applications filed for 13,166 seats in the freshman class of 2006 at all eight Ivy League colleges. Sure, there were multiple applications included in these figures, but it's clear that there were a lot of high-achieving kids who were very disappointed."
>
> *High school counselor looking at the numbers*

The Role of Your High School Counselor

In the best of all possible worlds, your experience with college counseling services at your high school would bear a strong resemblance to the following description:

Although formal college counseling does not begin until junior year, your counselor will prepare you for what is to come later by helping you select a challenging array of courses beginning in your freshman year and each year thereafter. A series of regular, one-on-one meetings with your college counselor will begin in February of your junior year. Your counselor has many years of experience guiding students through the college admissions process and has detailed knowledge about a wide range of public and private colleges both in the United States and abroad. Your parents will be invited to meet with your counselor at an early date so they can share their expectations and insights, and your counselor will keep them informed of your progress through regular written updates.

Your discussions with your counselor will cover a wide range of issues relating to college choice, focusing on your preferences and needs. You and your counselor will build on the relationship you have developed over the years and get to know each other even better. Over the course of several meetings you will develop a long list of colleges that tentatively meet your needs. Working with your counselor, you will use the spring semester to research each of the colleges on this list to determine whether or not a college should be included on your final list. If students from your school have applied to a particular college in recent years, your counselor will share data about the GPA and SAT scores of those who were admitted and those who were denied to help you determine the likelihood of your own acceptance. Throughout the spring, the counseling office will offer workshops on essay writing, interviewing, SAT preparation, and so on for those who want to get an early start on the application process. Your counselor will also help you decide whether an early decision or early action application makes sense for you.

You and your counselor will finalize your college list early in the fall of your senior year. Your counselor will work with you to ensure that you are aware of and meet all deadlines, including those for financial aid and scholarships. Your counselor will also help you identify your strengths and show you how to emphasize them in the application to maximize your chances of admission. Your counselor will provide feedback on your essays as appropriate, and will put you through mock interviews to prepare you for the interview process. Your counselor will personally prepare a well-written and thoughtful letter of recommendation for you that summarizes your achievements in detail, and will help your teachers write effective letters as well. Everyone writing on your behalf will assume the role of your advocate in the college admissions process.

Your counselor has good contacts with admissions officers at many colleges, and he or she will call the appropriate person at each of your colleges to make sure that all needed information has been provided and to ensure that your file is being interpreted correctly. Your counselor's goal is to ensure that colleges see your full array of strengths as your application portrays them. Your counselor will also provide colleges with any updated information that would strengthen your case.

In reality, very few high school guidance programs fit this description, and most don't even come close, especially in large public schools. Heavy workloads with hundreds of counselees simply make it impossible for many counselors, even the most dedicated and hardworking, to do everything they would like to do.

We believe you should take full advantage of the counseling services offered at school, realizing that those services may not fully meet your needs. There is no getting around the fact that the college admissions process is easier for students who have extensive, high-quality assistance from their high school counseling office. If help from your school is limited, the best approach is to be prepared to fill in the gaps yourself. Rest assured that you are far from the only student to do so. If you make the effort and continue reading this book, you will end up just fine.

A Word About Private Counselors

In many parts of the country, independent, fee-based counselors have become much more popular than they were even a few years ago. Most families seeking outside help find a counselor on their own, but some corporations such as Goldman Sachs and IBM have started to offer private college counseling for the children of employees as an employee benefit.

Private counseling services can range from an hour or two of help with college selection to multiyear "platinum packages" that provide extensive guidance, costing as much as $32 thousand, geared to preparing students starting as young as thirteen or fourteen years of age for admission to elite colleges. Most independent counselors, however, charge much more modest fees for less extensive services.

Who, if anyone, actually needs the services of an independent counselor? Many parents who employ them have children who attend excellent schools with fine guidance programs. In these cases, it isn't clear what additional benefit is derived from hiring an independent counselor except the feeling that one has done everything possible to ensure a successful outcome, however a family chooses to define "success." In reality, a private counselor can do nothing for you that you can't do for yourself, albeit with time and effort.

Be especially careful if you are thinking about getting extensive outside help, since college admissions officers warn that applications that are "over-packaged" as a result of professional handling are not well received. Colleges want an application to reflect an authentic

> " Ironically you want to look unpackaged and raw — someone like me can be behind the scenes and make someone look raw without over-packaging them. " [6]
>
> *Independent counselor who sees only half of the irony*

student voice. One independent counselor who specializes in $32 thousand multi-year packages recognizes this and promises to ensure that the student's application will be packaged in such a way that it appears "raw."

Although we believe that no one *needs* to secure the services of an independent counselor, there may be certain times when it can be helpful. When parents and student have limited time to explore college options, a good independent counselor can help a student quickly assess his or her needs and identify a list of "good fit" colleges for consideration. A counselor can also act as a gentle buffer between parent and child when it comes to deadlines— the counselor becomes the one who

> *"* It's not for me, but I understand some people might find the need to pay someone for services like this. I'd feel weird about it and want whatever college that accepts me to want me, not the hyped up image some stranger tried to create to look like a better version of myself.*"*
>
> *High school senior*

assumes the role of taskmaster, not the parent. And finally, an independent counselor may help a student "play to his or her strengths" in an application by suggesting that the student highlight specific activities or interests in his or her essays.

All of this is light-years away from the "platinum package" approach to college counseling that involves retaining an expensive, multiyear personal trainer who essentially makes admission to an elite college the center of every life decision made by her teenage client. We don't think that is a good investment of the few remaining years of childhood.

The Parents' Role

Parents, of course, play a role in their child's college admissions process long before an application is even filed. A loving home where education is valued is the most lasting, important gift a parent can give a child. When it comes time to seriously begin thinking about college, however, you can do lots of specific things to help your child deal with an unfamiliar and sometimes daunting process.

Teens differ in the kind and amount of help they will need and are willing to accept, however, so you will have to see what works for both of you. We'll provide specific suggestions for ways you can support your child in the chapters that follow. For now, we'd like to offer a word of caution about overinvolvement. Marilee

Jones, dean of admissions at MIT, has vividly described what can happen at the extremes when parents lose perspective:

> More and more, today's parents are getting too involved in their child's college admissions process, and in many cases, their actions and attitudes are getting out of hand. . . . At MIT we've been asked to return an application already in process so that the parent can double-check his/her child's spelling. We've been sent daily faxes by parents with updates on their child's life. We've been asked by parents whether they should use their official letterhead when writing a letter of recommendation for their own child. Parents write their kids' essays and even attempt to attend their interviews. They make excuses for their child's bad grades and threaten to sue high school personnel who reveal any information perceived to be potentially harmful to their child's chances of admission.[7]

Actions like the ones Ms. Jones describes are becoming increasingly common, although fortunately they are still far from typical. They send a clear signal to both the child and the college that he can't make it on his own. Neither message is a good one.

"A lot of parents—this annoys me as a student—do their kids' applications for them. I work at Starbucks and this dad will come in and say, "I was just doing Allison's applications today." They're really on their kids about what they want them to write and what they want them to do. I think applications are one of those things kids should do because they're also a learning process. I don't think you get as much out of it if your parents are doing it for you. Some people's parents are really too pushy. I was in a "gifted and talented" program in grade school. A lot of those kids are still under the same pressure they were in fourth grade. I know a group of girls from that class; they still hang out and if you ever talk to them, all they do is talk about college. Just being around them is stressful. Thinking about college all the time, when you should be hanging out with friends, is not fun. I think a lot of this is the parents' influence. My parents were more hands-off."

High school senior

Taking Responsibility

This book is designed to help you, the student, take charge of the college admissions process. The tools you and your family need to make good choices at every stage in the college admissions process are all contained in this book. What you have read up to now has set the context. The remainder of the book will help you and your parents make decisions and take actions that are the best ones for you. Read *Admission Matters* carefully, learn from it, and take an active role in achieving your goals.

How Colleges (and Students) Differ:
Finding What Fits

We all know some students who have thought about college since sixth grade and know exactly where they want to go. It may be mom's Ivy League alma mater or the highly regarded state university the student has heard about since he was a toddler. But scratch beneath the surface and ask those same students why a particular college is their first choice, and you might not get much of answer. Ask what other colleges they are considering if, heaven forbid, they are not accepted at their top choice, and you may find an unwillingness to consider such an unthinkable outcome.

At the other extreme are students, and we know lots of them, too, who have a hard time even beginning to construct a list of potential colleges. Not only do they not have a first choice, they don't have any well-defined choices at all, nor do they have a clear idea what they should be seeking. Most students, of course, are in between. They have some ideas about college choices but no good way to determine whether those choices are really the best ones for them. Regardless of where you are at this point in your thinking, this chapter and the next will help you build your college list with confidence.

So Many Choices: How Do You Begin?

For all of these students—even the ones who think they know what they want—the first step in developing a good college list is an honest self-assessment. A little later in this chapter we'll talk about what should go into a self-assessment. We'll then consider the many ways that colleges differ. Chapter Five will cover how to go about identifying specific campuses for your personal college list. Right now, though, we want to emphasize that as much as the viewbooks and campus tour guides would have you believe otherwise, there is no such thing as a "perfect" college. The college application process is all about fit—finding colleges that are a good match for you based on your interests, abilities, values, aspirations, and preferences, both social and academic. The more you know about yourself and the more you know about colleges, the better that fit can be. Although no "perfect" college exists, you can find many where you will be "perfectly happy."

Remember that deciding where to apply is one stage of the application process where you are in full control. Based on your research, you make the decision about the colleges to which you will be sending applications. The colleges do not make the decision for you. Make the most of the opportunity and select carefully. Later on in the college admissions process, control will shift from you to the admissions offices where the colleges decide who will be accepted. At that point you can only wait patiently for the review process to play out. Finally, at the end of the process, control shifts back to you as you decide which offer of admission to accept, ideally from among two or more fine choices that are a good fit for you.

But we don't want to get ahead of ourselves. We are still back at the beginning, laying the foundation for building a list of good-fit colleges. Thoughtfully considering your own preferences as well as how colleges differ, and then narrowing the list carefully to the right choices for you, are critical parts of the admission process. College rankings can't do this for you. And no matter how great your record, how eloquent your essays, and how full of praise your letters of recommendation, a college will never accept you if you don't apply! Doing your homework to identify a group of good-fit colleges is well worth the effort. It is easily half the battle.

Some Questions to Ask Yourself

Be honest with yourself as you try to answer each of the questions that follow. Most students find some of these questions are easy to answer and others much more difficult. You may have strong preferences or weak ones. Perhaps you have never thought about your preferences before, and maybe you just plain don't know. That's OK. You have lots of company regardless of which description fits you.

- **What are my academic interests?** Do you have strong interests in a particular field and plan to work in that field after college or pursue graduate study in that area? How specialized is that field? Are you undecided about a major and want to explore different options before making a commitment? Are you somewhere in between?

- **What kind of student am I?** Are you strongly self-motivated to achieve, or are you somewhat less ambitious academically (although you have done very well)? Do you thrive on intellectual engagement with bright and talented peers, or is that less of a priority? Do you need to be at or near the top of your class to feel good about yourself, or is lower down OK if the competition is stiff? Are you willing to seek out help or resources aggressively if you need them, or do you want them easily available without any special effort on your part?

- **How do I learn best?** Does the format of your classes matter to you? Do you prefer large classes where there is no pressure to participate actively, or small classes where you are expected to contribute to the discussion? Do you want some of both?

- **What activities outside of class matter most to me?** Do you enjoy being involved in a number of different activities at once, or do you prefer to focus on one or two? Are you interested in intercollegiate athletics? Intramural athletics? How specialized is your sport and what is your level of skill? Are any of your strong nonathletic interests specialized (and therefore available on some campuses only)? How involved do you want to be in community service? Do you have a strong drive to be a leader in whatever you are involved in, or is being a contributor OK?

- **How important is prestige to me?** Do you look forward to having people be visibly impressed when you tell them where you are going to college? Would you be disappointed if they never heard of your school or don't know much about it? If yes, just how important is this to you when balanced against other factors?

- **Do I want a diverse college?** Do you want to be on a campus that is highly diverse in terms of gender, race, ethnicity, and sexual and religious preference? Or would you prefer a campus that is more homogeneous? How important to you are campus programs that openly welcome and celebrate diversity?

- **What kind of social and cultural environment would I like best?** Are you looking forward to joining a fraternity or sorority, or do you plan to be an independent? Do you want a campus with a strong sense of community, or would you prefer to "do your own thing?" Do you like the feeling of knowing almost everyone, or are you comfortable with the idea of a large campus where most of the students will remain strangers to you? Do you prefer an "artsy" environment, a politically active one (liberal or conservative), or something else? Preppy or not? Do you want lots of options when deciding what to do on a Friday night, or will choosing among a smaller list of possibilities work for you?

• **Where do I want to live for the next four years?** Do you want or need to stay close to home, or are you interested in experiencing a new part of the country? Do big cities excite you, or do you prefer a small town, suburban, or country setting? Do you want a college that guarantees on-campus housing for four years, or are you eager to live off campus, maybe as soon as sophomore year? Do you want to be near skiing, near surfing, near lots of bookstores? What kind of weather do you like and what kind can you tolerate?

Try to keep these questions in mind as you learn more about colleges. As the selection process becomes more concrete, you may be surprised by the preferences that emerge as your list develops. But you may also be surprised by how flexible you really are. The self-assessment process is designed to help you identify your preferences so you can begin to consider colleges in a systematic way. You will also need to know the ways that colleges differ from each other so that you can narrow your college choices. We'll devote the rest of this chapter to discussing the differences among colleges. At the end of the chapter you'll find a questionnaire to help you record all of your preferences for later use in selecting and evaluating specific colleges.

Institutional mission—the goals a college sets for itself—is key to understanding how colleges differ. A good place to begin is the distinction between a liberal arts college and a research university. Most selective institutions fall into one of these two categories. The definitions for the different categories of educational institutions come from the work of the Carnegie Foundation for the Advancement of Teaching, a major higher education "think tank."[1] Like all simple classification systems, however, the Carnegie categories fit some campuses more neatly than others.

> " My original criteria for choosing a college were (1) it had to have cute squirrels (2) it had to be bigger than my high school and (3) PE should not be required. But my school does have PE, you have to take a whole year. Their squirrels are vicious. And it's about the same size as my high school. So I violated all three of my criteria. I'm sure I could have found my own niche somewhere else, too, but I absolutely love it here. "
>
> *College sophomore happy with her choice*

Liberal Arts Colleges

Undergraduate education is the primary, and often the only, mission of a liberal arts college. Colby College, Haverford College, Vassar College, Wheaton College (Massachusetts), and Claremont McKenna College are examples of selective liberal arts colleges. Liberal arts colleges award most of their degrees in the fields that compose the liberal arts, including majors in humanities, arts, social sciences, and sciences. This distinguishes them from colleges that have programs that could be considered applied—for example, engineering or business—although there are exceptions. Smith College and Swarthmore College, for example, have engineering programs in addition to their regular liberal arts degree programs. But these programs are small relative to the total number of degrees offered at those schools. Most liberal arts colleges enroll only undergraduates, but some

> *"I think you build self-confidence at a small college. You get the message you're special."*
>
> *Parent of student at a small liberal arts college*

may have small graduate programs, primarily at the master's degree level. Almost 90 percent of the over 220 liberal arts colleges in the United States are private.

A liberal arts college provides students with a sound foundation in core or basic disciplines such as English, philosophy, history, psychology, music, physics, and mathematics. Liberal arts colleges also offer interdisciplinary programs that draw from several fields, like women's studies and philosophy of science. Liberal arts programs distinguish themselves from others in that they are not career-focused. They are founded on the premise that a liberal arts education is excellent preparation regardless of an individual's later career choice. This premise has been shown to be sound.

Enrollment at selective liberal arts colleges typically ranges from about 1,200 to 2,500 undergraduates. Liberal arts colleges usually have small classes taught exclusively by faculty members. Small classes generally mean more opportunities to write and to contribute to class discussion. Classes often take the form of seminars rather than lectures, leading to greater student engagement.

Since many liberal arts colleges are located in small towns and in suburbs, student life tends to center around the college and the extracurricular activities it offers. The range of courses in a given field may be narrower than that offered in larger institutions, but students get to know their teachers and classmates well and form close bonds. A strong sense of community is usually an important part of life at a liberal arts college.

Many liberal arts colleges have athletic programs at the National Collegiate Athletic Association (NCAA) Division III level. The NCAA divides its member teams into three categories, Division I, Division II, and Division III, in descending order of athletic competitiveness. With fewer students and a less intense level of competition than that found at Division I schools, liberal arts colleges can offer a higher percentage of their students an opportunity to participate in varsity-level competition.

The same principle applies to other extracurricular activities. With fewer students vying for a newspaper job or similar activity, a greater percentage of students can get involved. But the scale of the activity may be smaller. The campus newspaper at a liberal arts college may be published just once a week, while a larger campus is likely to have a bigger paper that appears daily. There may also be fewer organized activities to choose from at a liberal arts college compared to a larger institution. Regardless of the absolute number, though, there are usually many options for student involvement at a liberal arts college. You'll keep bumping into your friends and acquaintances, even in diverse activities, because the community is small.

Research Universities

In contrast to liberal arts colleges, research universities have a three-part mission that includes research and public service in addition to teaching undergraduate students and graduate students. Research is the generation of new knowledge, while public service refers to efforts to share the knowledge generated through research with society at large. Faculty members at research universities are evaluated not only on the quality of their teaching, but also on the quality and quantity of their research and public service contributions. All of the Ivy League campuses, Duke University, the University of Michigan, and the University of Virginia are examples of selective research universities. The Carnegie classification system classifies an institution as a research university based on the number of doctoral degrees awarded each year across a number of fields. There are about 260 institutions in this category: two-thirds are public, and one-third are private.

> "For our faculty, research intensity is higher, and they are expected to continue research throughout their entire career. It's harder to stay current at a small school."
>
> *Dean at a large research university*

At the strongest and best-known research universities, many faculty members do research at the frontiers of their fields using well-equipped research laboratories and libraries. Faculty actively involved in research are a valuable resource for undergraduates, particularly those majoring in the sciences or social sciences where new research can rapidly change a field. It is exciting to learn from teachers who are doing

> *"* My mother kept talking about the small class size at Liberal Arts College, but I didn't care about that. I liked the idea of having just about every possible option open to me. *"*
>
> *Freshman happy at a large research university*

research that will appear in tomorrow's headlines and next year's textbooks and who can convey, first hand, what discovery and scholarship are all about. Research universities offer many opportunities for undergraduates to become involved in faculty research projects. Liberal arts colleges also offer many research opportunities, but their variety and scope will generally be more limited, particularly in the sciences.

Research universities come in all sizes. They range from quite small (Cal Tech, for example, has fewer than 1,000 undergraduate students and about 1,200 graduate students) to medium (Harvard University has about 6,500 undergraduates and 12,000 graduate students) to very large (University of Texas, Austin has about 40,000 undergraduates and 12,500 graduate students). Most selective research universities have 15,000 or more students enrolled, graduate and undergraduate combined.

Classes at research universities, particularly introductory classes, may be quite large, although smaller discussion sections usually accompany large lecture classes. Research university faculty generally teach fewer classes per term because of their other responsibilities, and may be less accessible to students than faculty at liberal arts colleges because of these additional responsibilities. Students at research universities will also probably find themselves in discussion sections or perhaps even classes taught by graduate students serving as teaching assistants (TAs). While often enthusiastic and committed teachers, TAs have less teaching experience than faculty, and they may not be around when it comes time to request letters of recommendation for a job or graduate school. Research universities vary greatly in the extent to which they use TAs for undergraduate instruction.

Research universities often have honors programs or other special opportunities that they offer to their most academically motivated and able students. These programs can be wonderful opportunities for highly qualified students to get the smaller classes and personal attention that characterize liberal arts colleges in a setting that gives them the advantages of a large research university.

4

How Colleges (and Students) Differ

What's in a Name?

Don't let the name of an institution mislead you. Wesleyan University, for example, is a liberal arts college, while Dartmouth College is a medium-sized research university. You'll need to look deeper than its name to determine a school's mission. It also pays to watch out for similar names that can be easily confused. As examples, Trinity College and Wesleyan University are both in Connecticut, but Trinity University and Wesleyan College are in Texas and Ohio, respectively. The University of Miami is located in Florida, but Miami University of Ohio is located—you guessed it—in Miami, Ohio. We could offer more examples, but you get the idea.

Other Kinds of Four-Year Institutions

Other kinds of four-year institutions exist, and depending on your career goals, one of these types of colleges might be right for you.

Master's Universities and General Baccalaureate Colleges

The most common alternatives to liberal arts colleges and research universities are master's universities and general baccalaureate colleges. Master's universities, public as well as private, typically offer bachelor's degrees in a wide range of fields, including business, engineering, education, nursing, and other applied areas, as well as the liberal arts, but award over half of their degrees to students enrolled in master's degree programs. They usually draw their undergraduate and graduate students from their geographic region. The more than 600 universities in this category are about evenly divided between public and private control. San Francisco State University, Morehead State University (Kentucky), and Jacksonville State University (Alabama) are examples. Their regional focus contrasts with selective liberal arts colleges and research universities that draw students from across the country and the world.

General baccalaureate colleges have a major emphasis on undergraduate education like liberal arts colleges, but they award more than half of their degrees in applied fields such as business, nursing, and education. About 85 percent of the approximately 320 institutions in this category are private. Examples include Elizabethtown College (Pennsylvania), Asbury College (Kentucky), and Linfield College (Oregon).

Master's universities and general baccalaureate colleges vary in selectivity, but few meet the definition of a selective institution that we are using; that is, a campus that accepts less than half of those who apply. Although master's universities and general baccalaureate colleges are not the focus of our book, we encourage you to become aware of them as part of your exploration of colleges. They can be affordable, accessible alternatives to a selective liberal arts college or research university and can be good choices to include in a college list.

Specialized Programs

Yet another kind of college is the highly specialized school such as a music conservatory (for example, Julliard and the New England Conservatory of Music), art institute (for example, the California Institute of the Arts), or undergraduate business (for example, Babson College in Massachusetts) or engineering school (for example, Cooper Union in New York, Rose Hulman Institute of Technology in Indiana, and Colorado School of Mines). These programs can be appropriate for students with highly focused, well-developed interests and clear career goals.

Other students may be better served by studying art or music as part of a program at a liberal arts college or research university that will allow them greater breadth in their education. The same is true for those interested in engineering or business. A research university that offers these programs will have a full complement of courses in other fields as well. It is easier for a student to explore them if the courses are readily available, and it is certainly easier to switch majors within a given university than it is to switch institutions. A lot depends on the student's level of commitment and talent.

Admission Matters is written primarily for students seeking an education at colleges that offer a range of programs across many fields of knowledge. The Resources section at the back of the book, however, provides links to information that will help you if you want to explore the option of more focused study. We include links to information about U.S. military academies as well.

Which Kind of College Is Best for You?

Is a liberal arts college or a research university best for you? Well, as with most things in life and in college admissions, it depends. It depends on your personality, your learning style, and your academic interests. Given the results of your self-assessment, do you have preferences that seem to fit better with one or the other?

"I didn't really enjoy visiting Elite University that much. I didn't like the campus. It seemed too big and impersonal. I didn't feel welcomed. When I went to Small Liberal Arts College they kept saying, 'What can we do for you?' and 'Here's a meal ticket for lunch,' and 'Here are five million people who want to talk to you.' It was just amazing. I felt like they really wanted me to attend their school and that they were happy to do things for me and make me feel at home. I know that Elite University gets so many applicants each year and it's not feasible for them to do what Small Liberal Arts College did, but I still didn't feel like it fit my personality type. My natural personality is to be hospitable, just to kind of hang out with people and be friendly. That's what made me realize I was a better fit for Small Liberal Arts College than for Elite University."

High school senior

If so, you have made a major step toward developing your college list. You may also find, though, that you do not have a clear preference. Many students feel comfortable in both settings, and their final choice turns out to depend on where they are admitted as well as the other factors that were tapped as part of their self-assessment. In the next section, we'll talk more about some characteristics of colleges to think about as you reflect on your own preferences.

Location, Location, Location

When you close your eyes and try to imagine yourself in your ideal college environment, what do you see? Do you envision a bustling city, with all of the excitement, anonymity, and diversity that accompany it? Or do you envision a more bucolic setting, perhaps near a small town, with expansive lawns and a slower pace? Or something in between? Perhaps you have no clear preference and you would be at home in any of these.

Despite the trend for students to think nationally rather than locally when considering colleges, the majority of students still go to college in the same part of the country in which they live—folks in the south go to southern schools, folks from the west tend to stay

> "I was really surprised by my son's reaction to certain colleges. The original Birkenstock-wearing California kid, he fell in love with Williams College, a small liberal arts college in rural western Massachusetts (enrollment 2,000) as well as Columbia University, a large research university, on West 116th Street in New York City (enrollment 23,000). Go figure."
>
> *Observation by surprised parent*

west of the Rockies, those in the northeast usually choose a school in that area, and so forth. Some students, however, see college as an opportunity to explore a different part of the country and factor this into their college search plans accordingly. For those strongly interested in the Ivy League, the geographical decision is an easy one: the Ivies are all in the northeast.

Each area of the country has its distinctive weather and culture. Try to keep your mind and options open, and don't automatically rule out a part of the country without carefully considering why. Be aware, though, a campus in rural Maine or the Upper Midwest that is gorgeous when you visit in the fall could be very unappealing in winter if you don't appreciate snow. And cultural differences can also pose a challenge for some. We know a young woman from the East who was determined to go to the most prestigious college that accepted her, no matter what. She chose to attend a super-selective college on the West Coast for that reason and ended up miserable because she thought it rained too much and that everyone was too laid back. Most people wouldn't describe Stanford University that way, but she did. The fit, for her, was a poor one.

If you find yourself drawn to colleges in other parts of the country, be sure to do your homework to determine what life would actually be like if you were to spend four years there. Be aware of possible differences in food, politics, weather, and lifestyle in general. In addition, colleges in remote locations present their own set of challenges when it comes to traveling home. Living in a different part of the country can be a wonderful experience if you are prepared to be flexible, or it can be a very long four years indeed.

> "At UC Santa Cruz, I thought 'This is so neat' but my son said, 'This is the boonies.' At UCLA, I thought, 'He'll get lost in a place like this,' but he came back beaming."
>
> California parent

Size

Academic institutions vary greatly in size. Some have fewer than a thousand students, total, and a handful have as many as 45,000 or more, with the rest somewhere in between. As a general rule, liberal arts colleges tend to be among the smallest, while the largest campuses are research universities, usually public. Size can play a major role in determining the feel of a campus. Michael Tamada, director of institutional research at Occidental College, has reflected on the differences. "A small college is like a small town; simply walking through the quad you will pass by faces which are at a minimum familiar and quite likely to be people who you know. A large university is more like a city; as you walk through the quad or hallways you'll mainly see faces of strangers, with an occasional encounter with someone who you know. These experiences can be comforting or stifling or liberating or alienating depending on your personality."[2]

Size affects not only the ambience of a campus, but often the educational experience as well. For one thing, a larger campus will usually have a broader choice of programs and courses. But the larger the campus, the larger the classes, at least at the introductory level. Exceptions to this, as we mentioned earlier, are the honors programs within a college or university. If class size is a concern for you, you'll want to find out about the size of specific classes you are likely to take. The student-faculty ratios that colleges often cite tell you very little about the size of actual classes, since all faculty are counted, even those who may do little or no undergraduate teaching.

> " My son grew up in a town with a big university, and that's what he's used to. When we toured small schools, he would say, '*This* is their union? *This* is their athletic facility?'"
>
> *Mother of college freshman*
> *happy at a large university*

There is no right or wrong when it comes to size. Fit will vary from person to person. Some students find it helpful to make visits to colleges near where they live, even if they are not interested in attending them, to experience what schools of different sizes are really like.

"I was trying to think of all the pros and cons of all these different places. I wasn't that excited about going somewhere that was the same size as my high school. My mom liked small schools because of class size, but I didn't really care about the small classes thing. I'm not an extremely opinionated person, so I don't talk a lot in class. I also wanted a place that was more diverse than my home town. I think it's good to go to a different town or city and try something new. I'm very happy at my large university. I've seen so many kids with parents who want them to go a specific school. I think it's good for the kid to decide. I have one friend whose parents wanted her to go to a certain school and when she didn't want to go they were really mad at her. They took away different privileges and stuff like that. That was an extreme case, I'd say, but it seems like so many parents are pushing their kid to go to a certain place or type of place because it's the "best" college or something. I think it's just good for the kid to decide."

College freshman

Curriculum and Requirements

Some students enter college with a clearly defined idea of what they plan to study, and others are completely undecided. How should this play into your consideration of colleges? If you are interested in special programs (engineering, dance, business, for example) it is important to determine where they are offered. It makes no sense to apply to a college that does not offer the program you want. However, it is also important to remember that the average student switches his or her major at least once before graduation. Ideally, you want to look for colleges that offer the kinds of programs that fit your interests, as well as the flexibility of being able to switch fields if your interests change.

Some schools offer special programs that allow students to obtain a bachelor's degree and a graduate degree in less time than it would take if the two were pursued separately. There are dual B.A.-M.D. programs where a student receives both degrees at the end of seven years, dual B.A.-J.D. programs that can be completed in six years, and dual B.A.-M.B.A. programs that take just five years. Dual programs save a year of time and a year of tuition. Similar programs exist for B.A.-M.A. programs in some fields at some schools. Smaller colleges offering these programs usually have cooperative arrangements with a university that offers graduate degrees, while large universities may offer both parts themselves. In either case, being accepted to a dual program means that if you do well, you don't have to go through a second admissions process to achieve your educational objectives.

Picking a Major

A student majoring in a particular field is required to take a certain number of credits in that field and in related fields as determined by the faculty. Some specific courses will usually be required for everyone in that major, while other courses are elective. Colleges often give students the opportunity to declare a minor, or a concentration in a different field requiring fewer credits. Double majors and occasionally triple majors, for the very energetic, are sometimes possible, and some schools give students a chance to create their own custom majors.

> "They're so right about freshmen changing their majors. I've changed from electrical engineering to computer science to pre-dental to political science — and I've only been here a semester."
>
> *Undecided freshman at a research university*

Be aware that some colleges, selective or otherwise, require you to declare your general area of interest when you apply, especially if the major is very popular and the college would be unable to meet the demand if the major were open to everyone. Such colleges may have higher admissions requirements for students interested in that major. If you are admitted to that college but not to the specific major, it may not be possible to switch later.

The college catalog and admissions materials will help you sort this out. We'll talk more about the college catalog in Chapter Five. If you still have questions about flexibility in choosing majors and when they must be declared after reading those materials, ask for help. A quick e-mail to the admissions office should get you answers to any remaining questions.

General Education Requirements

Another important aspect of the curriculum is how a college handles its general education requirements if, in fact, it has any at all. General education refers to an effort to ensure that every student, regardless of his or her major, will emerge from college with the background considered necessary to be an educated person. This means exposing the student majoring in the humanities to the social sciences and sciences, and the science major to the humanities and social sciences. Most colleges believe this is an important part of a student's education and build general education into the requirements for graduation.

General education requirements can vary from a Chinese menu-style approach where a student must take a certain number of courses in the sciences, humanities, and social sciences to more integrated approaches where special courses are required of all students. Sometimes the two approaches are combined.

College is often the last chance students have to be exposed to such a broad range of fields; the benefits of that exposure can be lifelong. When students must take courses to meet general education requirements, however, they may have fewer opportunities to take courses in their major or other areas of special interest. Some colleges, such as Amherst College and Brown University, believe that students should have complete freedom to choose their curriculum—those schools have no requirements other than the ones for various majors. At the other end of the spectrum, Columbia University has a highly structured, required core curriculum that receives high praise from students. Most colleges fall somewhere in between. Be sure to find out the approach taken by the colleges you are exploring so you won't be surprised or disappointed once you enroll.

Colleges with Special Affiliations

Some colleges have historical affiliations that appeal to students because of the distinctive environment they offer.

Religious Affiliations

Many fine institutions in the United States have a religious affiliation. Perhaps best known are the Jesuit colleges, such as Georgetown University, Boston College, and the University of Notre Dame. Davidson College was founded by Presbyterians, and Brandeis University has its roots in Judaism. There are hundreds more. Many colleges with religious origins welcome students of all backgrounds, but a majority of the students may be affiliated with the founding religion. Such colleges differ widely in the extent to which religion is a visible part of everyday campus life.

Although most campuses offer many optional religious organizations and religious services, some students seek a more central role for religion in their daily lives. You need to decide whether the presence or absence of a religious affiliation is a plus, a negative, or a neutral factor for you in choosing a college.

Historically Black Colleges

A number of colleges in the south have traditionally had a student body that is almost exclusively African American. Established at a time when many American universities were not open to African Americans, these colleges continue to provide an important educational option for African American students who would like a college experience in which they are part of a nurturing African American community. The historically black colleges provide a supportive environment and successfully launch students on careers of distinction. More information about historically black colleges can be found in the Resources section at the back of this book.

Women's Colleges

For most of the twentieth century, some of the best-known colleges in the United States were single sex. By the mid-1970s, however, much had changed. For practical as well as philosophical reasons, almost all formerly all-male colleges opened their doors to women, and colleges that had once been women-only became coed. Yale University, Williams College, and Amherst College are all examples of formerly male-only institutions that are now about 50 percent women. Vassar College, Connecticut College, and Sarah Lawrence College, former women's colleges, now welcome men.

A number of high-profile women's colleges have elected to remain open to women only, however, and as a group they are an academically strong and attractive option for students who would prefer the kind of supportive environment that a student body comprising only women provides. Women-only colleges include Smith College, Wellesley College, Barnard College, Bryn Mawr College, and a number of others. A list of women-only colleges and information about them can be found at www.womenscolleges.org.

The Intangibles

Size, location, and curriculum—all of these are readily observable and easily described and compared. More difficult to assess and compare are the many factors that contribute to the feel of a campus, both academically and socially. There is no right or wrong feel—each person will have his or her own set of preferences and needs. What is important is finding a set of colleges that feels right for you.

Where Do Students Live?

Most colleges with residential facilities require or strongly recommend that freshmen live on campus but are more flexible when it comes to sophomore, junior, and senior years. Where do most students live after freshman year? On or off campus? How far away do students live if they are off-campus? Do they seem generally satisfied with their housing options? Campuses where most students live on or near campus tend to feel more like a community than those where many students commute from a distance. Consider your own preferences and factor them into your decision making.

Campus safety can also be an issue. Is the campus well lit at night? Is an escort service available for a student who is working late at night in a library or lab and would prefer not to walk back to her dorm alone? Is access to dorms secure? Unfortunately, no campus is immune from crime, but a campus can take steps to reduce it. Every campus is required by federal law to publish an annual Clery Report providing statistics about crime on campus. Entering "Clery Report" on a college's home page will take you to that institution's report.

What's the Campus Social Life Like?

Do fraternities and sororities play a big role on campus? What percentage of students affiliate with a Greek organization, and how many live in a fraternity or sorority house? Do the answers fit with what you are looking for? Campuses also differ in terms of the ethnic, racial, and geographic diversity of their student body. Some are very diverse, others less so, and some quite homogeneous. Colleges readily provide information about the gender and racial mix of their student body, as well as the geographical diversity represented within it. These numbers can help give you a preliminary sense of the diversity of the student body. Other factors contribute to the social atmosphere as well. Some campuses are known for their liberal, eclectic student bodies, while others have a reputation for attracting more conservative students. Each type will have a different feel. Think about where you would best fit. Finally, how big a role does athletics play on campus? Is there a lot of team spirit, and does campus life tend to revolve around home games? Does this appeal to you?

What Is the Intellectual Atmosphere of the Campus?

Campuses differ in their reputations for academic intensity. Although there are always wide variations among students at a given college in terms of how hard they work, some colleges seem to have greater expectations for intellectual engagement among their students. And at some campuses, students seem to place greater demands on themselves. Campuses known for intellectual rigor and the work ethos of the student body can be exciting places in which to live and study. They can be perfect matches for some students—and a poor fit for others.

Ultimately, however, academic intensity is a subjective dimension. Different people will assess it differently from their own perspective. Rather than provide examples of colleges that offer greater or lesser degrees of academic intensity, we'd like to encourage you to do some thoughtful research along this dimension yourself as you investigate colleges. Your own assessment of a campus is, after all, the only one that really counts when it comes to finding a good fit for you.

How Do Students Spend Their Time Outside of Class?

A typical student takes fifteen or so credits each term, and that leaves lots of time outside of class, even after studying is over. How do students spend their free time? Do students have easy access to a wide choice of student groups? More important, are there groups in your areas of interest? Are the recreational facilities attractive and accessible? Will there be enough for you to do on Saturday night?

Campuses also vary to some extent in their tolerance for alcohol use by underage students. Excessive and abusive use of alcohol among college students is a serious problem at a national level and is not limited to one type of college or another. Although no college we know of condones the use of alcohol by under-age students, colleges differ in how strictly they enforce the rules and hence in how much drinking takes place on campus. Do students feel pressured to drink by their classmates, or is there freedom to do your own thing and abstain? Are alcohol and substance-free residence facilities available for those who want them?

How Easily Can You Get Help If You Have a Problem?

Students occasionally get sick or injured and need to go to the campus health center. Some experience psychological difficulties and need counseling or psychiatric care, and some just get lonely or homesick. Some have learning disabilities or may need to bolster their study skills or get extra help in some subjects. And almost all need help in selecting their courses, deciding on a major, and applying for jobs or graduate school. Campuses differ in the effectiveness of the support programs they offer to meet these needs. How good is the student advising program? What is the quality of medical care at the student health center? Where do students go to get help with study skills if they need it? What support services are available in residence halls? Overall, how well does the campus take care of its students? It is well worth asking current students these questions, probing more deeply into the areas that are of special interest to you. In particular, we strongly encourage parents of students with preexisting mental health problems or learning disabilities to contact the appropriate campus offices to discuss the support services that are available. You want to be sure that appropriate help will be there when it is needed.

What Makes for a Quality Undergraduate Experience?

Up to this point we have been talking about your preferences and interests and how you should identify colleges that match those preferences and interests. But what about quality? How can you assess the *quality* of the undergraduate education you would receive at a college?

The late Ernest Boyer, president of the Carnegie Foundation for the Advancement of Teaching, identified a number of key characteristics associated with a quality educational experience.[3] We've selected a few that we think are especially important. These criteria have nothing to do with the selectivity of a college, and they can be found at a liberal arts college or a research university, at a small or large campus, in an urban setting or a rural one.

- **Does the college do a good job of helping students make the transition to college life?** Is there a program for new students to orient them to life on campus? Is there a good advising system to help students throughout their college careers?
- **Does the college give priority to developing written and oral communication skills, not only in special classes for freshman but also across the curriculum?** Do students do lots of writing throughout their college careers? Are there ample opportunities for students to give oral presentations? The best way to learn to write and speak effectively and to think critically is to practice those skills; there are no shortcuts.
- **Does the college encourage quality undergraduate teaching through teaching evaluations, programs for faculty to improve teaching, and rewards for good teaching?** Are teaching evaluations obtained at the end of every course and used to provide feedback to the faculty? Do students feel challenged intellectually by their teachers?
- **Does the college encourage students to be active rather than passive learners?** Is independent, self-directed study encouraged? Do students have opportunities to participate in faculty research projects, small breakout sections of large classes, and internships?
- **Does the campus offer a wide range of activities—lectures, concerts, athletic events—that encourage community, support college tradition, and foster social and intellectual exchange?** Do students from varied backgrounds have enough extracurricular activities to choose from? Does everyone feel like a welcomed member of the campus community?

Although we will be the first to point out that no college is perfect, we suggest you keep Boyer's criteria in mind as you explore colleges and ask questions. The more a college meets these quality criteria along with your own personal criteria, the greater the chance that your experience there will be a good one.

Getting the Information You Need

This chapter was designed to help you learn more about colleges and more about yourself. While everything is still fresh in your mind, we encourage you to fill out the questionnaire, "Determining Your Priorities," that follows. Your answers will help you identify what you should look for in colleges that will be a good fit for you. Chapter Five will show you how to get information about specific colleges that match your priorities.

Determining Your Priorities

This questionnaire will help you identify what is most important to you as you think about choosing colleges. Questions are divided into three categories: Physical Environment, Academic Environment, and Extracurricular and Social Environment. Answer each question as accurately as you can. For each one, be sure to note whether your preference is very important (V), somewhat important (S), or not important (N) to you.

		Importance
Physical Environment	**Your Preference**	V S N

1. How far from home would you like to live? Close by? Easy or longer drive? Accessible by plane?
2. Do you prefer a large city, small city or town, suburb, or country environment?
3. Does weather matter to you? Is there an area of the country where you do not want to live?
4. What size college do you prefer: small (< 2,500), medium (< 10,000), large (< 20,000); very large (> 20,000)
5. Do you want to live on or off campus after freshman year?

Other:

Other:

		Importance
Academic Environment	**Your Preference**	V S N

1. Do you have a preference between a liberal arts college and research university?
2. Are there specific majors or courses that you want a college to offer?

Academic Environment	Your Preference	Importance V S N

3. Do you prefer small classes, large classes, or a mix?

4. Are there any special curricular features that you want (core curriculum, honors program, and so forth)?

5. What kind of intellectual environment do prefer? Exceptionally rigorous, midrange, less intense?

6. Do you want a "name brand" or prestigious college?

Other:

Other:

Extracurricular and Social Environment	Your Preference	Importance V S N

1. Are there particular extracurricular activities or special facilities that you would like to have available?

2. Do you want to participate in certain sports at the varsity level? At the club sport or intramural level?

3. How big a role should athletics play on campus?

4. Do you want fraternities and sororities to be available and an important part of campus life?

5. How diverse a campus do you want? What kinds of diversity are you seeking?

4

How Colleges (and Students) Differ

Extracurricular and Social Environment	Your Preference	Importance V S N
6. Do you want a campus with a special focus such as religious affiliation or women-only?		
7. Do you seek a particular kind of atmosphere? Artsy, politically active, cohesive community, other?		
Other:		
Other:		

Miscellaneous	Their Preference	Importance V S N
1. Do your parents have any requirements?		
Other:		
Other:		

List the preferences you have identified as very important or somewhat important in the spaces provided below. Then rank them in order of importance to you within each group. This list will guide you in identifying colleges before you apply and will help you in making a final decision once your acceptances are in.

Priorities Summary

The following preferences are Very Important to me:

_____   _____
_____   _____
_____   _____
_____   _____

The following preferences are Somewhat Important to me:

_____   _____
_____   _____
_____   _____
_____   _____

Where Should *You* Apply?

In Chapter Four, you began the process of building your college list by considering the ways colleges differ and identifying your own personal preferences. But there are over two thousand four-year colleges and universities in the United States. How can you go about finding the ones that fit your criteria?

We recommend starting with a "big book" that provides anecdotal and statistical information about a wide range of colleges. Fiske's annual *Guide to Colleges*[1] is our favorite, although there are other good ones as well. The *Fiske Guide* is updated and published each August and contains data for more than three hundred colleges on size, selectivity, the characteristics of the freshman class, and so forth, as well as descriptive and anecdotal information about the academic and social life on campus. The authors have interviewed students on each campus and include representative comments that give you a feel for the campus beyond the numbers.

We've found that having a copy (parents, this is a cue to you) lying on a table in front of the television is a good way to get the college selection process going in a low-key way. Another helpful book along similar lines is the *Insider's Guide to the Colleges.*[2] The *Insider's Guide,* published by staff at the Yale student newspaper, is a bit more irreverent than the one by Fiske, but it offers additional anecdotal perspectives about colleges that are worth considering. It is best used as a supplement to the *Fiske Guide,* not as a substitute.

Although it can be fun to browse, the big book is most helpful as a reference book to refer to when a specific college lands on your radar screen. Otherwise, it is a bit like trying to use the white pages of the telephone directory to locate a restaurant if you are not searching for a specific establishment. You can spend a lot of time looking at listings before you find what you want. That's why we recommend a key next step: talking to people who are in a good position to make suggestions. That will get you started, and you can branch out from there using many other sources of information.

Start at Your Counseling Office

Your high school counseling office is an excellent place to begin your college search. Your counselor may be able to combine his or her knowledge about a wide range of colleges with information about your academic record and personal preferences to help you generate a list of suggested colleges to get you started. The more specific you are about your preferences, the easier it will be for your counselor to help you. Although some counselors will know more about some colleges than others, they can all be helpful. If you haven't already built a relationship with your counselor, this is a good time to start. Remember that he or she will be preparing the secondary school reports for you once you are ready to apply.

The list you'll get from talking with your counselor is a good head start, but it is just that—a beginning point. You'll also want to talk with your parents, other family members, friends and classmates, and others who know you well who may have suggestions to offer. Don't worry if your list is long at this point. You'll have plenty of opportunities to narrow it down later.

Online Searches

Computer search tools can also help you identify potential colleges. Some high school guidance offices have software designed specifically to help students make college and career choices. There are also a number of free search programs online. The College Board Web site at www.collegeboard.com has a college search tool that will generate a list of possible colleges after you specify size, location, potential major, your GPA, your standardized test scores, and other criteria. It is easy to change your criteria and run the search again to get additional options. The U.S. Department of Education has a search tool, College Opportunities Online (COOL), which serves a similar function. You can find the link in the Resources section at the end of this book. Online searches are easy and fun to do. It's worth trying several to see what schools they generate for you. Pay special attention to colleges that appear more than once—they may be particularly good matches.

College Fairs

Attend a college fair in your junior year, if one is offered near you, and use it as a way to learn about different colleges. Usually held in the fall or spring, a college fair typically has dozens and dozens of colleges that set up individual tables staffed by admissions representatives. A college fair can be a very efficient way to gather information and get some questions answered. You can use it to learn about unfamiliar colleges, as well as to gather information about colleges already on your list. Sometimes, though, a fair can be a free-for-all with people crowding the booths of the most popular colleges. In this case, the best you can usually hope to do is take some marketing literature and add your name to the mailing list. Less well-known colleges will be much more accessible at the fairs. Use the opportunity to explore them in more depth.

College fairs usually feature presentations on different aspects of the college admissions process with an opportunity for you to ask questions. They are free and open to the public, and parents are often seen roaming the aisles as well. Your high school counseling office will have information about dates and locations of fairs in your local area. The National Association for College Admission Counseling also posts an up-to-date list of college fairs on its Web site, www.nacac.com.

College Representative Visits to Your High School

Try to participate in the visits that college representatives may make to your high school. Between Labor Day and mid-November, admissions staff travel to selected high schools to speak with small groups of students. If your school is among them, watch the schedule put out by your counseling office and try to attend those that are of greatest interest—if you can take the time from class.

Usually lasting about thirty to sixty minutes, these meetings are a chance for interested students to hear a short presentation by a college admissions representative and ask questions. Representatives will typically do four or five of these over the course of a day, so they don't spend a lot of time at one school. If you attend, your name will get on a list of students who have shown interest in the college and you'll receive mailings. When the groups are small, the admissions officer may jot down brief notes about the students he or she has met for later reference. Participating in a high school visit is an easy way to show interest. Most important, it can be a source of information that will help you decide whether the college is a good fit. Prepare a list of questions in advance based on what is important to you.

Occasionally, admissions representatives will conduct individual student interviews as part of the school visit. Although this isn't common, it does happen. These opportunities will be advertised well in advance.

The Visiting Road Show

A number of colleges sponsor regional events intended for parents as well as students in addition to, or in lieu of, high school visits. Regional events typically involve an opportunity for families to get materials about the college, hear presentations, and ask questions. Students who have previously expressed an interest in the college by requesting material may get a special invitation, but the events are usually open to all students who are interested in learning more about a school. They are most often held in the evening at a hotel with a meeting room that can accommodate a large audience.

Sometimes colleges combine their efforts and offer a joint session. Harvard University, Duke University, Georgetown University, and the University of Pennsylvania, for example, have traveled together across the country and coordinated their event for over ten years in a program called "Exploring College Options." It draws well over 20,000 students and parents each year. Families hear a short presentation on each institution followed by a question and answer session. Even if you don't ask questions yourself, you'll benefit from hearing the answers to questions asked by others. Colleges usually put the schedule of their regional trips on the Web. It is worth checking to see if colleges that interest you will be sponsoring a program near where you live.

Read Everything They Send You, But Don't Let It Go to Your Head

If you've already taken the PSAT or SAT and checked the box saying you would be willing to participate in the College Search Service of the College Board, you are probably finding your mailbox filling with glossy mailers from colleges. The sponsors of the ACT offer a similar service that sells the names and addresses of students willing to receive materials from colleges. Colleges buy this information about students who meet certain criteria (for example, scores above a certain point, interest in a specific major, or religious affiliation) and use the information to develop a targeted mailing list of students who might be interested in their institution. We suggest that you read the mailers you receive and then check out the colleges that seem interesting in your big book. The idea is to cast your net broadly at first—perhaps exploring as many as twenty to thirty colleges—and then narrow the list down based on more information.

"My mom got really excited when the letter from Elite Liberal Arts College arrived. It was personally signed by the dean of admission himself and really encouraged me to apply. I did pretty well on the PSAT so that's probably how they got my name. I had visited the college and liked it, and my mom said a personal letter meant they were very interested in me, too. I decided to apply. In May the thin envelope arrived—rejected. This time, the letter wasn't hand signed. A computer inserted the dean's signature. No big deal. I gave the letter to my mom, who files everything. When she was putting it away, she pulled out the original letter from the dean and noticed something strange. Both came from the same person, but the signatures were different. The light bulb went on. The dean hadn't personally signed the first letter. Staff members in his office probably took turns signing his name on thousands of 'personal' letters that went out. We read too much into it."

College freshman

Sometimes colleges send personalized letters, rather than brochures, to encourage students to seek more information and then apply. Be wary of reading too much into a personalized "search" letter from a college, particularly one from a highly selective college. These colleges send out thousands of letters to students who score well on the PSAT, SAT, or ACT, or who have other desirable demographic characteristics. They try to build a strong pool of candidates but can only accept a small percentage of them. The problem is that the letters are so flattering and encouraging that a student and his or her family can be led to believe that the student has an inside edge on admission.

The following phrases were taken from actual search letters:

- "I hope that this is the beginning of a long-term relationship between you and Williams and that you will be interested enough to keep us in mind as you apply to schools in the fall."

- "As you plan your educational future, we hope you will consider carefully the unique opportunities at Harvard."

- "We feel honored that you have expressed an interest in the University of Chicago."

- "I write to extend to you a special invitation to consider your educational future here at Chapel Hill."

In the vast majority of cases, search letters simply mean you are likely to be a viable candidate—no more and no less. They are nice to receive, certainly, but be sure that you keep them in perspective.

Reading a Catalog

Prospective students don't read college catalogs, also known as college bulletins, often enough. Designed primarily for current students who have already been admitted, a catalog is usually a no-nonsense document fairly free of the influence of marketing efforts that contains a wealth of information. The catalog describes courses and requirements for different majors and lists the faculty who teach in different areas, often with information about their educational background. Check out the courses and faculty in the departments of most interest to you. The catalog also provides details about other graduation requirements such as general education courses and a senior thesis, as well as information about dual degree programs and honors programs. Information about a school's academic calendar, housing policies, and honor code can also be found in the catalog. Use the catalog to read about the library, laboratories, and recreational facilities, opportunities to study abroad, internship programs, and other features of the campus. The catalog will also tell you whether the college is part of a cooperative arrangement with other colleges, known as a consortium.

Because of their size, catalogs are usually not provided free of charge to anyone who requests one. However, most campuses post their catalog on the Internet, making it accessible to all. Copies are also usually provided free when a student takes an on-campus tour. If not, a copy can usually be purchased in the campus bookstore for a few dollars.

College Web Sites

Clicking on "admissions" or "prospective students" from a college home page will lead you to lots of useful information about that college. You'll usually find statistics about the freshman class admitted the previous year, and a description of a college's entrance requirements and its academic programs. Links to academic departments will give you detailed information about faculty and their specializations. Colleges invest heavily in their Web pages to make them attractive and easy to use, since they know that many students and families use the Internet extensively.

Information about application deadlines and testing requirements is prominently featured on most sites, along with the application and detailed instructions, in a Web-enabled or downloadable form. You can also submit an online request to be added to a college's mailing list. You'll generally receive a viewbook with lots of pictures of the college, a paper application form and instructions, and information about financial aid. Depending on the college, you may get follow-up mailings as well. The admissions Web page is also a good place to learn about visiting the college, including information about nearby hotels and travel arrangements. Increasingly common are admissions chat rooms that allow prospective students to talk to admissions officers and current students. Admissions Web sites post the details of these chat sessions, which anyone can join. Most colleges also have their student newspapers online. It is worth checking them out to get a feel for what the "hot" issues are on campus.

Other Sources of Information on the Web

As you can probably tell from our discussion of college rankings in Chapter One, we think rankings are a pretty useless tool for selecting colleges, since they distract you from focusing on fit. That doesn't mean, though, that some of the measures that go into ranking formulas aren't helpful. The best known purveyor of rankings, *U.S. News and World Report,* provides online access for a modest fee to a wealth of factual data about colleges (www.usnews.com). Examples include the percentage of students who graduate within six years of entering and the percentage of classes with enrollment under twenty students. You can usually find this information on your own by using a big book and college Web sites, but the *U.S. News* database makes the job easier and allows you to sort colleges by specific measures.

Another good source of online information is the free College Board Web site at www.collegeboard.com. We mentioned earlier their college search feature that lets you enter specific criteria to look for colleges that meet your needs. The Web site also offers key information about many colleges in an easy-to-use, uniform format. You can check out majors, application deadlines, admissions criteria, and many other facts about individual colleges simply by entering the name of the college into the "search" feature.

The College Visit

Once you have learned as much as you can about a preliminary list of colleges from indirect sources, you will find campus visits to be extremely helpful in narrowing your list further. Some students take a college tour to look at several colleges, usually with parents or with an organized group, during spring break in their junior year. A tour at that time has the advantage of letting you see campuses while classes are in session and the campuses are fully alive. A campus visit usually includes an hour-long group information session led by an admissions officer and a group tour led by a student tour guide. Both are great ways to get a quick overview of a college and a good way to get some questions you may have answered.

> "On paper every college looks more or less the same. But when you go there, you get a totally different feel. You have to see whether you like the atmosphere. If you can imagine yourself there, then maybe it's for you."
>
> *College sophomore who went to school far from home*

Don't limit your visit to the formal tour and information session, however. Try to spend some time on your own exploring the campus. The student union and the library are good places to check out. Have lunch in the union and get a feel not only for the food but also for the pace of the campus. Read the notices posted on the bulletin boards. Walk through the library and see how the students are studying. Are they studying at all, and if so, are they mostly working alone, or are they interacting in small groups? Is the library well lit with lots of comfortable places to sit? As you walk across campus, do people seem to make eye contact, or are they inwardly focused?

> "I had a bench test. At the end of every campus visit I found a bench and sat on it. I thought, 'Is this the place for me?'"
>
> *High school senior*

> "We went to visit a campus. It was on a hill. It was a great place, but I didn't want to climb a big hill every day. These little things make an impression on you."
>
> *College student happily enrolled on a flat campus*

Most important, look around at the students and try to imagine yourself among them. And don't hesitate to ask questions. A tour guide's job is to answer them, but most students you will meet on your visit will be happy to offer their perspectives as well. Keep your list of questions handy—the ones that are important to you and that are not answered in written materials—and don't be shy about asking them. Everyone has an opinion if you are willing to listen! Remember also to take some notes about what you see and your impressions. If you visit several colleges, you'll need them to keep everything straight in your mind not only

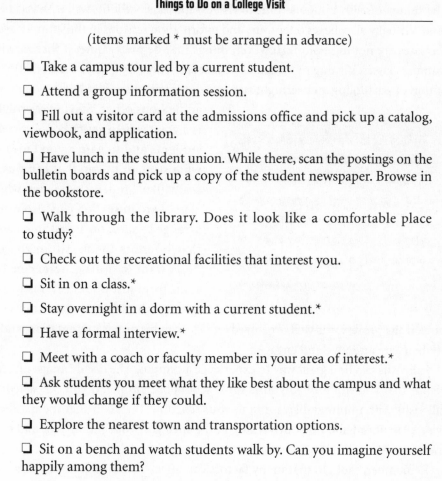

Things to Do on a College Visit

(items marked * must be arranged in advance)

❏ Take a campus tour led by a current student.

❏ Attend a group information session.

❏ Fill out a visitor card at the admissions office and pick up a catalog, viewbook, and application.

❏ Have lunch in the student union. While there, scan the postings on the bulletin boards and pick up a copy of the student newspaper. Browse in the bookstore.

❏ Walk through the library. Does it look like a comfortable place to study?

❏ Check out the recreational facilities that interest you.

❏ Sit in on a class.*

❏ Stay overnight in a dorm with a current student.*

❏ Have a formal interview.*

❏ Meet with a coach or faculty member in your area of interest.*

❏ Ask students you meet what they like best about the campus and what they would change if they could.

❏ Explore the nearest town and transportation options.

❏ Sit on a bench and watch students walk by. Can you imagine yourself happily among them?

now but also when you have to make a final decision about where to attend. Taking a few photos can also help.

Depending on your particular interests, you may also want to try to speak with a coach in your sport or a professor in your major field of interest as part of your visit. The admissions office can tell you how to arrange such meetings, which should be set up ahead of time.

Timing Your Visit

The summer is also a popular time to visit campuses, since it fits well with vacation time. Virtually all colleges offer tours and information sessions in the summer even if classes are not in session. However, things may be pretty quiet if there are no summer classes. Visiting in the fall of your senior year may give you the additional option of scheduling an overnight stay in a dorm with a student host through the admissions office. Staying overnight is a great way to get to know current students and to gain a good idea of what student life on that campus is really like. Students who visit when classes are in session can also often arrange to sit in on a class in an area that interests them. Although you don't want to draw general conclusions from just one class, it is worth noting whether the class starts on time, if the professor is well organized and clear in his or her presentation, and if students are attentive and engaged.

> "I recall an incident when we visited Elite U. A very articulate and personable kid led the tour around campus. Near the end, one parent asked the guide if he could describe the college's negative side. The kid stopped dead in his tracks and said, 'Look, what do you take me for? I'm a tour guide. Do you really think they pay me to tell you what's wrong with Elite U?'"
>
> *Parent who accompanied his daughter*

Fall visits can be a great way to experience a campus. The disadvantage of a fall visit is that you will probably miss some school back home. If you can schedule fall visits with minimal disruption to your schedule, then consider them; otherwise, plan ahead and do your visiting in the spring of your junior year and over the summer.

Remember, though, that many factors can affect your initial impression of a campus, not the least of which are the personality of the tour guide and the weather while you are there. Colleges know that students relate best to other students, and that is why students are chosen to lead campus tours. Tour guides are usually energetic, enthusiastic students who enjoy their college and are eager to present it in the best light. Sometimes, though, a guide may be poorly trained and less than an ideal ambassador for a campus. In such cases, try to keep an eye on the bigger picture. Similarly, a campus seen in beautiful weather has a big leg up on one seen in the pouring rain. Try to keep this in mind as you compare and contrast your impressions of different colleges.

"My first-choice school invited me to a weekend program even before I was formally accepted. I had visited the campus once before, but now I was going to stay overnight. I didn't know what to expect, but I was excited about going. I was put in with this pretty crazy girl, and she and her friends were doing all this drinking and stuff. I was really scared because I wasn't expecting that. I had no experience with alcohol. I think the workshop leaders knew what was going on, but they just said things like, 'Be careful at night,' and stuff like that. I came home and thought, 'I don't really fit in at that campus.' Later I learned I was in the part of the campus known for party dorms. I wonder if I had been with a different roommate, if I would have had a different feeling. Anyway, I chose another school, and I like it so much here that I didn't want to come home for Christmas."

College freshman

How Can Parents Help?

Although some students visit colleges on their own or with groups of other students, most visit colleges with their parents. Whether the trip is part of a vacation or scheduled specifically for the purpose of looking at colleges, the parent perspective can be a very valuable lens through which to view colleges. As a parent, you can provide an extra set of eyes and ears on the visit and serve as a sounding board for reactions. Virtually all campuses invite parents to join their children on the formal tours, but

> "We're just starting the search all over again. If I had known it would be this exhausting, I would have had my children further apart."
>
> *Mom of two*

be sure to give your child plenty of freedom to look at what interests him and to ask the questions he wants to ask. Bowdoin College has started to offer separate tours for parents to encourage students to be more open with questions on tours geared just for them.

What If You Can't Visit?

What if scheduling or cost prevents you from seeing a campus firsthand? Fortunately, many resources can help fill that gap, such as viewbooks, catalogs, and virtual online tours available on campus Web sites that we discussed earlier in this chapter. Some colleges will send you a free video if you ask. Asking for one not only lets you see the campus but also helps you demonstrate interest. Many high school counseling offices maintain a library of commercially produced college tour video-tapes, and there are businesses that sell them directly to families. Although not a complete substitute for an in-person visit, these tapes can give you a good sense of the campus.

Consider sending an e-mail with short questions about campus life (including "What do you like best?" and "What would you most like to change about your campus?") to several current students. Admissions officers are usually happy to provide the names and e-mail addresses of current students willing to respond to such queries, as well as answer questions that you pose directly to them. Take advantage of these opportunities to fill in the gaps in your knowledge.

Selectivity and Your College List

A wise student distributes his or her college choices among three categories based on the likelihood of admission. The first category, which we will call *good-bet* colleges, includes those where you are almost certain to be admitted. The next category, which we will call *possible* colleges, involves chances that can range from "pretty likely" to "fifty-fifty" to "not too likely." It is the broadest of the categories. The final category, which we call *long-shot* colleges, includes those where the college's acceptance rate in conjunction with your own record makes admission unlikely but not impossible. These three categories correspond to terminology with which you may be more familiar: safety, target, and reach colleges. We feel that our terms—good bet, possible, and long shot—more accurately capture the current reality of college admissions.

How Long Should Your College List Be?

In general, it is a good idea to develop a college list with one to three good-bet colleges that you would be happy to attend. It is critical to spend significant time and energy selecting these colleges. Too often they are selected as an afterthought, a method that proves problematic if, at the end of the admissions process, a student must choose one of them. A good list of good-bet colleges is a wonderful cushion in what can otherwise be a very uncertain process. Two to four possible colleges and two to three long shots can round out the final list.

These guidelines lead to college lists ranging in length from five to ten. But some students apply to fewer than five colleges, and others to twelve, fifteen, or even more if they are especially eager for acceptance at possible or long-shot colleges. Shorter lists are fine as long as they include at least one or two good bets that a student would be happy to attend.

Depending on circumstances, applying to more than ten colleges may be a wise investment or a waste of time and money. Some high schools, private as well as public, limit the number of applications a student can file by restricting the number of counselor recommendations they are willing to send in for a single student. By limiting the number of recommendations it will send on a student's behalf, a high school is indirectly encouraging students to research their choices carefully and to make each one count.

> "I wish I had applied to more 'middle range' schools. I feel like I overshot on most of my schools and then didn't like the others."
>
> *High school student in spring of senior year*

> "I know girls in my class who have applied to fifteen schools. Even in my sister's year (two years ago) I don't think people applied to as many schools. With my eight or nine I still think, 'Oh, my gosh, what if I don't get in anywhere?' You want to do the reaches but you also want your maybes, then you get insecure about your maybes and think maybe you should have more backups and I think that's how people get up to fifteen."
>
> *High school senior*

In Chapter Seven, we will discuss early acceptance programs (specifically early decision and early action) that involve identifying one college as your top choice and submitting an application to that college by an early deadline in exchange for early review by that college. Under the right circumstances there can be significant advantages to submitting such an application, but it doesn't eliminate the need to develop carefully your full college list and in many cases have applications already prepared. If you are not admitted early to your first-choice college, you will have your carefully researched list of alternatives ready to go.

Determining Your Chances

How can you tell what your chances of admission are at different colleges? Here's where it helps to have the most current edition of the big book that we recommended at the beginning of this chapter. The big book provides data for each college for the most recent year available from the Common Data Set (usually two years earlier than the year listed on the book cover) showing the SAT range (or ACT range) for the middle 50 percent of freshmen, as well as the percentage of freshmen ranking in the top 10, 25, and 50 percent of their high school classes when that can be determined.

The middle 50 percent of SAT scores is a much better indicator of what the student body looks like than the average SAT score, and it helps you place your own scores in better context. The data in the big book also include the percentage of applicants accepted. If you significantly exceed the midrange of SAT scores of incoming freshmen and have a GPA that places you at the high end of the freshman class the prior year, the college can be considered a good-bet for you, if its overall acceptance rate is at least 50 percent. The higher the acceptance rate, the lower your SAT or GPA can be relative to the midrange of freshmen for the college to be considered a good bet for you.

> *"My son seemed to narrow down his list very quickly. Columbia, NYU, UCLA. Five other top schools. Just one safety would have been a good idea. I wasn't as engaged as I should have been."*
>
> *Father of son denied everywhere who is now "completely happy" at a school that wasn't on his list but should have been*

A possible college takes many forms. It can be one where your grades and GPA scores place you in the middle range of the freshman class and where the admissions rate is 50 percent or higher. Another possible college would be one where your scores significantly exceed the midrange of freshmen, but where the admissions rate is around 35 percent. The higher your scores relative to the average freshman, the lower the admissions rate can be and still have the school be a possible one for you.

Finally, long-shot colleges are ones where, given your profile, you have less than a 35 percent chance of admission. For almost all students, even

> *"A few years ago I had a student—#3 in his class—who was bringing in his applications one by one. I saved them up for a while without looking at them, then took them home over the weekend to work on them. As I filled out one after another I thought to myself, 'Oh, no, he hasn't applied to seven schools, he applied to the same school seven times.'"*
>
> *High school counselor referring to a student who did not have a range of colleges on his list*

those with terrific "stats," all colleges falling in the super-selective category with admissions rates of 20 percent or less should be considered long shots. The many factors that affect the admissions decision make it difficult to predict the outcome at such schools. Colleges in the "highly selective" category that admit 35 percent of applicants or fewer are also long shots for most students, although they can be possible colleges for those with exceptional academic records that place them well into the top quarter of the freshman class.

Some Cautions About Data

With growth in the number of high school graduates, GPA and SAT scores at selective colleges have been increasing every year. To be sure you are using current data, buy the most recent edition of the big book. As we mentioned earlier, even the newest editions of the big books may be out of date, since they contain data from two years earlier than the year on the cover. Web sites such as www.collegeboard.com also have this built-in lag.

The best sources of up-to-date numbers are the Web sites of the colleges themselves. Most colleges put the statistics for their entering class on the Web by the fall. These numbers are for students who actually enrolled that year. The previous spring, most colleges issue press releases, also found on Web sites, that give data about the students who were just offered admission. These numbers are often more impressive than the numbers for enrolled students that will appear in the fall, since many colleges accept top applicants who choose to go somewhere else. Just be sure you know what data are being presented: are they for admitted students (all of those who received offers of admission) or enrolled students (freshman who actually accepted offers of admission the previous spring)?

Scattergrams Can Help

Although big book data can be very helpful to you in assessing your chances of admission to a given college, important additional information on your chances of admission can be obtained from admissions scattergrams from your high school. A scattergram is simply a graph of the GPA and SAT (or ACT) scores of students who were accepted, denied, or wait-listed at a college over a period of time. It is an easy, visual way to determine where your own credentials fall in the context of other students at your school who have recent application experience at that college. You usually need about five data points (from five students who have applied to a college) for the scattergram to be really useful, however, so if your school has not had many students apply to a particular college recently the information will be of limited value.

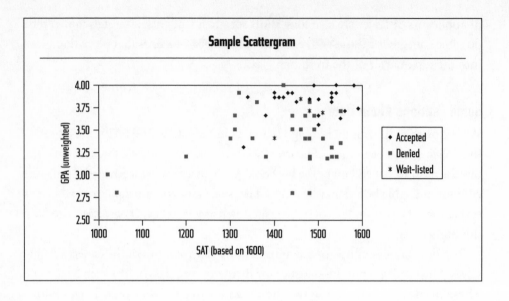

Sample Scattergram

Keep in mind, though, that your GPA and standardized test scores are only part of your application. The other factors—extracurricular activities, letters of recommendation, essays, and special talents, for example—may be critical to the outcome and help explain why a student with the lowest GPA and SAT scores in a group was accepted by a particular college while others with higher scores were not. Remember that institutional priorities play an important role in admissions decisions. The sample scattergram vividly illustrates this point. It is loosely based on real applications from students at a high-performing high school to a selective private university and shows that although admission offers tended to go to students with the highest GPA and SAT scores, that was not always the case. Clearly other factors played an important role in determining the outcome in some cases.

Some high schools do not actually transform GPA and SAT data into scattergrams but maintain them in lists that show the GPA and SAT data for each student who applied to a given college, along with the outcome. In either form, this kind of information is probably the single most important tool you can have to help you determine your chances of acceptance to a given college. It allows you to "calibrate" your own record more accurately than you could if you were using only the summary admissions data from the colleges.

	Sample College Application Outcomes List		
GPA	**SAT** **(based on 1600)**	**Early Application?**	**Outcome**
4.00	1580	❑	Accepted
4.00	1490	❑	Accepted
4.00	1420	❑	Denied
3.92	1400	☑	Accepted
3.90	1530	❑	Accepted
3.90	1390	❑	Denied
3.83	1480	❑	Accepted
3.83	1470	☑	Wait-listed
3.68	1510	❑	Wait-listed
3.70	1560	❑	Accepted
3.50	1490	❑	Denied
3.50	1310	❑	Denied
3.20	1200	❑	Denied
3.18	1520	❑	Denied
2.85	1020	❑	Denied

Private schools with good counseling departments maintain extensive data on the admissions experiences of their students from prior years. Public schools are less likely to have the resources to do this, although more and more are making it a priority. Students should ask their counselors early in their junior year whether such data are available. Even if your school does not collect these data systematically, your counselor may be able to give you information about the recent admissions experience of students from your high school who applied to specific colleges. Scattergrams and similar data provide ballpark, not definitive, information. But given the nature of college admissions, that's probably the best you can get.

Have Eight First Choices

The key to developing an appropriate list is to be sure that all of the colleges on it are ones that you could actually see yourself attending, and attending happily. It is certainly reasonable to acknowledge that you would like to attend some more than others, but the outcome of the college admissions process can be surprisingly unpredictable, and you want to be sure that you will have at least one or two choices that you are happy with in the good-bet category. In fact, Joyce Mitchell, a former admissions officer who is now a high school counselor, advises students to have eight first choices—assuming that they are submitting eight applications, of course![3] This makes good sense.

It also makes good sense, and is common courtesy all around, to apply only to colleges you would seriously consider attending. Sometimes students get caught up in a prestige game and decide to apply to colleges in which they have no real interest just to see whether they will be admitted. This phenomenon is so common, in fact, that counselors have a name for it: trophy hunting. Parents sometimes directly or indirectly contribute to trophy hunting. Though seemingly harmless except for the waste of time and money, trophy hunting may hurt the chances of other students at your high school.

> "We went to Harvard. I didn't want to apply. I thought, 'Harvard's going to be stuck up and it's not going to be very nice.' But Dad said, 'No, you're going to apply just to apply.'"
>
> *Student who says, "Harvard had a really nice rejection letter."*

As we discussed in Chapter Two, colleges want to accept students who will actually attend. Colleges also want to have a diverse student body, and the number of students a given college will accept from one high school may be limited. If you apply to a college knowing you would not attend and you are accepted, you may inadvertently cause the denial of another student at your school who is seriously interested in that college. And there is the possibility that future students from your school may be adversely affected if your school develops a reputation for generating applicants who never accept the college's offer of admission.

Self-Assessment and Research: The Keys to a Good College List

Developing a college list can be an exciting process for you and your family. We encourage you to begin with a careful self-assessment using the "Determining Your Priorities" questionnaire at the end of Chapter Four. Make special note of characteristics that are very important or somewhat important to you. Then use the results of your assessment to develop a list of possibilities, narrowing that list as you learn more about the schools themselves and their degree of selectivity in relation to your own record. You'll find a "College Research Worksheet" in Appendix A that will help you organize what you learn as you do your research. Make photocopies of the worksheet and use it to record key information about the colleges that you are exploring. A good college list is the result of a lot of thoughtful introspection, as well as thorough research about colleges.

A Word About Finances

At this point, we would like to introduce another factor in the equation as you consider colleges: finances. Although some students are able to cover the cost of their education from family resources, many more need financial aid to cover all or part of the cost. A great deal of financial aid is available, with the largest amounts going to those with the lowest incomes to make it possible for them to attend college. Middle-class and upper middle-class families eligible for aid are often asked to assume loans for part of their college expenses. How much is your family willing and able to contribute to your education? How much borrowing is comfortable for you and your family? Finances shouldn't dictate your college list, but they shouldn't be ignored, either.

Chapter Nine will give you some important information about financing a college education and direct you to online calculators that can give you a sense of the amount of need-based aid you may expect to receive from colleges. Colleges use complex formulas to determine financial aid in an effort to be fair and equitable. But sometimes a college will not give you and your family as much as you feel you need. Just in case financial aid does not work out as well as you had hoped, it is a good idea to include on your list a college you know you can afford and where you are very likely to be admitted.

Your goal should be to have an array of college choices so that your admissions experience will end happily regardless of the admission or financial aid decision that is made by any given college.

The Big Tests

If you are interested in applying to one or more of the hundred most selective liberal arts colleges and research universities in the United States, you already know—or soon will find out—that most require applicants to submit scores from one or more standardized tests. You probably also know that these tests—what they actually measure and what role they play in your getting accepted to college—are at the heart of the most anxiety-provoking part of the college admissions process.

In this chapter we will help you understand what the SAT, the best known and most controversial of these tests, is all about and why there is so much controversy surrounding it. We'll talk about how the SAT has changed, and continues to change, over time and how selective colleges weight SAT scores in the admissions process. We'll discuss how you can prepare for the test. Understanding all of this will help you put

> "The SAT has become a symbol of all the anxieties, concerns, fears, and frustrations in the college admissions system." [1]
>
> **Lee Bollinger, president of Columbia University**

the SAT in perspective and approach it more confidently. This chapter will also consider the ACT Assessment, ACT for short, which is an alternative test widely accepted in place of the SAT. The ACT is best known in the midwest and south, although its popularity is growing in other parts of the country.

Where Did the SAT Come From?

Your parents may remember when the SAT was called the Scholastic Aptitude Test. First developed in the mid-1920s as an adaptation of the Army Alpha test used to assign duties to recruits during World War I, the Scholastic Aptitude Test became widely used as an important tool in college admissions after World War II. Colleges facing unprecedented numbers of applications from returning veterans needed an efficient way to evaluate them. The idea of testing "aptitude" for college as part of the admissions process became popular as the number of applications soared.

> " On the one hand, [standardized tests] are portrayed as an evil that should be purged from our society; on the other, they're viewed as a trustworthy measure of the academic standing of students, schools, and communities — perhaps even the quality of American education." [2]
>
> *Rebecca Zwick, professor of education at the University of California, Santa Barbara and former Educational Testing Service researcher*

Over half a century later, a version of the Scholastic Aptitude Test is still widely used in the admissions process at most selective institutions, although with considerably more caution. The Scholastic Aptitude Test, originally designed to measure just what its name suggested, morphed into the SAT I: Reasoning Test (with the new name deliberately not an acronym for anything). We'll refer to this test as the SAT for short. The name change took place in 1995, the same year that the College Board "recentered" scores on the test so that the average score on each of the two parts would once again be 500. According to the College Board, the nonprofit organization that owns the SAT, the renamed test measured "verbal and mathematical skills that you develop over time through the work that you do in school and on your own." In 2005, as we will discuss shortly, the test was revised and renamed once again.

Concerns About the SAT

The SAT has been challenged as culturally biased and unreliable in predicting success in college. Critics point to the substantial disparities in average scores of African Americans and Hispanics compared to white or Asian students, as well as strong correlations between socioeconomic status and performance on the SAT. Critics also cite data showing that high school GPA is a better predictor of first-year college grades than the SAT.

For those who appreciate history, it is more than a little ironic that the arguments *against* the SAT are basically the same ones offered *for* the SAT by those who promoted its use after World War II. Educators at that time knew that economically disadvantaged students rarely had access to classes and instruction of the caliber offered at prep schools. Thus, they argued, these students would be at a disadvantage on subject matter tests that had traditionally been part of the college admissions process. Tests of reasoning ability like the Scholastic Aptitude Test, however, would presumably not be closely tied to high school experience, thus allowing good students to shine regardless of their educational background. Additional support for using the SAT came from statistical studies at that time showing "that general verbal and mathematical ability tests predicted college grades better than did achievement tests in particular subjects."[4] Recent research now shows the opposite.

> "Aptitude tests like the SAT have a historical tie to the concept of innate mental abilities — that such abilities can be defined and that it is possible to measure them. Neither notion has been supported by modern research."[3]
>
> Richard C. Atkinson, former president of the University of California system

Fifty years later, in 2001, the president of the University of California proposed that the prestigious multicampus public university system abandon the SAT as a requirement for admission altogether. Richard C. Atkinson, himself a distinguished psychologist, called instead for the University of California to focus on subject matter tests, including the one-hour exams that the College Board offers in different subjects such as U.S. history, mathematics, foreign languages, and physics. First called the Scholastic Achievement Tests, and then the SAT II Subject Tests, these are now known simply as the SAT Subject Tests. Atkinson argued that students (and often their high schools) were spending too much time and energy on preparing for the SAT, a test whose usefulness remained in serious question. Although scores on the SAT did predict first-year college grades to some degree, SAT Subject Test scores were an even better predictor. And since the SAT was not directly related to the curriculum, Atkinson noted, preparation for it came at the expense of learning what students were in school to learn in the first place.

The New SAT

In response to these concerns as well as the potential financial consequences of losing the tens of thousands of SAT test-takers who apply to the University of California each year, in 2001 the College Board announced a major revamping of the SAT that took effect in March 2005. The changes include new types of questions, elimination of some existing question types, and an entirely new section on writing. The old SAT was divided into two parts, verbal and math, each of which was scored from 200 to 800. The test is now known as the new SAT and has three parts.

The verbal section has been renamed "critical reading" and the word analogies that were part of the old SAT verbal section were dropped as a result of criticism that they were unrelated to anything ever taught in the high school curriculum. Replacing the analogies are short reading passages that are included along with the longer reading passages that were already part of the test. The math section has been expanded to cover additional math concepts; the questions now assume that a student has studied Algebra II and Geometry in addition to Algebra I. The newest section, writing, requires students to write a short essay in response to a prompt as well as to answer multiple-choice grammar questions. The prompt consists of either a pair of quotations or a short paragraph from a real text. The writing assignment focuses the student on the issues addressed in the quotations or paragraph. Since each of the three sections on the new SAT is scored from 200 to 800, the test has a maximum possible score of 2400 instead of the familiar 1600. The new SAT is about three hours and forty-five minutes of actual test time, about forty-five minutes longer than the old version.

These changes, the College Board has argued, more closely align the new SAT with the high school curriculum and allow students to demonstrate what they have learned to a greater extent than did the earlier version of the test. But not everyone is happy with the changes. The new writing section is of particular concern to nonnative speakers of English, who believe that it puts them at a disadvantage. In addition, even those who support a test of writing skill question the predictive validity of an essay written from start to finish in twenty-five minutes and graded in two minutes (or less).

The essays are handwritten but later scanned into a computer and scored on a scale from 1 to 6 by two independent readers who read them off a monitor. Essays that do not respond to the prompt (that is, essays that don't answer the question) will receive a score of zero, no matter how well written they are. The scores from the two readers assigned to a student's essay are added together to obtain the student's essay score ranging from 2 to 12. If the ratings of the two readers differ by more than one point, the essay goes to a third reader. The essay score is combined with the score on the multiple choice portion of the writing test to produce a scaled score between 200 and 800. Colleges will receive the actual essay itself along with the regular score report.

Is the SAT Coachable?

For most of its existence as the Scholastic Aptitude Test, the test was promoted as a test of a student's ability to think and reason critically that could not be coached. Students registering for the Scholastic Aptitude Test received a booklet describing the test along with some sample questions, but no more. Test questions were guarded jealously, both before and after a test. Until 1957, in fact, students did not even receive their scores directly. Results went first to high school counselors who then used the information to "guide" students in the direction of appropriate colleges.

But not everyone believed that the Scholastic Aptitude Test was not coachable. While still a high school student in Brooklyn in the 1940s, a young man named Stanley H. Kaplan began tutoring friends to prepare them for the test. Word of his effectiveness spread, and he eventually built a thriving business in the 1960s and 1970s doing what the College Board still insisted wasn't possible. Years later he sold that business to the *Washington Post–Newsweek* group for $50 million. It still operates under Kaplan's name.

A turning point came in 1987 when New York State passed a Truth-in-Testing law that required the College Board to make available old exam questions with answers. Up to that time, coaching businesses like Kaplan's relied on exams that mimicked the Scholastic Aptitude Test. With the new law, they gained access to the real thing. Soon after, the College Board itself began to refer to the test as "teachable" and to sell test preparation materials.

How Much Does the SAT Count?

"OK," you say. "That little bit of history is interesting, but what does all this mean for me? Just how important is the SAT and how should I approach it?" We quoted David Erdman, admissions dean at Rollins College, in Chapter Two as saying, "At most institutions, standardized test scores count less than students think and more than colleges are willing to admit." This is a pretty accurate summary of the current state of affairs, which continues even with the introduction of the new SAT.

At many selective colleges, SAT scores count significantly in the evaluation of a student's academic strengths but less than GPA, class rank (if available), and the rigor of the student's coursework. Admissions officers also know that many factors affect how well a student will do on the SAT, and they try to take these factors into account. They are most interested in your achievements relative to the opportunities you have had. Parental education and income correlate positively with a child's scores on the SAT (more education and higher income are associated with higher scores), so admissions officers expect to see higher scores from the prep school–educated son of two professional parents than from the inner city educated son of working class, immigrant parents.

In general, the more selective a college, the higher the scores of students falling in the middle 50 percent of the freshman class. College A, for example, may report that the middle 50 percent of its freshman class had SAT math scores ranging from 550 to 650. This means that 25 percent of freshmen had math SAT scores below 550, 25 percent had a score of 660 or above, and the remaining 50 percent had scores in between. College B may report that the middle 50 percent of its freshman class had SAT math scores of 660 to 760. Comparing the two sets of numbers, we can see that 75 percent of the freshmen at College B had a math score of 660 or above (all of those in the middle 50 percent plus those in the top 25 percent), while only 25 percent of the students at College A achieved that score or higher. A score of 550, placing you right at the 25th percentile for College A, would place you at a much lower percentile at College B.

What Does the SAT Midrange Mean?

College A—Math Midrange of 550 to 650

25% of students scored less than 550	50% of students scored 550 to 650	25% of students scored 660 or more

College B—Math Midrange of 660 to 760

25% of students scored less than 660	50% of students scored 660 to 760	25% of students scored 770 or more

Of course, many factors other than SAT scores play a role in admission to the most selective colleges, so scores are just one part of your total profile. Scores in the bottom 25 percent of a school's freshman class will not by themselves disqualify you. By definition, 25 percent of the students in the class have scores that fell at or below the twenty-fifth percentile and they obviously were admitted. But realistically, lower scores will not help your case. Many of the students in the lower quartile probably had a special admissions hook that offset their scores.

High scores, of course, can help an application. How high is high depends on the college and its SAT distribution. Using the example above, a score of 660 on the math portion of the SAT would be considered relatively high at College A, but relatively low for College B. In general, scores falling in the top 25 percent of the range at a college can reasonably be considered high for that college.

As an applicant to a selective college that requires or recommends the SAT, you have no way of knowing how much of a role your SAT score will play in the college's decision. The smart approach, then, is the obvious one: try to obtain the highest score you can with *reasonable* preparation.

How Does the PSAT/NMSQT Fit into the Picture?

Each October, the College Board offers an abbreviated version of the SAT called the PSAT/NMSQT. Though rarely spelled out, this mouthful stands for Preliminary SAT/National Merit Scholarship Qualifying Test. The PSAT/NMSQT is basically a shorter version of the SAT with three parts: verbal, math, and writing. The writing section consists of multiple choice grammar questions, but no actual writing is required. Scored on a scale of 20 to 80 for each section, the test has a maximum score of 240. The College Board reports that the results of the PSAT correlate highly with what a student's SAT score would be if the student took the SAT at that time. The rationale behind the PSAT is to give students an idea of their potential strengths and weaknesses on the SAT early in their junior year so that they can prepare appropriately for the real thing. The PSAT has been revised to reflect the changes in the new SAT. No essay is included, but the other questions are based on the same subject matter and have the same format as the new SAT. Students register for the PSAT through their school rather than through the College Board directly. The test takes place in mid-October, and students receive their scores, along with their test booklet and an analysis of their correct and incorrect answers, in mid-December.

The PSAT serves as the screening test for the National Merit Scholarship Program, a large scale, nonprofit scholarship and recognition program. (The test is also used to identify students for the National Achievement Scholarship program and the National Hispanic Recognition program for African American and Hispanic students, respectively.) Each spring, the National Merit Scholarship Corporation contacts the 50,000 high school juniors who score in the top 2 percent of those taking the PSAT nationwide the preceding October, and invites them to identify two colleges they would like the National Merit Corporation to notify of their honor. The cutoff score for notification is usually around 200 out of 240 and is the same for all states in a given year.

In September of their senior year, about 16,000 of the 50,000 students notified the previous spring are informed that they have been selected as National Merit Scholarship semifinalists. Eligibility for semifinalist status varies from year to year and is determined on a state-by-state basis, with the cutoff score based on the top 1 percent of scores in each state. For 2004–05, the cutoff score ranged from a low of 203 in Wyoming and Mississippi to a high of 222 in Massachusetts, the District of Columbia, and Maryland. It was 216 in California and Texas and 218 in New York. The cutoff figures for different states may vary slightly from year to year and are not widely publicized. However, you can call the National Merit Scholarship Corporation's offices at (847) 866-5100 to get the most recent cutoff score for your state if you are curious. The remaining 34,000 students who are not named semifinalists are referred to as "commended students" by the National Merit program.

Semifinalists are invited to submit an essay, transcript, SAT scores, and a school recommendation to be considered for finalist status. About 90 percent of semifinalists become finalists, and about half of those subsequently receive some monetary award either directly from the National Merit Corporation itself or from colleges eager to have National Merit Finalists enroll at their college. A National Merit Finalist who receives a scholarship through the program, either directly from the National Merit Corporation or from a participating college, is known as a National Merit Scholar. Too many students are named finalists for such an honor to carry much weight at the most selective colleges, however, and many very selective colleges don't award any money of their own through the National Merit Scholarship Program. Additional details about the program can be found at www.nationalmerit.org.

For many years the National Merit Corporation administered its own selection test independent of the PSAT. Now that the PSAT serves as the screening test for the National Merit program, some high schools no longer see the PSAT as the practice test for juniors that it was originally intended to be. Private schools and high-performing public high schools usually offer the PSAT to sophomores and occasionally even to freshmen. The idea is to give them practice on the practice test they will take as juniors.

When Should You Take the New SAT?

The new SAT is offered seven times during the school year: October, November, December, January, March, May, and June. It is generally a good idea for a student to take the SAT for the first time in the second half of the junior year; January, March, and May are good dates. The whole registration process can be done very efficiently online at www.collegeboard.com by using a credit card. The test is offered at many sites, but the sites available depend on when you plan to take the test. Information is available online on the College Board Web site and in the printed registration booklet. Some test sites fill up quickly, so it is a good idea to plan ahead and register early to get the site of your choice. If you wait too long, you may have to take the test at a less convenient location.

Scores are mailed about three weeks after the test date, or are available by phone or online two weeks after the test. Online scores are available free; a fee is charged for scores by phone. The same Web site where you register for the test will have your scores—password protected, of course. You can also register, either before or after the test, to receive a copy of an answer grid showing your pattern of correct and incorrect answers as a function of question type and difficulty level. For some test dates, but not all, you can even get a copy of the actual test you took. The latter can be especially helpful to students who want to study before repeating the test.

How Many Times Should You Take the Test?

Once you get your first set of SAT scores, you can decide whether you want to retake the test later in the spring of your junior year or in the fall of your senior year. The College Board keeps track of your scores and reports them to colleges you specify. All of your scores are reported, including any you have taken from ninth

"I definitely wanted to do well on the SAT, but my parents were totally supportive of me and told me that they would be proud of whatever score I got, so I wasn't too scared. What I know now is—having gotten a good score but wishing I got a great score—I wish I had studied my behind off. I bet I could have gotten an amazingly outstanding score if I had pushed myself that much harder. I improved my math and verbal scores by taking it a second time; my overall score went up 90 points, so I wonder . . . if I had taken it a third time, especially with studying, how would I have done?

On the other hand, taking the test was not a defining moment in my life. I'm at the college where I wanted to be, so the test didn't hurt me or change my plans for the worse or anything, so it was a pretty unremarkable event. But I still want to go back and take it again, to kill my old score and get a better one. Maybe that darn number just stays with you."

College sophomore

grade on—you can't request that some scores be omitted. But most selective colleges, particularly private ones, will typically "count" only the highest critical reading, math, and writing scores you have ever received, regardless of whether they come from the same test date or not. There are some exceptions, however. All campuses of the University of California, for example, currently use the highest total score from a single test date.

You can take the new SAT as many times as you want, but three times is a reasonable practical maximum, and most students take the test just once or twice. Taking it more than three times can make a student look a bit desperate. And at about $40 a test, the cost can add up. You can take practice tests as many times as you want on your own, of course. The College Board publishes a book, *The Official SAT Study Guide for the New SAT*, which contains eight practice tests and is ideal for this purpose. It costs about $20. Just try to limit your official testing to a maximum of two or three times, unless there are special circumstances.

Obviously, the idea of repeating the SAT is to do better—we don't know of anyone who has ever claimed to do it for fun. How can you maximize your chances of doing well on the SAT, regardless of how many times you take it? The fact is that for most students, preparation will help. And for some, it will help a lot.

Does Test Preparation Help?

Test developers know that a person's score on a given test is based on three factors. The first factor is how much the person knows about the subject matter being tested. If a question requires a certain kind of calculation, you are unlikely to get it right if you don't know how to do it. The second factor deals with test taking skills—how comfortable you are taking such tests in general and how familiar you are with the construction of the test. And finally, and most disconcerting, each test score has a random component—the luck of the draw—on the day of the test. No exam can exhaustively test your knowledge. It can only sample it at a certain point in time. The questions on a given test may or may not be representative of your knowledge more broadly. And you might not be feeling your best that day.

If you look at a SAT score report, it shows a score for each part, as well as a "score range." A math score of 650, for example, has a score range from 620 to 680. By reporting a score range, the College Board is making it clear that if you took different editions of the test within a short period of time, your performance would be likely to vary a bit but fall within a 60 point spread. This variation would be expected independent of any attempts to improve your score through studying or familiarizing yourself with the format of the test. Colleges ignore the score range and count the score itself, just as students do.

What Goes into Preparing for the Test?

Preparation for the SAT usually focuses on both subject matter and test-taking skills. The shorter the prep program, the greater its emphasis on test-taking skills, since subject matter preparation generally takes longer. Both approaches can be helpful, however. If you don't have a rich vocabulary, for example, it can be hard to answer questions that require you to know the meaning of unfamiliar words. Building a vocabulary is an important part of SAT preparation, although there are far too many words in the English language to learn them all. Preparation programs put their efforts into ensuring that students master the words that most commonly appear on the tests. They also teach something about the Latin and Greek roots from which many words are derived.

Similarly, knowing simple mathematical formulas may be critical to solving some of the math problems. SAT preparation courses focus on the basic math concepts that test takers are assumed to have mastered, which can be especially helpful for students who have not had recent experience with them. With the introduction of the new writing section, practice on writing and grammar is also included.

But for many good students with strong verbal, math, and writing skills, the most valuable part of SAT preparation deals with test-taking skills. Practicing tests under timed conditions can be important, as is learning how to approach various questions. Although obviously differing in detail, questions tend to fall into predictable categories, and test prep teaches ways to approach efficiently different kinds of questions. As an extreme example, reading comprehension questions on the SAT can sometimes be answered correctly without reference to the paragraph on which the questions are based simply by analyzing the answer choices. In addition, the people who develop SAT questions also know the kinds of answers that careless mistakes produce—and you can be sure those are going to be among the multiple choice options. Helping students identify the kinds of repeated, careless errors they tend to make can raise scores significantly just by itself.

What Kind of Test Preparation Works Best?

Test preparation comes in many forms. Successful preparation can be done with a $20 book or software program (Kaplan and Princeton Review, the two largest companies offering classroom-based SAT preparation, both publish books they claim contain much of the same material covered in their courses) or a $900 course meeting twelve times for three hours each, all the way to individual one-on-one tutors, a few of whom charge well over $300 per hour for their services. Still other options include online courses for those wanting the structure of a course but greater flexibility in timing. At elite private schools and high-performing public schools on the east coast, almost all students do significant test preparation, often with private tutors. Many of those schools also arrange for a test prep company to offer a course right on campus.

Companies offering prep courses sometimes guarantee that a student's score will increase by a certain number of points. But note that only rarely do they offer a refund. A student who does not improve by the guaranteed amount simply gets a chance to take the test prep course again for free—not exactly what anyone is really eager to do.

Which approach is most effective? The fact is that no one knows for sure. The kind of large-scale, carefully controlled research that would be needed to evaluate the effectiveness of different preparation approaches compared to each other and to no preparation at all hasn't been done. There are a few studies, but the conclusions that can be drawn from them are very limited. The fact that test takers can learn to select correct answers to reading comprehension questions without even reading the material on which the questions are based shows, just by itself, that test preparation can help increase scores. And common sense suggests that as long as the content being taught is similar, the particular method of preparation shouldn't matter as long as the student is willing to commit the time and effort needed to slog through the program and do the practice exams that appear to be critical to success in improving scores.

> "Several years ago my son went up 240 points from January to March (with expensive one-on-one tutoring and doing lots of practice tests that he then reviewed with the tutor)."
>
> "1240 beginning of junior year; 1410 in April, 1500 in May. Test prep works! Just don't pay money for a tutor. Just use the book with practice exams and you'll be fine!"
>
> *Different perspectives on test preparation posted on an Internet discussion board in 2003*

This is where you need once again to do some honest self-assessment. If you have the self-discipline and motivation to work from a book or software program consistently and diligently in a timely manner, you can save yourself and your parents literally hundreds of dollars and get results similar to those you would have obtained from an in-person course or tutor. But the key is applying yourself. The course or tutor has the advantage of providing structure for you and, in the case of the tutor, personalized structure and instruction.

What Kind of Results Can *You* Expect?

How much of an improvement can you expect? An informal survey of a sample of college-bound seniors at our local high school in 2003 showed that over 60 percent took a formal SAT prep class or committed significant time to using a book or CD on their own. Self-reported improvement ranged from 0 to almost 300 points total, with the average gain being about 80 points. No one method emerged as obviously superior. One student improved his scores by 120 points by doing extensive preparation solely from a book and achieved an almost perfect score of 1590 out of the then maximum 1600.

The few formal studies that have been done on the effects of test preparation usually report modest increases of 30 to 40 points, while the test prep companies have claimed increases of upward of 100 points out of 1600.

"I was on this incredible emotional teeter totter about the SAT. On one hand, I wanted to do well. On the other, I felt that my SAT score does not make or break who I am. It was a strenuous time because I tried to have a balance of a good social and academic life. Should I go watch a movie with my friends and have fun, or stay at home and study for the SAT two more hours? Most of the time I chose the academic path. However, I do remember being at a school dance (I had to work at the dance since I was in student government) the night before the SAT. I was sitting in the coat room with a fat SAT book and my friends kept coming up to me saying, "You're studying at a dance? Oh, come on!" Needless to say, they convinced me to put the book down and I never regretted it. It's simple: if you don't know the material already, you're not going to learn it in a few hours, so there's no use cramming. It was for this same reason that my band teacher never let us play the day of a concert. If you don't know it by now, you're not going to."

College junior

But all of these reports, including the informal survey just cited, are based on averages, and averages don't tell you anything about how *you* will do. Your scores may go up very little (or even decline a bit, because of the random error that is inherent in any test), or they may go up a lot (but this won't happen if your scores were already very high, since there isn't much room for them to go up!). It just can't be predicted. As a result, we believe the best approach is to prepare in a reasonable way that doesn't disrupt your ability to do well in school and to be involved in your extracurricular activities. Preparation is *not* reasonable if it takes over your life.

Considering the ACT

The ACT is another standardized college admissions exam that is well known in the midwest and south. Unlike the SAT, which began as the work of a Princeton psychologist in the mid-1920s, the American College Testing Program began in 1959 through the efforts of a University of Iowa statistician who had worked on a statewide testing program for Iowa high school students. The ACT began with a different philosophy—it was closely tied to specific instructional goals, while the SAT was more abstract and contained only verbal and mathematical sections. Virtually all colleges in the United States that require a student to take a standardized admission test will now accept scores on either the SAT or the ACT, although historically the SAT has been the most widely used test on the east and west coasts and at

New SAT–ACT Score Comparisons

SAT Score Critical Reading + Math	ACT Composite Score
1600	36
1560–1590	35
1510–1550	34
1460–1500	33
1410–1450	32
1360–1400	31
1320–1350	30
1280–1310	29
1240–1270	28
1210–1230	27
1170–1200	26
1130–1160	25
1090–1120	24
1060–1080	23
1020–1050	22
980–1010	21
940–970	20
900–930	19
860–890	18
810–850	17
760–800	16
710–750	15
660–700	14
590–650	13
520–580	12
500–510	11

According to the College Board, scores on the critical reading section of the new SAT are comparable to scores on the former verbal section, and scores on the math section of the new SAT are comparable to scores on the former math section. The previous SAT–ACT comparison table, shown here, is still appropriate for the new SAT.

selective colleges everywhere. It is to your advantage to know how the ACT differs from the SAT so you can determine whether it makes more sense to take one or the other, or maybe even both. High school sophomores can take a preliminary version of the ACT known as PLAN.

The ACT has traditionally been known as more content-oriented than the SAT. The questions on the ACT are tied more to what a student has learned in school in grades 7 through 12 than to critical thinking and problem solving in general. The ACT focuses on four areas—English, math, reading, and science reasoning.

The test consists of four sections corresponding to these four areas. Actual testing time is about three hours (with breaks the test takes about three and a half hours) and all questions are multiple choice. Results are reported as a composite score as well as scores on each of the four sections, with each part, as well as the composite, scored on a scale from 1 to 36. The national average composite score is around 21, just as the average SAT score (old version) is about 1000 (500 on each of the two main sections).

Most students who have taken both tests feel that the ACT is more straightforward and less tricky than the SAT. Another important difference is that students can decide which ACT test sitting to submit. If a student takes the test three times, for example, he or she can submit the highest score from a single sitting. The College Board, in contrast, automatically reports all SAT scores ever received by a student from ninth grade on. As we noted earlier in this chapter, most colleges that use the SAT will actually count just the highest subtests, regardless of whether they were obtained in the same sitting or different sittings.

In spring 2005, the ACT began offering an optional essay similar to that in the new SAT. Each college is free to decide whether to require it of ACT test takers. The essay adds an additional thirty minutes of testing time.

Which Test Should You Take?

In general, there is a high correlation between performance on the SAT and ACT. Although most students perform at similar percentile levels on both tests, sometimes a student does significantly better on one of them.

Some students choose to take the ACT fairly early in the junior year to see how they do compared to their scores on the SAT that they will take in the spring. This

Standardized Tests at a Glance

	New SAT	ACT
Sections	Math	Math
	Critical Reading	Reading
	Writing (includes essay)	English
		Science Reasoning
		Optional Essay
Scoring	Each section 200–800	Each section 1–36
	Maximum total 2400	Maximum Composite 36
	Essay scored 2–12	Optional essay scored 2–12
Test Length	Approximately 3 hours and 45 minutes including essays	Approximately 3 hours without essay; 3 hours and 45 minutes including essay
Essay Details	Required part of test	Optional part of test
	Essay written at the start	Essay written at the end of test
	25 minutes total	30 minutes total
Format	Multiple choice and completion (for some math questions only)	Multiple choice only
Question Order	Questions presented in order of difficulty within each section	Questions randomly ordered within each question
Scoring Basis	Random guessing penalized	No penalty for random guessing
Online Information Test Registration	www.collegeboard.com	www.act.org

gives them the option of concentrating on the test that is likely to yield the highest percentile score for them (if indeed there is much of a difference at all). Some students choose to submit scores from both tests. At the University of Pennsylvania, for example, about 50 percent of the applicants for the class of 2008 submitted the ACT in addition to the SAT. At Yale University, the percentage was about 15 percent. Students usually submit results from both tests when their ACT places them at a higher percentile than their SAT. Submitting *just* the ACT to a college where a majority of students submit the SAT, however, especially if you live in a part of the country where the ACT is not common, may cause admissions officers to wonder what happened on the SAT. Yale University's Dean of Admissions and Financial Aid Richard Shaw has said that if an applicant "is in a primarily SAT state and only submits the ACT, it would make me pause."[5]

Students living on the east or west coast who want to explore the ACT option may have to seek out the information themselves, since the ACT is still not widely used in those regions of the country. Some counselors, particularly at public high schools, may know little about it. Students in the midwest and south will almost always have ready access to counselors fully knowledgeable about the test. But complete information about the test, as well as online registration, is readily available to everyone on the ACT Web site, www.act.org, and test prep books and online courses are available nationwide. The test is administered six times a year, and students can register online using a credit card just as they can for the SAT.

The Special Case of Special Accommodations

The organizations that administer the SAT and ACT know that some students require special accommodations to overcome challenges that would otherwise negatively affect their performance. Blind or visually impaired students are the most obvious example, but also included are students with other kinds of physical impairments that make it difficult or impossible to complete the test in the standard way. With appropriate documentation submitted in advance by the student's school, special arrangements can be made to address the student's needs.

Physical impairments represent just a small percentage of cases requiring such accommodations, however. Most special accommodation requests are for extra time to compensate for learning disabilities that would otherwise make it difficult for a student to perform up to his or her ability. Here, too, documentation of the learning disability satisfactory to the testing agency must be submitted in advance of the test. Accommodations can range from time and a half (the most common) to untimed testing, depending on the severity of the learning disability. Just as an exam in larger typeface may be provided to a student with visual problems, extra time accommodations for learning disabilities are an attempt to level the playing field for otherwise able students.

Traditionally, the College Board noted the use of special accommodations right on the student's score report. "Score flagging," as it was called, was dropped in 2002 in response to a federal lawsuit filed by a disabled test taker seeking to have the flag removed from another standardized test. At the same time it dropped flagging, however, the College Board began requiring more detailed evidence of a disability before an accommodation was granted to ensure that only those with documented disabilities would receive extra time. For years, there had been concerns about possible abuse of the system because requests for extra time were coming disproportionately from public and private high schools in wealthy areas, in some cases with questionable documentation.

If your child has a disability that would require special accommodations on the SAT or ACT, you should contact his or her guidance counselor as early in the student's high school career as possible to begin the process of documenting the disability following the new guidelines. The actions of a small percentage of families to manipulate the college admissions process to their advantage have made it more difficult for those who truly need accommodations. Planning ahead is crucial in dealing with the more stringent documentation requirements now in effect.

The SAT Subject Tests

As we noted earlier in this chapter, the College Board offers one-hour subject matter tests in addition to the SAT in subjects ranging from biology to Hebrew. Like each of the three parts of the new SAT, the SAT Subject Tests are scored from 200 to 800. About 150 colleges require or recommend that students submit scores from one or more of these tests, including almost all colleges that are selective by our criterion. Some of these allow students to submit ACT scores in lieu of both the SAT and the SAT Subject Tests in recognition of the content-based nature of the ACT. Most colleges requiring the SAT Subject Tests have traditionally asked students to submit scores from three tests.

With the arrival of the new SAT in 2005, the College Board eliminated the SAT Writing Test, since it overlapped with the new SAT itself. Some colleges have subsequently modified their SAT Subject Test requirements, giving students more flexibility in the tests they submit or asking for fewer of them to be submitted in the first place, or both. The University of California, for example, no longer requires a total of three SAT Subject Tests, including writing and mathematics. Students must now submit scores from just two exams, both of the students' own choosing.

In contrast to its position on SAT coaching, the College Board has always encouraged preparation for the SAT Subject Tests. As content-based tests, they are designed to measure a student's mastery of a specific subject. Studying and reviewing can result in big improvements. The major test preparation companies offer courses to prepare students for some of the SAT Subject Tests and, of course, private tutors are eager to help. Many test prep books and software programs are also available. The latter two can work just as well as more expensive alternatives, if a student is willing to put in the time and effort to use them.

On any given test date, students are allowed to take the SAT by itself or up to three SAT Subject Tests. You don't even have to specify in advance which test or tests you are going to take. The new SAT is offered on all test administration dates, but SAT Subject Tests are not offered on the March date, and some specific tests are offered on certain dates only. It pays to check the College Board Web site at www.collegeboard.com to find out for sure. You can't take both kinds of tests on the same day.

Students should choose their SAT Subject Tests carefully and plan to take appropriate tests when subjects are freshest in their minds. Most students take the SAT Subject Tests at the end of their junior year. However, depending on which ones you plan to take, you may want to take one or more a year earlier if you have the right preparation. For example, if you take chemistry as a sophomore and feel you have mastered the subject, it makes sense to take the SAT Chemistry test at the end of your sophomore year rather than wait until you are a junior. Colleges will typically "count" your highest scores, although the College Board will report all of your scores for the SAT and SAT Subject Tests when it sends your score reports. You can get a booklet about the SAT Subject Tests from your guidance office; the same information is posted on the College Board Web site. Read it carefully and decide which tests make the most sense for you, keeping in mind the requirements of specific colleges in which you have an interest.

As a final note, it is certainly possible to take three SAT Subject Tests on the same day, but it can be a tough morning. You may be able to spread out your testing if you plan far enough in advance.

A Special Word to Parents About Standardized Tests

There is a lot of anxiety about the SAT and ACT. High school students sometimes feel that their future and their self-esteem depend on the outcome of one, four-hour test taken on a Saturday morning. This is not healthy for them, nor is it true. Please help your children understand that the SAT and ACT are just tests, and flawed ones at that. Encourage them to prepare thoroughly for the tests in a reasonable way and to do their best, but try to keep standardized tests from becoming an obsession for you or them.

Some students dread getting their scores for fear of disappointing their parents or, at the other end of the continuum, providing their parents with a reason to brag or embarrass them. Avoid both extremes. We hope that reading the history of the SAT at the beginning of this chapter has helped you gain the perspective you need to be the supportive parent your child needs and that you want to be. The history of the ACT is less colorful, but the same caveats apply.

A Postscript on the Future of the SAT

Even after the major revamping of the SAT that went into effect in the spring of 2005, more changes are likely. The fact that test preparation—some of it geared solely to test-taking tricks—can be very effective in some cases argues strongly that the SAT may rapidly be losing whatever value it had as a predictive tool in college admissions. Add in concerns about cultural bias inherent in the test itself, and it is not too difficult to see that the SAT's lifespan in its current form will probably be limited.

The College Board, in fact, is actively funding research to develop new kinds of tests that will assist in the college admissions process. They don't intend for the new tests to replace the SAT but rather serve as a supplement to them. Robert Sternberg, a cognitive psychologist at Yale University, notes that the SAT tests well for memory and analytical skills but that important creative and practical skills go unmeasured. Sternberg is conducting research he calls the Rainbow Project that is aimed at assessing those additional skills.[6] In work supported by the College Board, Sternberg and his colleagues are measuring creative intelligence by asking students

The SAT

If someone had told me when my children were applying to college that "the SAT exam is a teaching tool" I would have said, "What are you talking about? It's a big, nasty test that favors some kids over others, and I don't like it."

I might still say that, but it turns out that both things are true: it *is* a big test, but students do learn from it.

When I interviewed young people about the SAT, most mentioned stress, and many expressed disappointment in themselves for not studying more. But they also learned things, not just multi-syllabic vocabulary words, but how privilege works and what they value in themselves and others.

One said, "Students who come from affluent families have free time and the resources to take test prep courses. Other students might work or care for siblings. In my opinion, there is more truth in personal statements and recommendations than on any answer sheet or test booklet."

Another commented, "A test prep class improved my scores, but I didn't become more intelligent. I just learned how to capitalize on some key test-taking concepts."

"I didn't feel the SAT measured intelligence but rather one's ability to take a test," wrote one student. "Overall, I think the SAT is more about being able to manage time and stress than about being smart."

An alumnus said, "After I went to college and witnessed various learning styles, standardized tests began to lose legitimacy in my eyes. I saw people who were very intelligent but didn't test well and people who seemed ordinary but tested like superstars."

In the long term, even students who were upset by the testing experience regained their equilibrium, not by denying the importance of the SAT, but by reaching real wisdom about the testing process, especially its inequities.

It made me proud and happy to learn that students can separate test results from their own value as a person.

My fondest wish for them is that they can do the same for the whole college admissions experience.

M. F.

---

to write cartoon captions and to think up a short story based on a picture collage. Practical intelligence is being measured with problem-solving vignettes, such as "You've been assigned to work on a project for a day with a fellow employee whom you really dislike. He is rude, lazy, and rarely does a proper job. What would be the best thing for you to do?" Long-term studies are under way to see whether performance on these experimental tests correlates with success in college and later life. If it does, the tests may be useful in developing additions to the SAT some time in the future.

For now, the SAT (or the ACT) is a very real part of college admissions at most—but not all—selective colleges. Slowly, over time, an increasing number of colleges are eliminating the SAT or making it optional, leaving it up to students to decide whether or not to submit scores. The ACT is positioning itself as an alternative test with fewer problems than the SAT, but not everyone agrees with that assessment. The National Center for Fair and Open Testing (commonly known as FairTest) is very critical of standardized testing and sees little difference between the ACT and SAT. It remains to be seen how the testing wars will play out. As we noted in Chapter Two, a list of the colleges that do not require standardized tests, or that make them optional, can be found online at www.fairtest.org/optional.htm. The www.fairtest.org site gives additional background about the controversies surrounding the whole issue of standardized tests in college admissions. It makes for fascinating reading regardless of the conclusions you may ultimately draw.

> "We know the value of a test of analytic ability. But we also recognize that there are other kinds of intelligence, and that schools would want to know more about them because they are important to students' performance, and to their careers." [7]
>
> *Wayne Camara, vice president*
> *for research, College Board*

Deciding About Early Decision and Other Early Options

Although most students apply to college by January 1 of their senior year and make choices from among their options once decisions are announced the following spring, more and more are taking advantage of early acceptance programs. Early acceptance options require you to apply to a college early in the school year, typically by November 1 or November 15, in exchange for an early response from that college, usually by December 15.

The programs offered by different colleges vary in important ways. Some, known as *early decision,* commit you to attending if you are admitted. You can apply early decision to only one college since acceptance is binding. Another kind, *early action,* allows you to get the college's decision early, but lets you have until May 1 to make your final decision. Most early action programs permit you to apply early action to other colleges as well and even submit one early decision application. A third

> "There are so many early options to keep straight and choose from. I think the whole thing should be called 'early confusion.'"
>
> **Parent of a high school junior**

type, *single-choice early action,* does not commit you to attending if accepted, but it does restrict you from applying early action or early decision to any other college. If you feel you need a scorecard to keep all of this straight, you are not alone.

About 500 colleges, including virtually all those that would be considered selective by our criteria, offer at least one of these options. About thirty-five colleges
have both early action and early decision programs: Tulane University, Rice University, St. Olaf College, Earlham College, Wells College, and Hampshire College
are examples. About sixty colleges, including Smith College, Reed College, Claremont McKenna College, Bowdoin College, Vanderbilt University, Wesleyan University, and Tufts University, offer only early decision but have two different dates:
ED I with an application date around November 15, and ED II with an application date around January 1. And a few even offer three options—Dickinson College, for example, offers two early decision dates as well as an early action option.

Early acceptance programs, and early decision in particular, have been the subject of a great deal of discussion and controversy. In this chapter we will tell you
what the early debate is all about, guide you in sorting out the options, and help
you decide whether an early acceptance program is right for you.

The Pros and Cons of Early Decision

On the surface, the rationale for early decision admission programs is simple. If a
student has a clear first-choice college, the student can express that preference by
applying early and committing to attend if admitted. In exchange, an acceptance
will allow him or her to bypass much of the drawn-out anxiety lasting into the
spring that can accompany regular decision applications. If the college's answer
is "no" (a denial), or "we are not sure" (a deferral of the decision until the regular
application cycle), the student can still apply to other colleges in time to meet the
regular cycle deadline.

Some Advantages of Early Decision

An advantage to early decision from a college's perspective is that it enrolls students
who are exceptionally eager to attend. The college also gets a good start at assem-
bling a well-rounded class, since it knows that each student who is accepted early
decision will indeed matriculate in the fall. There is no guesswork involved in the
"yield" from the pool of early decision acceptances: it is 100 percent. Early decision
reduces enrollment uncertainty for a college. It can help a college minimize the awk-
wardness and cost associated with underenrollment or overenrollment, since it is
impossible to predict the yield for regular decision admits with certainty. The

process appears to be an efficient way to match students who want a given college with a college that wants them, and it looks like everyone wins. But as with everything else in college admissions, the situation is not that simple.

Early decision programs have become highly controversial, even rivaling debates over the SAT and affirmative action in college admissions. Although early decision programs at some colleges have been around for decades, they have spread and become more popular in the last ten years. James Fallows, editor of the influential *Atlantic Monthly* magazine, has forcefully expressed his view that early decision is bad policy. In an article entitled "The Early Decision Racket," he writes that early decision programs "have added an insane intensity to middle-class obsessions about college. They also distort the admissions process, rewarding the richest students from the most exclusive high schools and penalizing nearly everyone else. But the incentives for many colleges and students are as irresistible as they are perverse."[1] These are strong words. Why has a program so seemingly well-intentioned and straightforward generated this kind of reaction?

> "I just want to go to sleep until December 15th."
>
> "I've taken up praying. I don't even believe in God."
>
> "I'd sell my soul—if I still had one."
>
> "Either the best moment in life, probably better than sex, or the worst moment, even worse than death."
>
> *Student comments about early decision and early action posted on an Internet bulletin board*

The Major Problem with Early Decision

Critics of early decision point out that it has become something it was never intended to be—an admissions *strategy* that increases the chances of being accepted to an elite institution. Some elite colleges have admissions rates two or three times higher for early decision applicants compared with regular decision applicants, and fill from one-third to one-half of their freshman classes from the early pool. As a result, the much larger pool of regular decision applicants ends up competing for fewer slots well after the much smaller group of early applicants has secured their place. Some colleges have also been up-front in telling legacy applicants that their legacy hook will only be considered if they apply early, reinforcing the idea of early decision as a strategy. The Johns Hopkins University, the University of Pennsylvania, and Cornell University are among the colleges and universities that tie the legacy preference to an early application.

Does Applying Early Help Your Chances?

It has been common knowledge for many years that the percentage of students accepted via early decision is usually higher, sometimes much higher, than the percentage accepted during the regular cycle. Colleges have traditionally asserted that although exactly the same standards are used to evaluate the early and regular applicant pools, the files of early applicants are stronger as a group than those that arrive for regular review and that differences in qualifications account for differences in acceptance rate. A group of researchers at Harvard University, however, has recently shown that this is not the case.

In *The Early Admissions Game,* researchers present an analysis of admissions data for 1999–2000 from fourteen of the most selective colleges in the country (all of which agreed to participate under the condition that the names of the colleges would not be revealed).[2] The data show that early decision applicant pools, overall, were academically weaker than regular decision pools. The investigators conclude that an early decision applicant on average receives an admissions "boost" that is roughly equivalent to an increase of 100 points on the SAT. The admissions rate for early decision candidates equaled that of regular admissions cycle applicants whose SAT scores were 100 points higher. These findings are directly in conflict with what most colleges have been saying publicly for years about their early decision programs.

> "I was surprised there was such a consistent result—that all of the colleges were favoring early applications. I was also surprised by the magnitude of the advantage."[3]
>
> Christopher Avery, professor of public policy at Harvard University and coauthor of The Early Admissions Game

Students at high schools with strong guidance programs have known for a long time that colleges have not been candid about the boost given to those who apply early decision. They and their counselors have watched classmates with equivalent records have very different outcomes in the admissions process as a function of when they sent in their applications. As a result, the number of early decision applications has gone up dramatically over the last decade, increasing at a faster rate than the number of applications overall.

Counselors cringe when they hear your classmates say, "I want to apply early—I just don't know where," because it shows that students are under great pressure to make a choice, perhaps prematurely, to maximize their chances of admission to an

"I didn't really know about early decision until I started hearing other kids talking about it in late October. They were all moaning about having to ask for letters of recommendation and worrying that the teachers wouldn't send them in on time. I couldn't see the point of all that drama, until someone explained to me that I might have a better chance if I applied early admission . . . like maybe if the college knew I wanted them, they would want me. So I started to feel pressure to 'want' some place, but really I hadn't visited many, and the only place I really liked, I liked because my buddy was going there. I visited him once and we went to a cool party. I mean, maybe that means the atmosphere was right for me — you know, people I could get along with — but I don't know. And my parents flipped out when I said that maybe I'd just apply early decision to Jerry's school.

Anyway, I didn't apply early decision anywhere, so now it's March and I'm getting awfully antsy because I don't know where I will be going in the fall yet. But that is better than picking a school for the wrong reason, getting in, and then having to go there because you applied early decision. I just wish I had gotten started earlier on the whole thing."

High school senior

---

elite college. Once students do pick a school, the pressure continues, often intensely, up through the decision date. Students tend to think, often correctly, that an early decision application is their best shot at their dream school. Acceptance is greeted with great joy, while denial and deferral all too often are met with despair.

Everyone agrees that you should be absolutely sure of your first-choice college before applying early decision because it is binding—you can't change your mind after being accepted. The best way to be sure, of course, is to learn as much as possible about colleges and to visit them in person, ideally when they are in session and well before the early decision application deadline. To be a good candidate for early decision, you need to begin early, preferably no later than the spring of junior year, informing yourself about early decision options and deadlines. It also helps considerably to have the time and money to visit schools to see whether one emerges as a clear front-runner.

The Early Advantage for Legacies

In Chapter Two we noted that legacy status—being the child (or in some cases the grandchild) of an alum—can boost your chances of admission at a selective private (and occasionally public) college. Some of those colleges, however, make it clear that the legacy advantage applies most strongly to students who elect to apply early. Essentially they are saying that legacies lose the advantage if they apply as part of the regular decision pool. As we'll see later in Chapter Eight, the same situation sometimes applies for recruited athletes—they are told that they will lose their hook if they don't apply early. Be aware of this, but don't let it drive your final decision. An early decision acceptance is binding; it is only an advantage if you know with certainty that the early decision college is, in fact, your first choice.

> *"Children and grandchildren of alumni who wish to receive maximum consideration for the legacy affiliation are urged to apply Early Decision."*
>
> *University of Pennsylvania instructions to undergraduate applicants for the class of 2008*

More Concerns About Early Decision

Critics of early decision have argued that early decision programs favor students who do not need financial aid and who have access to a support system that will assist them in identifying a top-choice college by early in the fall of the senior year and submitting their application materials by the early November deadline. Students with limited financial means who disproportionately attend poorly funded and overcrowded public schools are much less likely to meet these criteria than students from private schools or high-performing high schools.

> *"I wish I would have known how early early applications were due. It seemed as though the year had just begun and I was already applying for college."*
>
> *Comment made in the spring of senior year*

Students who are accepted early decision are also potentially limited in terms of their financial aid options. Although in principle a student is released from an early decision commitment if the financial aid package offered by the college is inadequate, early decision does not give students who need significant financial aid a chance to compare financial aid packages from several schools, and perhaps even negotiate a more desirable package at one school based on the offer from another. Students whose families are prepared to pay the full sticker price of admission, in contrast, don't have this concern. And the importance of having family and counseling support to pick that one "right" college early and submit an application in time for early decision review is often underestimated.

The Move to Single-Choice Early Action

Educators increasingly argue that early decision is out of control. Yale University President Richard Levin has been the most vocal. In a December 2001 interview with the *New York Times*, he said, "If we all got rid of it, it would be a good thing. It pushes the pressure of thinking about college back to the junior year of high school, and the only one who benefits is the admissions officer."[4] Thomas Parker, dean of admission and financial aid at Amherst College, has echoed Levin's sentiments. "With some of the elite schools taking higher and higher percentages of their students early decision, a growing number of kids are strategizing about where to apply, rather than looking for the place that is right for them."[5]

In 2002, Yale University and Stanford University announced that they would replace their early decision programs with an early action program beginning with the selection of the Class of 2008. Although less common than early decision, early action has been offered for many years. A major difference is that students accepted through early action can wait until the spring to decide whether to attend—it is not binding. In the meantime, students are free to apply to other colleges through the regular process and are able to compare financial aid packages before making a final choice. Early action colleges have traditionally also allowed students to apply to other early programs—a maximum of one early decision college as well as other early action schools.

> " Early decision was established for legitimate reasons, but it has grown beyond all reasonable bounds. Students are pressed to apply early decision to increase their chances, locking in college choices six crucial months earlier than otherwise. And colleges and universities can't resist ever more early decision admits to boost their admissions statistics and rankings, as well as for the convenience of spreading out the admissions process from one decision point to two. But along the way we increase application anxiety, encourage false and premature decisions (not exactly the best grounds for starting an educational interaction), and also decrease potential diversity. " [6]
>
> *Anthony Marx, president of Amherst College*

> " In an ideal world we would do away with all early programs. We'd go back to the days when everyone could look at all their options over the senior year. Students, parents, and high schools would be very grateful. Philosophically, and in every other way, it would be so much better if we all could make the change. " [7]
>
> *William Fitzsimmons, dean of admissions at Harvard University*

In fact, both Yale University and Stanford University had early action programs until 1995, when they switched to early decision. Now they have switched back in an effort to ease pressure on students and allow them to compare financial aid offers. Their new early action programs, however, are now "single choice," that is, a student wishing to apply early action to Stanford University or Yale University may not apply early action or early decision to any other college. Stanford, however, makes an exception for students who want to apply early action to public institutions.

By making their early action programs "single choice," Yale University and Stanford University are saying that they want early applications from students who consider one of those campuses their first choice. Although they no longer require a student applying early to attend if admitted, they want to be sure a student is serious about them. Harvard University followed suit and now has single-choice early action as well. Over time, other colleges may join them.

	Comparing Early Application Options (Be sure to check the instructions for specific colleges)		
	Early Decision (ED)	**Early Action (EA)**	**Single-Choice Early Action (SCEA)**
Binding?	Yes (except if financial aid is inadequate)	No	No
Allows comparison of aid packages?	No	Yes	Yes
Allows other early applications?	Yes (EA applications only)	Yes (EA applications and one ED)	No (exception may include EA and rolling admission to public colleges)
Allows regular decision applications?	Yes (these must be withdrawn if the student is admitted ED)	Yes	Yes

One immediate effect of these changes has been a significant increase in the number of early applications at institutions that have made their early program less restrictive. Stanford University, for example, went from about 2,500 early decision applicants for the Class of 2007 to around 4,000 single-choice early action applicants for the class of 2008. Yale had a similar increase. Harvard's switch from unrestricted early action to single-choice early action, however, led to a decrease in early applications, since single-choice early action is more restrictive than ordinary early action. Harvard University saw its early applications for the class of 2008 drop almost 50 percent, from 7,600 to 4,000.

Students who apply early decision or single-choice early action are expected to honor the commitments associated with those application choices. For early decision, you commit to attend the college to which you are admitted unless the financial aid package is inadequate. With single-choice early action, you commit yourself to an early application at one college. Colleges offering either early decision or single-choice early action have students sign a statement as part of their application indicating that they understand and agree to the terms of that program. Some colleges require a parent and the student's high school counselor to sign the statement as well.

Should You Apply Early Decision or Early Action?

Early decision programs can work to your advantage if you (1) have a clear first choice college that emerges after careful research, (2) don't need grades from first-semester senior year to bolster your academic record, (3) have the support from your parents and counselor needed to submit a strong early application, and (4) are not concerned about comparing financial aid offers. If all of these conditions are satisfied and the result is a "fat" acceptance packet come December 15, your college admissions process can be brought to a happy conclusion months before it otherwise would. Add the bonus of an increased chance of acceptance to begin with, and early decision becomes, in Fallow's words, almost irresistible. Early action, single-choice or otherwise, is more flexible, since an acceptance does not imply commitment. You are free to apply to other colleges via regular decision if you wish and eventually compare financial aid offers in the spring.

But there is a downside to an early application of either sort that we haven't yet talked about. The pressure to identify a single college for an early application can be intense. It can also reinforce the idea that there is only one college that is a "perfect fit" for you and that your job is simply to discover it and go after it with vigor. As more students choose to apply early, however, more will be disappointed by denials or deferrals. For some students, the buildup has been so great and so much seems to be at stake that either of these last outcomes can be a major blow. Perspective can easily be lost as students face, often for the first time in their lives, what they perceive as significant failure. In contrast, at regular decision time, denials or wait-listings will be buffered by some good news as well. Applying to several colleges also tends to negate the idea of a perfect match—you see several colleges as a good fit.

> "Not everyone gets into Elite U, but even so it's not like the 5,000 students at Elite U are the only ones who are happy with their college and will go on to success in life. While I eagerly hope for my deferral to turn into an acceptance, I know that I have to look at my other options as a definite possibility so my college experience is not haunted by 'the ghost of Elite U.'"
>
> *Comment made on December 16 by student deferred at an Ivy League college*

> "The advantages of applying early are sufficiently great that you should at least consider applying early to a first-choice college where you would be a long shot for regular decision. [But] you can easily convince yourself that you actually have a chance of being admitted as an early applicant to a school that is well out of reach. An early application will not help you at a college where you are not close to being a competitive applicant." [8]
>
> *From* The Early Admissions Game

So where does this leave you? Well, it depends. If you have a clear first-choice college and satisfy the criteria for early decision or early action we have noted, you should seriously think about applying early. If you would be a competitive applicant, there are clear advantages to applying early. But please remember what we have said about the downside of early applications. Don't let your enthusiasm for a college let you succumb to early acceptance syndrome—the belief that there is one, and only one, college where you can truly be happy.

Is Early Decision Right for You?

❏ I have a clear first-choice college and am completely confident that it is a very good fit for me.

❏ I have done careful research about the college that supports my choice, including most of the following: visited in-person or on the Web; studied the catalog, viewbook, and other material in detail; reviewed the college's profile in a "big book"; talked with current or former students in person, through online chat, or e-mail, etc.).

❏ I will probably be comfortable with the financial aid that is offered to me and won't have to compare financial aid offers.

❏ My grades from first-semester senior year will not be significantly better than the rest of my record.

❏ I have taken (or will take) my standardized tests so that the scores will reach my early decision college in time for early review.

❏ My overall record places me within the admissible range for this college.

❏ I will be able to prepare and submit my application by the early decision deadline, including letters of recommendation from my teachers and counselor.

❏ I would like the extra admissions boost that early decision candidates appear to get.

❏ I would like to know for sure where I will be going to college as early as possible.

❏ I will do careful research on the rest of my college list and prepare applications to them in case I am deferred or denied early decision.

❏ Despite the fact that my early decision college is my clear first choice, I realize that I may not be accepted and that there are other colleges where I will also be very happy and get a fine education.

7

Deciding About
Early Decision and
Other Early Options

More Things to Consider

It is important to remember that much of what we have just presented may change, and change rapidly. As more students become aware of the early admissions boost, more are choosing to try to take advantage of it. At the same time, some colleges are cutting back on the percentage of the freshman class admitted through the early cycle. It's like the situation where word starts to spread far and wide about a wonderful neighborhood restaurant that always has free tables. The restaurant can soon find itself needing to take reservations that become harder and harder to get as word spreads. The early admission boost may decrease or even eventually disappear.

> " You can say, 'look at the bigger picture,' blah, blah . . . but that doesn't help our depression in getting rejected if we've focused so much on a single school. You can't deny that you'll be crushed if you don't get in. That is just a fact."
>
> *Senior commenting on how she and her friends will feel if their early applications are denied*

But what everyone else is doing or not doing shouldn't really matter. If you think a college is truly your first choice, whether there is an advantage to applying early shouldn't make any difference in your decision. We also want to emphasize that even if you apply early decision or early action to your first-choice school, you should carefully consider where else to apply. December 15 is too late to decide on other colleges and begin your applications in the event #1 declines or defers your application.

> " Crud. I guess I have to shell out 75 bucks to Stanford. It's a conspiracy, I tell you. I find out whether or not I had to spend my money *after* I've already spent it. Pleeeaaase, MIT, accept me!"
>
> *Bulletin board post by student applying early action to MIT who just learned that MIT would send its decision after the Stanford University regular application deadline*

One of the arguments often offered in favor of early decision is that it can eliminate the need to complete additional applications. This just doesn't hold up in reality for most students. Some colleges require a pre-application, along with an application fee, that needs to be filed before the application itself. These are usually sent in well before the December 15 early action or early decision notification date. And remember, most regular decision applications are due January 1 or soon thereafter. Beginning an application after December 15 during the holiday season isn't an

Early Acceptance

I belong to a family of planners, and we like to have things resolved. What time is dinner? Who's taking out the trash? What pet are we getting? While other families decide such things on the spur of the moment, we plan, and if PETCO has only gerbils and not our choice (hamsters), we go somewhere else.

For people like us, early acceptance is compelling. Choose early? Hear back in December? Sounds wonderful—if you accept that you won't be able to compare financial aid packages.

Our family also enjoys travel, so it's no surprise that our college tours began early. My daughter checked out schools as a sophomore and gave hints to my son, who traveled junior year. Both found "favorite" colleges. By November 15th, the paperwork was done.

Then came the waiting.

Brain power that could have been put to better use polishing essays for other applications (in case of denial or deferral) went into analyzing everything from postal service competency to the walking speed of our mail carrier.

Finally, the decisions came. My daughter was accepted and life got a whole lot easier.

Three years later, my son was not as fortunate. After expending what for him was tremendous energy on his application (an audition tape was particularly daunting), he learned that he had been "deferred."

He wasn't prepared to wait.

He knew which college was his second choice. They offered a second early decision program and he jumped for it. In February he was accepted, and that's where he enrolled.

Meanwhile, I kept waiting for him to feel bad. His first-choice school was eight miles from the beach. Second choice was in a freezing climate, 2,000 miles from his girlfriend. If he had held out for regular decision, the first-choice school might have accepted him.

But the anguish I awaited never came. He bubbled with college plans.

If the beach school had been swept into the ocean, I don't think he would have noticed.

I conclude that loyalty to a college you have never attended isn't really all that strong.

M. F.

appealing option, especially after receiving a disappointing decision from a first-choice college.

Teacher and counselor recommendations and transcripts, as well as SAT or ACT scores, also need to be requested well before the due date. As a result, many students find themselves applying regular decision to their full array of college choices, although they have an early application pending. If the early application is successful, they must withdraw those additional applications. The extra effort and expense gets written off as the cost of "insurance."

As we noted earlier, a number of colleges have two rounds of early decision, ED I and ED II. The date for ED II often coincides with the date for regular decision applications, but of course the ED II applicants get their decisions earlier and are committed to attending if they are accepted. Colleges offering two rounds of early decision say that they do this to give students more time to decide on a first choice. Although this is no doubt an important consideration that helps many students, an additional reason for a college to have a second early decision round is to receive applications from students denied or deferred on December 15 by another college. This approach gives both colleges and students two shots at making an early match.

Likely Letters and Early Notification

Colleges differ in the timing of their regular decision cycle notifications, with most notifying students between March 1 and early April in time for a choice to be made by May 1. But a few students who apply regular decision get letters early—sometimes very early—that don't formally tell them they are accepted but instead tell them that they are very likely to be accepted. Known in admissions circles as *likely* letters (and sometimes as *wink* letters), these early notifications allow a college to adhere to the official notification date while signaling to a select group of students that the college is especially interested in them.

Colleges hope that a likely letter will increase the chances that the student receiving it will accept the official offer

> "Congratulations! Every once in a while in the midst of reading hundreds of files, an admissions officer will be so excited about a student's application that he or she will come to ask if we might reserve a place in next year's class for that student. I am very pleased to tell you that this has happened in your case, and that we are provisionally reserving a place in the Class of 2008 for you. Such an offer before the normal notification date is highly unusual: from the record number of 17,700 applications we received this year, not even 100 applications inspire us to send this sort of early notice."
>
> *From an Ivy League likely letter*

of admission when it arrives later. Likely letters often go to people the college is especially eager to recruit—athletes, members of underrepresented groups, and others who present credentials that make them truly distinctive.

Still other colleges have early notification programs where they formally admit some regular decision cycle applicants a month or so earlier than others. Swarthmore and Williams are two such colleges. Students do not apply for this kind of early notification. It is up to the college to decide. Yet another program is "early evaluation." Wellesley College offers students the option of formally requesting an early assessment of the likelihood of admission. If they apply by January 1 rather than the regular deadline of January 15, students who request early evaluation will receive a letter at the end of February that lists their chances for admission as "likely," "possible," or "unlikely." The large majority of those accepted, however, at the Ivy League and elsewhere, receive their first and only notification on the previously announced formal reply date. Regardless of the timing of notification, students all have until May 1 to make a final decision.

The Advantage of Thinking Early Even If You Decide Against Applying Early

Many students have the long-standing habit of cutting things close to the wire, and they extend that habit to the college application process. But even if you do not plan to apply "early" to a college, there are advantages to getting your application in well before the deadline. The most obvious case is where a college uses rolling admissions to select students as their applications come in, rather than waiting until they can compare applications to each other. Used at many state universities and some less selective private colleges, rolling admissions allows a college to accept qualified students up until the freshman class is full. Clearly, applying early is better than applying at or close to the deadline to ensure that your application will be considered while there is still room.

But there are advantages to getting your application in well before the deadline for other colleges as well. Even if you are applying regular decision to a college with a January 1 deadline, you

> "One of the most comical things is that close to half of our applications come in during a two to three day period right before the deadline. If you come here around December 30, you'll see the FedEx truck, Airborne Express, UPS, all lined up out here. We literally have buckets and buckets of mail that come in."[9]
>
> *Thomas Parker, dean of admissions and financial aid at Amherst College*

can submit your application as early as you want once the applications are available.

Getting your materials in early even if you want regular cycle review means that they will arrive earlier than the deadline "crunch" and be filed and acknowledged earlier (and be more likely to make it successfully to your folder rather than go astray). You will get notification, online or via postcard, that your file is complete, and you won't have to worry about whether a letter or test scores will get there on time. And if something does end up missing, you'll have lots of time to get a replacement sent.

Because admissions committees start reading files that are complete soon after the closing date, you'll get a reading by staff members who are fresh and not yet burdened by the many hundreds of files they will read during the winter months. It's impossible to know, of course, if that will make any difference in the final decision, but it can't hurt. Getting applications in early also means that you can enjoy the holiday season with your family, rather than spend it worrying about applications. We think you (and your family) will be glad you took our advice.

And Humor Always Helps Keep Things in Perspective

Mike Mills, director of admission at Miami University, penned the following parody for the *Journal of College Admission*. We enjoyed it and hope you will, too.

From an Application in the Future

Term applying for: Fall 2012 ___ Spring 2013 ___ Application Fee: $250

Applying for:

Priority Decision[1] ___ Regular Decision[2] ___ Precision Decision[3] ___

Division Decision[4] ___ Revision Decision[5] ___ Provision Decision[6] ___

Derision Decision[7] ___ Rescission Decision[8] ___

[1] Yes! Beyond the tangible benefit of earlier notification, I want to receive all other attendant (albeit ambiguous) benefits of applying under this plan. I also want to keep my options open while avoiding the stigma of applying under the Regular Decision plan.

[2] I want to keep all my options open and I refuse to be a pawn in your silly admission game.

[3] This is *exactly* the school I'm looking for and I will enroll if accepted.

[4] My parents and I fought long and hard over whether I should apply to this school and it is your job to figure out who won.

[5] I like this school, but I may opt to attend a better school should I be admitted to one.

[6] I like this school and will attend provided you ante up with some significant scholarship dollars. I know you have the endowment to do it.

[7] I'm applying, but don't fool yourselves—you're definitely my back up school.

[8] I'm applying, but I may and likely will cancel my application at some point in time.

Adapted from Mike Mills, "Applications We Hope Never to See." *Journal of College Admission,* Winter 2004, Number 182. Reprinted with permission. Copyright 2004 National Association for College Admission Counseling.

Applying Well

If you've read to this point in *Admission Matters*, you know that a lot of important self-reflection and research needs to take place before the actual process of applying to college can begin. But once that work is done and you develop an appropriate list of good-bet, possible, and long-shot colleges, the next step is tackling the applications themselves. You'll want to present your qualifications to college admissions committees in a way that will distinguish you from many other applicants with similar credentials. This chapter will help you do just that. We'll guide you through

- Writing a personal essay that can make a difference
- Obtaining strong letters of recommendation
- Preparing an activities list that sets you apart
- Shining in your interview

Plus, we offer tips for athletes and those with special talents.

Preparing a strong college application is a lot of work. There's no way of getting around that. A typical application asks many questions, and your answers tell a lot about your academic abilities, background, talents, and interests. It's less obvious that your answers also send subtle messages about your degree of interest in a college and how much time and effort you have put into determining whether it is a good match for you. The best applications make a strong case on both fronts.

Getting Off to a Good Start

Although the competition for admission to selective schools is greater than ever, the actual process of filing an application has never been easier. More and more colleges not only accept, but actively encourage, electronic submission of applications. Some waive their application fees if you submit online. Colleges differ greatly in the extent to which they use technology in the application process, but the trend is clearly in the direction of a paperless process where materials are submitted electronically and read from a computer screen. Even colleges that do not accept electronic submissions usually give you the option of completing your application on the Web and then printing it out for mailing. And for applicants who still prefer to fill out a paper form and are good at cut-and-paste, word processors have made revising essays and producing clean copies much simpler.

Gone, fortunately for good, are the days when the only way to prepare an application was with a typewriter and a bottle of correction fluid. Many parents reading this will remember how hard it was the old-fashioned way. It is a major advantage to be able to easily update and edit your application right up until it is submitted. Your application can now be as complete and accurate as you can make it, without having to go through the agony of starting everything over because you forgot to include something or changed your mind about how to phrase an answer.

Fight the Urge to Procrastinate

We'll be the first to admit that completing a college application is not fun. It is hard to answer all those questions and distill yourself into little boxes on a form. Not only that, it takes time, something often in short supply in senior year. And on top of it all, just thinking about college, as exciting as it may be, can make you nervous. Where will I be next year? Will I have friends? Will I be happy?

The natural tendency in a situation like this is to put off dealing with it as long as possible. Our simple advice is *DON'T.* Do your research on colleges early, and begin the actual job of applying. Fight the urge to procrastinate. Everyone experiences it—including us, the authors of this book, as we tackled the job of writing and found that things didn't always go as smoothly as planned. But procrastination never helps, and it can really hurt. It can mean that your college list is put together hastily and does not really fit your needs, or that you rush to meet a deadline and don't make it. Procrastination can result in missed opportunities, such as when

"I've always left things to pretty much the last minute and it's never been a problem. In character, I left my most important college application to the day before it was due. I planned to rework an essay I had written for a college that had an earlier deadline, so I wasn't too worried. After spending all day Sunday putting everything together, I was ready to submit my application electronically at 9:00 P.M. Then I realized the program cut off the last seven sentences of my essay. No matter what I did I couldn't get the whole thing in. My mom looked at the essay and we agreed that it would be really hard to cut. She suggested I look at the paper app — maybe it would fit in there. It did. I then spent the next two hours filling out the paper app by hand and doing cut-and-paste onto the form for my essay. It was after 11:00 P.M. when I finished. I had school the next day, but my mom mailed it for me and met the postmark deadline. I was accepted and am now a sophomore. But even I agreed I cut things too close. I could have really blown it."

College sophomore

your favorite teacher says she won't have time to write your letter of recommendation because you asked too late. It can mean less thoughtful answers to questions, since you won't have time to carefully review and edit them, or benefit from feedback from others. Most important, it can mean that you don't have a chance to make your best case for admission.

The wise student starts early, makes a time line indicating what is needed and by when, and then sets about the task of getting it done.

Neatness and Completeness Count!

The ease with which an application can be submitted electronically or filled out online can lead to carelessness in proofreading and failure to double-check everything for accuracy. The natural desire is to hit the "send" or "print" key and be done with it. Resist the urge. Typos, omissions, and other errors can mar an otherwise good application. In particular, you want to avoid having your great response to the question about why you want to attend Amherst College mention that you find Columbia University's core curriculum exciting. Errors of this kind, and worse, routinely happen when word processors are used to cut-and-paste from one application to another. Electronic applications make the process easier, but they can also make it easier to make mistakes.

Mistakes can also happen when you are hastily filling out a lot of applications close to a deadline. An error-filled, incomplete application practically shouts, "I didn't take this application seriously." Why, then, should the college? Before submitting an application, be sure to carefully proofread everything yourself and have a friend or parent proofread as well. And then proofread it again.

> "For years, parents, teachers, guidance counselors, school administrators, and members of the school board have been urging teenagers to abstain from sex or to use condiments."
>
> At least the student used spell check. . . .
>
> *Actual sentence from a college application reported by an admissions officer[1]*

Follow Directions

Be sure to read the application carefully and answer the questions that are asked, not other ones. In an effort to economize on work, you may want to recycle answers from one application to another. This is fine, as long as you make sure that the same questions are being asked and, as we just noted, you double-check to be sure to remove any specific references to the first college in your answer!

You should be especially careful in responding to questions asking why you believe a certain college is the right match for you. A good answer shows that you have carefully researched the college and given thought to what you would get from, as well as contribute to, the college. A vague answer shows lack of real interest or knowledge.

Following directions also means being aware of limits on the length of responses and the number of recommendation letters. We'll talk about how to approach these limits later in this chapter.

Should You Use the Common Application?

The Common Application is an application form accepted by over 250 colleges and universities across the country. It was designed to simplify the college admissions process for students who would otherwise have to provide identical information in different formats to each college. Some colleges offer applicants a choice between their own form and the Common Application, including Princeton University, Pomona College, and Carleton College. Other colleges use the Common Application exclusively, including Harvard University, Cornell University, Dartmouth College, Haverford College, Tufts University, and about sixty others.

Regardless of whether they use the Common Application exclusively or not, most selective colleges that use it require a supplemental form that asks certain college-specific questions. There are still some selective institutions that don't accept the Common Application at all. Included among that group are Columbia University, Stanford University, the University of Chicago, and most public universities. The University of Chicago takes great pride in calling its form "The Uncommon Application" because it asks unusually distinctive essay questions. But over 60 percent of the institutions that meet our definition of "selective" use the Common Application, and the percentage is growing.

Using the Common Application will save a lot of time, since you need only complete a single application—either online or on paper—regardless of the number of schools to which you apply. The Common App Online (www.commonapp.org) is particularly time-saving because you don't even have to print and mail an application. And many schools also allow you to submit your supplement online as well. A copy of the Common Application for 2005–06, along with all related forms, is included in Appendix B. Look it over carefully. It will give you a good idea of what college applications are like in general. The latest version of the Common Application, with full instructions, can be found online through the Common Application Web site.

Students sometimes ask whether colleges prefer their own form, and if submitting the Common Application will imply that students are less interested in a college than they might really be. The fact is that colleges that accept the Common Application pay a fee for the privilege. They also pledge to treat all applications, the Common Application and their own, in the same way. On rare occasions a college's own form may ask a question that is not included in either the Common Application or the college-specific supplement. Even though the college will, in fact, treat both the Common Application and their own form equally, you may decide that your answer to that specific question will strengthen your case for admission given your particular circumstances. In this rare circumstance, it may be worth completing the college's own application form. Carleton College, for example, asks a few questions on its own form that are not included on the Common Application. No one is going to stop you from filling out a college's own form when it is available. The choice is yours. But overall, we encourage you to take advantage of the reduction in paperwork that the Common Application allows.

Writing an Effective Personal Essay

Many college application forms, including the Common Application, require one essay or personal statement of about 500 words in length, as well as paragraph-length answers to several short questions. In some cases, two essays are required. Next to the SAT, the essay is the most dreaded and perhaps most misunderstood part of the college application process. In this section, we'll show you how to approach the essay as an opportunity, not just as an unwelcome assignment. Although colleges differ in the emphasis they place on the essay, it can make a difference.

> *"*What exactly do admissions officers want to know when they ask you to write the college essay? No matter which question, we are asking what is really important to you, who you are, and how you arrived where you are. The whole college application process is really a self-exploration and the essay is a way to put your personal adventure into words.*"* [2]
>
> *Delsie Phillips, former director of admissions at Haverford College*

Why Do Colleges Ask for Essays?

Think of the essay as a way for you to personalize your application and give it life. That's the way colleges view it. Along with your letters of recommendation, your essay helps admissions officers differentiate you from many others with similar records. It is a chance to share something special about yourself that will help the reader conclude that you would make a wonderful addition to the next freshman class. It can also demonstrate to a college that you've mastered the ability to express yourself effectively and persuasively in writing—a skill that is crucial for success in college. Henry Bauld, author of a delightful book on college admissions essays, sums up the essay as follows: "It shows you at your alive and thinking best, a person worth listening to—not just for the ten minutes it takes to read your application, but for the next four years."[3]

The Three Types of Questions

Sarah McGinty, a consultant specializing in workshops on writing college essays, points out that most college essays boil down to one of three types: some version of "tell us about yourself," some variety of "why us?" in terms of college or career choice, or a "creative" question that asks you to reflect on some topic that may appear to be

"Tell Us About Yourself" Essays

What is the one thing you would bring with you to Colgate? Why?
(2004–05 Colgate University)

What event, work of art, book, activity, or experience has had the greatest influence on your development? In what ways did you change as a result?
(2004–05 Bowdoin College)

"Why Us?" Essays

Please tell us what you find most appealing about Columbia and why.
(2004–05 Columbia University)

Please describe your reasons for applying to Hamilton.
(2004–05 Hamilton College)

"Be Creative" Essays

Have you ever walked through the aisles of a warehouse store like Costco or Sam's Club and wondered who would buy a jar of mustard a foot and a half tall? We've bought it, but it didn't stop us from wondering about other things, like absurd eating contests, impulse buys, excess, unimagined uses for mustard, storage, preservatives, notions of bigness . . . and dozens of other ideas both silly and serious. Write an essay somehow inspired by super-huge mustard.
(2004–05 University of Chicago)

On Mars, the latest TV fad among the native life forms is Trading Bodies. You're picked to play. Whose body would you inhabit and why?
(2004–05 University of Virginia)

---

only tangentially related to the college admissions process, if at all. In her book, *The College Application Essay,* McGinty emphasizes that regardless of the form of the question, each is trying to get information about *you.*[4] What you choose to write tells the reader a great deal about how you think, what your life experiences have been, and what you value.

In writing your essay you shouldn't concern yourself with trying to figure out what colleges want to hear. Focus instead on what you want them to know about you. Think about the qualities you want to convey, and then think about how to represent those qualities in your answer to the question. Ideally, your essay should illustrate your points through personal example, rather than simply state them; in other words, your essay should *show,* not just *tell.* Be sure, though, that you answer the question that is asked, not some other one. Even though the questions are all asking about you, directly or indirectly, they vary in the way they frame their inquiry. The only essay we are aware of that gives you total latitude in responding is the Common Application essay option of "Choose your own topic." If you are responding to a more specific prompt, your essay should address the question the way it is asked. An essay written for one prompt can often be reworked to fit another one, however, so you may be able to use a good essay in different ways for different colleges, saving a lot of time and effort. Just be sure to modify your essay carefully, as appropriate, each time you reuse it.

Helping Your Case

Think back to Chapter Two and the discussion of how application files are evaluated. The admissions officers or readers assigned to your file will take anywhere from ten to thirty minutes to read it, and it is one of perhaps thirty or forty files that they will read that day. Your job is to try to make your personal essay as interesting as possible at the same time that it sheds light on who you are as a person. The more your essay stands out positively, the greater the chance it will help your application. The specific topic you choose to write about isn't so important—how you develop the topic *is.*

> "My son's girlfriend was hanging around the house bemoaning the fact that she had nothing to write about in her essay. I said, 'But you like reading. You like the classics. I remember how upset you were when other kids said they didn't like *Jane Eyre.*' I knew if she wrote about books, her essay would show real passion."
>
> *Former writing teacher who knows that many high school students don't enjoy the classics*

It is not surprising that certain themes appear with great frequency in college application essays. Among them are, "How My Summer Trip to _____ Changed My Life," "Winning the Race (or

Game, or Election)" or "The Death of My Beloved _____." These topics, and others that appear with similar frequency, are not necessarily bad. In fact, there are no bad topics—just bad essays. A bad college essay is one that tells the reader little about what makes the writer an interesting, unique person. The more common your essay topic, the greater your burden in writing something different from what the large number of other applicants tackling the same topic are writing. A topic more unique or personal to you, no matter how "small" the topic may be, is often easier to make distinctive and interesting. Good essays have been written on topics as simple as thoughts about a weekly walk with an aging grandparent, reflections

---

Essay Don'ts

- Don't write an essay that any one of a thousand other seniors could write, because they probably will.

- Avoid writing an essay that will embarrass the reader. While you definitely must risk something personally in order to write an effective essay, the risk should not place a burden on the reader.

- Don't try to sell yourself. Rather than persuading the college that you are great, just show them who you are, what you care about, what the pivotal points in your life have been so far.

- Don't try to write an important essay—the definitive statement on the Middle East or race relations in America. These essays tend to come across as much more pompous than authors intend.

- Don't set out to write the perfect essay, the one with huge impact, the one that will blow the doors to the college open for you. Think instead of giving the reader a sample of yourself, a slice of the real you, a snapshot in words.

Adapted with permission from "What Not to Do and Why" by William Poirot, former college counselor, in C. Georges and G. Georges, *100 Successful College Application Essays*, New York: Penguin, 2002. Copyright © The Harvard Independent.

on working with young children in a summer camp, and cooking a meal for a special friend.

Some topics, though, are best avoided altogether, no matter how distinctive your approach. Essays dealing with sexual experiences, rape, incest, and very controversial political and social issues such as abortion are usually best avoided. You don't know who your readers will be, and it makes little sense to write about a topic that may well make one or more of them uncomfortable. Not everyone will agree with us on this, but we believe you should at least think twice (and maybe three times) before proceeding along these sensitive lines.

What Kind of Help Is Appropriate?

Colleges expect that the essays you submit with your application are your own work. This doesn't mean that you can't brainstorm ideas for the essay(s) with your family and friends, and it doesn't mean that you can't get comments from others once you have written a draft. In fact, most professional writers go through several drafts and get comments and reactions from others along the way. It makes good sense to write a draft, put it away for a few days, and then revisit it. Do this two or three times and then get some feedback. Your English teacher can be especially helpful in making suggestions about your essay, and parents can often be helpful as well. The important point, however, is that the end product should be your own work and sound like you, not someone else two or three times your age.

Parents can sometimes lose sight of this and set about the task of trying to rewrite their child's essay. Although help with brainstorming and editing is good, wholesale rewriting is not. It can hurt much more than help. It can rob a student of his distinctive voice—something that admissions officers really want to hear—and signal that the parent doesn't think the child can do the job himself.

Steps to a Successful Essay

- Brainstorm about the personal qualities that you would like to convey in your essay. Involve family and friends in the process of helping you identify what makes you special.

- Read the essay topic(s) carefully and think about ways to convey these qualities through the essay.

- If you have a choice of topics, select the one that is the best match for what you want to say.

- Outline and then draft your essay. Be sure to show by example, not just tell.

- Set your essay aside for a couple of days, and then revise it. Repeat as needed until you are ready to show it to others.

- Ask your English teacher or counselor or both to read and comment on your essay. Your parents will probably be eager to read it as well.

- Incorporate the best suggestions into another draft. Set it aside for a couple of days and then reread, making changes until you have a final draft.

- Proofread your essay carefully. When you think you are finished, proofread it again.

The Resources section at the end of this book lists several excellent books that focus on writing the college essay. We've given you a good start here, but we encourage you to consult one or more of these sources if you would like more detail about essay writing.

Pay Attention to the Shorter Essays

As we noted earlier, the typical application includes one or two 500-word essays and a few questions that can each be answered in a paragraph. Many students focus all their effort on the long essays, leaving the shorter ones to the very end when they are rushed and trying to meet a deadline. The fact is that shorter questions are important as well, because both short and long essays give the reader insights into who you are. Pay attention to the shorter questions, and edit and proofread them just as you would the long essays. The Common Application contains just one short question: "Please describe which of your activities (extracurricular and personal activities or work experience) has been the most meaningful and why." Common Application supplements usually contain several additional questions requiring paragraph-length answers.

Do I Have to Count Every Word?

Finally, applicants often wonder how strictly they need to adhere to a word limit. In fact, admissions staff do not have the time to count words, even if they wanted to. Use the word limit as a general guideline, not a rigid rule. In most cases, make your essay as long as it needs to be, within reason. Remember that those reviewing your file have many others to read as well. An overly long essay, no matter how wonderful, will not be appreciated. Remember, too, that electronic applications may limit the length of your essay. Sometimes the program will allow you to type in a longer than average essay, but will truncate your essay before it can actually be submitted. Be sure to "preview" your electronic applications before submitting them to avoid this happening to you.

Getting Great Letters of Recommendation

Most colleges that require letters of recommendation ask for two from teachers and one official secondary school report, usually prepared by a guidance counselor. These letters, along with your essay, can make your application distinctive. Especially valuable are anecdotes that bring a paper file to life and transform numbers into a real person. Admissions officers also welcome context—descriptions of special challenges a student has faced and overcome, an explanation of erratic grades or other unusual aspects of the record, an evaluation of the student relative to classmates, among other things. All of this helps the admissions officer develop a fuller mental picture of the student and distinguishes a student from many others with similar "stats."

Whom Should You Ask to Write?

Although you obviously have no direct control over what your counselor or teacher writes in a letter, there are things you can do to increase the chances that the letters will be helpful in making your case for admission. The most important is approaching the right teachers. Students often have a difficult time deciding which teachers to ask for a letter of recommendation. The most helpful letters are those written by teachers who know you the best—not necessarily the teachers who gave you the highest grades, though it is nice if both are true. A well-written letter of recommendation should include specific examples of your contributions and achievements. Like a good personal statement, it should show by example rather than simply tell. Being an active contributor to class discussions is one way to ensure that teachers will be able to provide specific examples about you when it comes time to write your recommendation.

Some schools with strong college guidance programs provide training for teachers in how to write effective recommendations. Most schools, however, leave it up to the teachers to figure it out for themselves. Given that reality, savvy students seek out teachers who seem particularly thoughtful, who know them well, and who are themselves strong writers.

How Should You Approach a Teacher?

It can be hard to know how willing a teacher will be when asked to write a letter of recommendation. You should approach your teachers early (at least one month before a letter is due, ideally more) and give them an easy way out if they have reservations about writing for any reason, including time constraints. A good approach is to tell a teacher that you plan to apply to several selective colleges and ask whether the teacher feels that he or she knows you well enough to write a supportive letter of recommendation. The response you want is an enthusiastic "Sure," "Yes," or "Of course!" If there is any hesitation, it is probably best to pick up on the cue. Thank the teacher for considering your request, but indicate that you'll be happy to ask someone else. A reluctant letter writer is unlikely to provide a letter that will be helpful, so it is best to move on to another teacher if you can.

Providing Background Information

Recommendation writers need as much information about you as possible to write an effective letter, and it is your job to be sure they have that background. Many schools have students fill out a multipage form that provides teachers and counselors with information about their college plans, extracurricular activities, GPA, standardized test scores, intellectual interests, hobbies, and other general background information that highlights what makes them different from other students. Your letter writers will refer to this form, so be sure to complete it accurately and thoroughly. If your school does not provide a form for this purpose, you can use the one provided in Appendix C or make up one of your own. It is also a good idea to supplement the general form with specific information for each teacher to help refresh his or her memory of you in the classroom.

It will help a lot if you provide your recommendation writers with everything they'll need at one time in a large envelope: your personal information form, the individual recommendation forms with the identifying information at the top completed by you, and due dates clearly indicated for each school. Be sure to include a stamped, pre-addressed envelope for each recommendation. Most recommendation forms are similar to the one used with the Common Application. They ask for a teacher to provide a written evaluation as well as complete a checklist of characteristics that compare you to other students the teacher has known.

Colleges offer teachers the option of attaching a letter to the reference form rather than completing the form itself to save time. Usually, the form should still be attached, however, with the top portion filled out, to be sure that the letter reaches your file and is treated as one of your official letters, not an optional extra one. Although some high schools collect the letters of recommendation from teachers and submit them, most have teachers send their letters directly to the colleges.

Waive Your Right to See the Letters

The Family Educational Rights and Privacy Act, known as FERPA, gives students the right to see their permanent college record unless they voluntarily waive the right to see parts of it. Since letters of recommendation can become part of your permanent record once you are accepted and enroll, some college recommendation forms contain a statement that you can sign that waives your right of access to them. Colleges believe that teachers will be more candid if access is waived, and most students readily sign the statement. The recommendation form that is part of the Common Application, however, does not contain the waiver statement, so there is nothing to sign when using that form.

How Many Letters Should You Submit?

Sometimes a college will offer students a chance to submit an optional third recommendation from a coach, employer, or anyone else who knows the student well, in addition to the two required letters from teachers. A few colleges—Williams College and Dartmouth College, for example—even invite a letter from a peer. Consider taking advantage of sending in an extra letter if you have someone in mind who could share valuable information about you. Ideally, the writer makes it clear that he or she knows you well and provides specific examples or anecdotes to back that up. But don't worry if you don't have someone who fits this bill. Most applicants, including most of those who are accepted, don't submit an extra letter. And few extra letters make much of a difference.

What if you have one or two additional recommendations you are dying to include but the application itself asks for only two? An extra letter or two from people in a position to provide a meaningful supplement to your application will be accepted and considered by most colleges even if the form doesn't explicitly say so. Be sure, though, that the writer includes your full name and social security number prominently at the top of the letter so that it can find its way to your file.

Resist a letter-writing campaign, however. College admissions officers cite an old adage, "The thicker the file, the thicker the student," meaning that weak students have traditionally tried to pad their applications with multiple letters of endorsement. The only really helpful letters are from people who know you well and can add something substantive to your file. A letter of support from your uncle's lawyer who met you once years ago, no matter how rich or how prominent he may be, will at best be ignored and at worst be an annoyance that reminds admissions staff of the old saying. Limit your extra letters, if you send them at all, to one or two.

The Secondary School Report or Counselor Letter

Colleges also typically require a letter from your counselor, known as the secondary school report. The form asks your counselor to rate the rigor of your program relative to that of your classmates and to provide an overall evaluation of you as a student. Colleges are aware that students from large public high schools usually do not get to know their counselor well, so their expectations for the level of detail in such letters are not high. However, a detailed letter can help, so it is to your advantage to get to know your counselor to the greatest extent possible. This is especially important if aspects of your record or background would benefit from explanation. For example, if your first-semester grades in your junior year suffered because you had a serious illness, be sure your counselor knows. Your counselor can only explain your situation if he or she has the needed information. The secondary school report or Common Application supplement may ask your counselor to indicate whether you have ever been suspended in high school, and if so, why. It goes without saying that it is best if your counselor can truthfully answer "no." The background information sheet that you prepare for your teachers should also be given to your counselor. The more your counselor knows about you, the better.

The counselor report is usually sent to colleges in the same envelope as your transcript and the school profile we mentioned in Chapter Two. You'll need to provide your counselor with a stamped, pre-addressed envelope along with the appropriate form for each college just as you do for your teachers who will be writing recommendations. Be sure you put on enough postage.

Shining in Your Interview

Schools vary widely in the importance placed on interviews. As we briefly discussed in Chapter Two, some require an interview as part of the admissions process, some make it optional, and some don't offer it at all. Just how important are interviews anyway, and how should you view them?

If a college doesn't offer interviews—for example, Stanford University—then obviously interviews don't play a role in the admissions process. But what if they are offered? Our best advice is to take advantage of an interview, prepare for it, and take it seriously. But don't expect it to carry too much weight in the final outcome.

> *"The best interview is a good conversation."*
>
> *Alumni interviewer*

The Difference Between Informational and Evaluative Interviews

There are two main types of interview: informational and evaluative. Informational interviews are a way for colleges to provide applicants with personalized information about their program. The main goal of informational interviews is recruitment—getting students excited about the college and its offerings. They are usually offered by local alumni who volunteer to help their alma mater, but they can be offered on-site at the college as well. Informational interviews let you ask questions and learn more about a college; they also give you a chance to demonstrate your interest in the school.

Evaluative interviews are trickier. Here the college is up-front about saying that the results of the interview will be part of your admissions file. Evaluative interviews may be strongly encouraged or merely optional, and they are usually offered both on-site at the college by admissions staff or college seniors specially trained for the task or by alumni close to home. Most interviews are conducted in a student's hometown by an alumni volunteer. The alum can be a recent grad or someone who graduated thirty-five years ago, or somewhere in between. The variability among interviewers—admissions staff, seniors, and, especially, alums—can make it difficult for colleges to place great weight on interview results, even when they are intended to be evaluative.

How to Approach Your Interview

The admissions office may describe your interview as evaluative or informational, or maybe no distinction will be made at all. Regardless of how it is described, plan to show up on time. Don't arrive early at an interview in someone's home—just

---

Some Frequently Asked Interview Questions

1. What are you looking for in a college? What attracts you to this college?

2. What are your top two extracurricular activities and why do you like them?

3. What sort of challenges have you faced in your life so far?

4. What is your favorite subject in school and why?

5. How would you describe yourself to a stranger?

6. What is your favorite pastime?

7. How did you spend last summer and how did you grow from it?

8. What book have you read that has left a lasting impression?

9. What have you enjoyed most about high school?

10. Do you have any questions I can help answer?

---

be there when you are supposed to be. Expect the interview to last about forty-five minutes, plus or minus fifteen minutes, depending on the interviewer and how the discussion goes. Dress neatly and look presentable, but you do not need to dress up for the occasion. If someone drives you to the interview, be sure he or she parks nearby to take you home promptly after the interview. You don't want to find yourself awkwardly hanging out in the interviewer's living room while you wait for your ride.

> "Somebody I interviewed once said he wanted to major in accounting. I said, 'You know, that's not a major at Harvard.' It went downhill from there."
>
> *Harvard alumni interviewer*

In preparation for your interview, give some thought to how you would answer the questions you are most likely to be asked. Some commonly asked questions are shown in the box on this page. You may be asked a different set of questions, but thinking about your answers to the ones we have provided will help you be well prepared. In addition, have several prepared questions ready to ask when given the opportunity. Make sure that your questions are

Tips From an Alumni Interviewer

I am an alumni interviewer because I care about students, and I believe I can give them a good interview experience. Since alumni interviewers are basically untrained, unknown "staff," I realize that our opinions do not count highly in the selection of students. We're there to report the few bad apples and to be friendly contact people to everyone else.

These tips are drawn from my experience.

1. It's fine to ask logistical questions in advance of the interview. Take down the interviewer's phone number, in case you have further questions or get lost. Don't be surprised if, for safety reasons, your interviewer suggests meeting in a public place, like Starbucks, which could be busy and noisy.

2. Don't assume that your interviewer knows much about you. Colleges differ in how much information they dispense. I never receive any information about grades or SAT scores and, frankly, I prefer not to know. An interview gives the student an opportunity to be more than a number.

3. Although it is helpful to prepare for a few obvious questions, don't spend hours on this task. Use your time, instead, to prepare thoughtful questions about the college that can't be answered by the catalog or Web site.

4. Ask your interviewer about his or her own experience at the college. This gets you off the hot seat for a while, and you may gain a new perspective on the school.

5. Remember that the interview is not only to evaluate your potential and make friendly contact. Admissions offices want to know you are really interested in the school. If you don't show any prior knowledge of my college, I may assume that it's not near the top of your list.

6. Don't be afraid to let your passion show. I still remember one student who said, "I know it sounds crazy, but I want to be the next Stephen Spielberg." I wrote a report to the college that captured his dreams.

Final note: I consider it a privilege to interview the wonderful applicants who come my way. When they get denied, I'm disappointed, too.

M. F.

---

ones that can't be readily answered by looking at the catalog or application materials, such as, "Do you have an engineering program?" Questions that show you have read the material provided by the college and thought about it are the best kind.

When the interview is over, thank the interviewer for his or her time and ask for a card or otherwise make note of his or her name and e-mail or snail-mail address. A short thank-you note or e-mail sent after the interview is a nice gesture.

Interview Checklist

❑ Make sure you have the exact details of the interview time and location and arrange reliable transportation.

❑ Carefully review the material you have about the college (online and paper) to make sure you know about its programs and special features.

❑ Think about your answers to possible questions, including the most important, "Why are you interested in this college?"

❑ Prepare your own thoughtful questions about the college to ask your interviewer.

❑ Dress neatly and appropriately for the setting. Dressy clothes are not necessary, but jeans and shorts are best avoided.

❑ Shake hands when you meet the interviewer and try to maintain eye contact throughout the interview.

❑ Try to relax and enjoy the conversation.

❑ After the interview is over, thank the interviewer for taking the time to speak with you. Shake hands again and ask the interviewer for a business card or other contact information.

❑ Send a short thank-you note in the next few days. A written note is nice, but e-mail is fine, too.

Highlighting What You've Accomplished

As we discussed in Chapter Two, extracurricular activities, community service, and work experience are important ways that students can demonstrate their passions, initiative, and leadership skills. Depending on exactly what your activities are, however, the typical college application form can make it hard to convey your strengths to full advantage. Most forms, including the Common Application, have a small grid that asks you to note the name of each of your activities, the grades during which you were involved in them, and the number of hours per week and weeks per year you spent on them. The grid also asks you to fill out any positions held, honors earned, or letters awarded for each activity.

8

Applying Well

Activity Sheet Format

A separate activity sheet gives you the flexibility to organize your information the way you want and to present detail where it would be helpful. We provide suggested categories below. You can decide to include some categories as-is, combine others, and simply omit those that aren't relevant to your situation. When detail is needed, limit it to a couple of sentences or a short paragraph at most.

Categories to consider are

Extracurricular activities (includes athletics)	Awards and honors
Hobbies and special interests	Summer activities
Work experience and internships	Community involvement
Other activities	

Be sure your activity sheet has your name, address, and social security number at the top. Arranging information in columns makes it easy to follow. The format below (we've included a sample entry) works well for most categories, although you'll need to modify the headings somewhat for a couple of them.

Extracurricular Activities

Activity	Grade (9, 10, 11, 12)	Hours per week, weeks per year	Description
French Language and Culture Club	10, 11, 12	5/40	Secretary (11); president (12). Led development of foreign language semi-annual newsletter at high school

The boxes are tiny, however, and it may be hard to do your activities justice in such a small space. The solution is simple. You can create your own supplementary form that presents the same information in a more user- and reader-friendly format. If the application form is adequate for your needs, however, don't feel you have to produce a separate activity sheet. Use one only if you need it, and don't include one if the instructions specifically tell you not to do it. Some forms, including the Common Application, request that you complete the application grid even if you submit a separate activity sheet.

If you do prepare a separate activity sheet, keep it short—one or two pages if possible—and follow the general format used on the application itself. But take advantage of the fact that you have more room to write two or three sentences that capture the essence of your involvement in each activity if it is not obvious from its name. Be sure to note "see separate activity sheet" on the application form so that the reader will know to look for it. An easy-to-read activity summary can be a valuable addition to a college application. Just be sure it is compact and neat and clearly identified by your name and social security number.

If you submit your application online, you may have to send in your activity sheet by regular mail. Be sure to attach a note requesting that this supplementary information be added to your application file.

Special Talent

Students seeking admission to selective drama, art, music, theater, or dance programs are expected to audition or submit portfolios and tapes for review. These programs vary widely in their intensity and selectivity. Many liberal arts colleges and research universities have strong arts programs as part of their regular curricular offerings. In addition, a number of schools specializing in the performing and visual arts offer degrees in the arts that are part of an arts-focused liberal arts program. And some highly specialized schools, known as conservatories, have as their sole mission the training of professionals at the highest level. Programs vary widely in their requirements for admission, so you should check into specific requirements as early as possible. The beginning of junior year of high school is not too early to begin to prepare.

But what if you simply want to bring your special talent to the attention of an admissions committee? Colleges differ in the approach that works best for them. Pomona College and Williams College, for example, explicitly ask on the application whether the student wishes to submit special material for review and invites the student to send such material with his or her application. Some colleges are quite detailed about what you should send. Although tapes and portfolios may be sent to the admissions office, the relevant academic department reviews them. When the evaluation comes back to the admissions office, it becomes part of the student's file and is considered part of the overall application. Other campuses, such as Colgate University, ask students to send their materials directly to a specific faculty member for review. The evaluation is then sent to the admissions office to be included with the application.

Regardless of how the review is obtained, the result is the same. In each case, the admissions office receives a professional assessment of your materials. If the evaluation indicates exceptional ability in a given area, your talent may serve as a significant admissions hook, especially if it is in short supply at the college. If the evaluation of your work isn't particularly strong, however, it won't play much of a role at all.

If you are in doubt about how to submit evidence of your talent, you should call or e-mail the admissions office. At campuses that assign officers to regions of the country, you will most likely be put in touch with the officer assigned to your area who will be able to answer your questions. The earlier you do this the better, since it often takes a good deal of time to prepare your portfolio or audition materials. Although planning ahead is a good idea for everyone, it is especially important if you want to make your special talent part of the application process.

The Special Case of the Student Athlete

As we noted in Chapter Two, athletic talent can be the biggest "hook" of all when it comes to admission at a selective college. If you are exceptionally strong in your sport and want to play in college, you should read this section.

The over 800 colleges that are part of the National Collegiate Athletic Association (NCAA) are divided into three divisions. Division I houses the most athletically competitive programs and, with eighteen exceptions, all offer athletic scholarships. The Big Ten schools are all Division I, as are Stanford, schools in the Ivy League, and many others. Division II schools, which offer some scholarships, are less competitive both athletically and academically than most Division I schools. They tend to be regional universities like the University of Wisconsin, Parkside, and California State University, Chico, as well as private colleges that draw students primarily from their local area. Division III schools are more selective academically than Division II schools but less competitive athletically. Liberal arts colleges like Bowdoin College, Amherst College, and Lafayette College are in Division III. So are some selective universities like the University of Chicago, New York University, and Carnegie Mellon University. A complete list of NCAA membership by division can be found at www.ncaa.org.

Coaches at academically selective schools are always looking for athletic talent. Sometimes that talent is brought to their attention when high school students are nationally ranked in their sport or when they receive other sports-related honors. Coaches keep track of such students with an eye toward actively recruiting them when it comes time for college admission. Still other students bring themselves to a coach's attention through correspondence expressing interest and by providing relevant athletic and academic statistics.

The NCAA sets rigid guidelines that govern student eligibility as well as the process by which coaches can recruit players. There are rules that govern when and how often a coach can contact a prospective athlete, as well as rules on what can and cannot be reimbursed if an athlete comes to campus for an interview. The rules are designed to ensure that eager coaches do not overwhelm young athletes. You can find all the guidelines that govern the division you are interested in at www.ncaa.org.

> *"* Dealing with college coaches in the fall of your senior year is flattering but nerve-wracking. A coach may call and write every week, insisting that you're the 6'2" center she needs for her basketball team . . . but you don't know how many other 6'2" centers she has on her call list as well, and she only needs one for next year. If you delay, and another of those players commits, your phone will go stone cold and you'll never even know what happened.*"*
>
> *College freshman heavily recruited to play women's basketball*

At many colleges, coaches are given a number of slots they can fill with their highest-priority recruits. They can submit additional names, but those athletes won't get priority from the admissions office above and beyond what their non-athletic credentials would merit. The problem for recruited students, however, is that they rarely know in advance where they rank on a coach's list. Coaches have to recruit more students than they actually need, since there is no guarantee all will enroll. And they don't know their full potential talent pool until the recruiting season is over. A student who is high on the list at one point in time may be bumped down by talented late arrivals.

> "There was a young athlete at my child's private school who was superb in her sport. An Ivy League coach showed intense interest and encouraged her application to the extent that the private school's counseling staff thought it was a done deal. The girl was denied early decision. Turns out that the coach was new and inexperienced, and had encouraged the girl without checking with admissions to see if she had an admissible profile. The Ivies have a formula for athletic admits, and she didn't make the grade."
>
> *Mother of two athletic recruits*

In Chapter Three we talked about the Academic Index (AI) used by Ivy League colleges. Computed from SAT or ACT scores and class rank, the AI is used to ensure that a recruited athlete's academic record falls within the broad parameters of the prior year's freshman class. Ivy League colleges have agreed that the average AI for all athletes admitted to a specific college must fall within one standard deviation of the mean of the entire class admitted the year before. In addition, only a few individual athletes whose AI falls more than 2.5 standard deviations from the mean of the previous year can be admitted.[5] Although Ivy League admissions processes give a big boost to athletes on a coach's list, Ivy League colleges have agreed to place constraints on just how big that boost can be.

If you are a strong athlete interested in playing in college, we advise you to talk to your high school coach about your level of ability no later than early in your junior year, and preferably earlier. Begin your college search early so that you can identify colleges that meet your academic and social needs and that offer the opportunity to play your sport at the right level for you. Contact college coaches, providing a short athletic and academic résumé, by the end of your junior year if you

> "Recruiting puts kids under tremendous pressure to apply ED. Most coaches told my daughter that the only influence they had was in the early decision cycle — if she waited and applied regular decision, they could not help her. I don't know if that was the truth, or just a ruse so that the coach would know which students were serious enough about the college to merit further attention."
>
> *Parent of a heavily recruited athlete*

are not contacted first. And be sure to register with the NCAA Clearing House at www.ncaa.org by the end of your junior year to ensure your eligibility if you plan to play in Division I or Division II.

The NCAA Web site provides a wealth of information about the athletic recruiting process. You and your parents should read it carefully so that you will know what to expect and what is expected of you. You may ultimately find that a college coach will only guarantee you a place on his list if you agree to apply early decision. Do so if you know you want to attend that school and will be happy there. Otherwise, placement on the coach's list is no bargain. A strong athlete who is not recruited may be able to play as a "walk-on" to the team once he or she is admitted via the regular admissions process.

Details, Details

It is often said that the devil is in the details. The last thing you want to happen is for your thoughtful, carefully prepared case for admission to be sabotaged by minor details. Review this list before you apply, and then double-check it along the way.

• **Be sure to spell your name exactly the same way on all of your application materials and correspondence.** If you use your middle initial, use it every time on every form for every college-related purpose. Get into the habit of doing this right at the beginning and avoid the hassle of having three copies of every college mailing arrive at your house, or SAT scores or recommendation letters that don't find their way to the right file. If your social security number is required, be sure you enter it correctly each time.

• **Make sure your e-mail address reflects your maturity.** Save Imtoosexy@ internetprovider.com for communication with your friends, and get another address, from a reliable provider, for the business of applying to college.

• **Keep a copy of everything you send in, including online applications and other written and e-mail correspondence.** Make sure you submit all parts of the application, along with the application fee if one is required, by the indicated deadlines. Don't wait until the last minute to file—unanticipated problems have a habit of appearing at that point.

• **Give each person who is writing recommendations for you everything he or she needs to submit them on time.** Make up packets that include the appropriate recommendation forms (with identifying information legibly filled out at the top). Sign the waiver if the forms have one. Consider putting a Post-it® on each form with the due date. Include a stamped, pre-addressed envelope for each form, but leave the return address blank. Your school or letter writer will fill that in. Put all the letters and envelopes in one big manila envelope, and write your name and the due date for each recommendation clearly on the outside. Do the same for the secondary school reports that you give to your counselor. Arrange to pay for the transcripts that colleges typically request.

• **File your financial aid forms promptly, even if you and your parents have to use estimated figures.** Keep copies of everything you use to fill out the forms. You may need to produce them as part of the data verification process.

• **Ask the College Board or ACT, or both, to send your scores to the colleges of your choice.** Remember that the College Board will send all the scores from tests you have taken from ninth grade on. The ACT will send only the scores you ask them to send. Each gives you a limited number of free score reports if you provide the names of the colleges at the time of testing. Later reports can be purchased online, by mail, or by phone. Be sure you send your test results in time. Allow three weeks for regular delivery of scores. You can pay for rush delivery, but it is expensive and should be unnecessary if you plan ahead, except for November scores if you apply early.

• **Be sure to keep all correspondence that may come from your colleges after you apply.** Some may come by snail mail and some via e-mail. You will probably get a password to access the status of your application online, as well as the final decision. Keep your password in a safe place and, just as important, remember where you put it.

• **Check the status of your application about three to four weeks after everything was sent.** It can take quite a while for forms to be opened and sorted, and information is not always immediately posted online. If a college doesn't have a Web site where you can check your application's status, give the admissions office a call to see whether everything has been received. If something is missing, arrange to send it again.

• **Stay alert for phone messages or e-mail from alumni interviewers if your colleges offer such interviews.** Read the college material to see whether you have to formally request an interview (and by what date) or if you will be contacted automatically (and when). If you do not hear from someone in the time frame indicated, call or e-mail the admissions office.

- **By mid-January, request that your high school send your fall semester grades to each college that requires them as part of the regular decision application process.** These colleges typically include a "midyear report" form in the application package for this purpose. Some high schools send a new transcript; others submit the grades right on the form itself. The midyear report form also usually invites the counselor to note any significant additions or changes to the applicant's academic, extracurricular, or character record. This is a place where good news can be added or problems noted. Once again, provide a stamped, pre-addressed envelope for each submission.

- **If you have a new major honor or accomplishment after you apply, send a note to the admissions office (with your name and social security number clearly indicated at the top) requesting that this information be added to your file.** But don't add something that is insignificant. It can make you look as if you are trying too hard.

Now What?

Completing your applications is a major milestone in the college admissions process. Although you will still have a few things left to do (for example, checking on the status of your application and participating in interviews), the bulk of the work is behind you. Take a deep breath and celebrate!

If you have done your job of building your college list well, you will have at least one and probably several good choices come April. Now is the time to get back to being a fully engaged student, working to do well in your classes and continuing to be involved in meaningful activities. You are about to enter your last few months as a high school student. It has been a long haul, but you're almost there.

Paying the Bill

The news is mixed when it comes to paying for college. The good news is that for many students, the cost of tuition, fees, room, and board printed in the college catalog is only loosely related to what the student actually pays. Although no one pays more than the "sticker price," many students pay less, sometimes much less, depending on their family's financial situation and their campus's financial aid policies. The not-so-good news is that financial aid can be complex and confusing, and in some cases disappointing, if you don't understand how it works both in general and at the specific colleges where you are applying.

This chapter will give you the tools you need to understand the different kinds of financial aid and how they are awarded. We'll show you how you can roughly calculate how much aid you might expect to receive, and we'll explain why the actual amount may be more or less depending on a college's financial aid policies and practices. We'll also share some thoughts about the role of financial considerations in developing a college list and in making a final decision. If your family can easily cover the cost of your education, you can safely skip this chapter. If not, it will pay to read it carefully.

> "Financial aid allowed us to send our daughter where she wanted to go, a private school in the east. With three children, we couldn't have done it without that help. Financial aid really helped our middle-class family."
>
> *Parent of college sophomore*

How Do Colleges Determine Your Financial Need?

Need-based aid is financial assistance awarded on the basis of the difference between the cost of attending a college including tuition and fees, room and board, and books and incidentals (cost of attendance) and what a student and his or her family can reasonably afford to pay (expected family contribution, or EFC for short). The difference between these two figures is known as *demonstrated financial need* or simply *financial need.* Need-based aid is designed to reduce or eliminate financial need as a barrier to attending college. The determination of what a family can afford, however, is not left up to the family, for obvious reasons. There are objective ways of measuring how much a family can reasonably

> " I thought we would qualify for need-based aid, but the calculations showed we didn't. It was probably just wishful thinking on my part. "
>
> *Parent disappointed by the results of the need analysis*

contribute to their child's education. An underlying principle is that parents and students have a primary responsibility to contribute to the cost of a college education, according to their ability, before receiving financial aid.

The Free Application for Federal Student Aid (FAFSA)

All students applying for need-based aid are required to fill out the Free Application for Federal Student Aid, or FAFSA. The FAFSA is a need analysis form that all colleges use to calculate the expected family contribution for purposes of determining eligibility for federal financial aid. It is also used to determine eligibility for most state-based aid, for many private awards, and for institutional-based aid at many colleges. The FAFSA includes some parts of a family's income and assets

---

The Key Equation for Financial Aid Based on Need

Cost of attendance
− Expected family contribution

= Financial need

---

and excludes others. For example, while the FAFSA uses all parent and student income, it does not take into account the income of a noncustodial parent in the case of divorce, nor does it consider home equity as an asset. The FAFSA includes questions about the size of the family and the number of family members currently in college, and it assumes a certain basic level of household expenses. Calculation of need using the FAFSA is known as *federal methodology.*

> " I didn't find the FAFSA as daunting as some people said it would be. It's time consuming, but it's not difficult. You need to gather all your records and your tax returns in one place. From there on it's pretty straightforward."
>
> *Mother of twins who had to file twice*

The FAFSA can be submitted between January 1 and June 30 of the year a student plans to start college. It requires detailed information from the parents' and student's federal income tax return for the previous calendar year, as well as the list of colleges to which a student will be applying. Although the FAFSA will be accepted up until June 30 for a need analysis for aid for the following year, many colleges have much earlier dates by which a student must file, often as early as February 1.

It is a good idea to file the FAFSA as early as you can, even before your tax returns are completed. The FAFSA allows you to use estimates of the figures that will appear on your tax return; you can amend the estimates when you have the final figures from your returns. You then submit the FAFSA online or in paper form directly to the government agency that processes it. The online version is easy to use and gives you immediate feedback about any errors you may be making in entering your data. Confidentiality is assured whether you submit your form online or through the mail.

After your FAFSA is filed and processed, you will receive your Student Aid Report, or SAR, indicating your expected family contribution based on the federal methodology. It can take three to four weeks to get your response if you submit your FAFSA by mail, but a week or less if you do it online. Once you receive your SAR, review it carefully for any errors and report them immediately. Complete information about the FAFSA, along with forms, can be found at www.fafsa.ed.gov. You submit your FAFSA just once; copies of your SAR are sent electronically to the campuses you designate on the form. You can add more later if you wish.

CSS PROFILE

Several hundred private colleges as well as a small number of public colleges also require financial aid applicants to complete a form known as the College Scholarship Service Financial Aid PROFILE, or CSS PROFILE. The PROFILE is used by these colleges to determine eligibility for aid from college-based resources. Some states and a number of foundations and other groups that award special scholarships also require students to complete the PROFILE.

The PROFILE takes into account all the sources of income and assets used in the FAFSA, but unlike the FAFSA, it asks about home equity, trust funds in the name of siblings, a student's summer earnings, and the income and assets of a non-custodial parent. These additions generally increase the expected family contribution in those cases where they apply. On the other side of the ledger, however, the PROFILE considers medical and dental expenses and private school tuition for siblings as family obligations that can decrease a family's ability to pay for college. These expenses are not considered by the FAFSA. A need calculation using the CSS PROFILE is known as *institutional methodology*.

The College Board, the administrator of the SAT, also administers the PROFILE. Information about the PROFILE can be found at www.collegeboard.com. Unlike the FAFSA, which uses the same form for everyone, the PROFILE is customized for each family with additional questions requested by the colleges to which the student is applying for aid. Individual colleges can choose from among a large number of additional questions dealing with things such as foreign assets, business loans, or details of divorce settlements. The extra questions that appear on a student's form will vary depending on the colleges a student lists when registering for the PROFILE.

The PROFILE can no longer be filed in paper form; the College Board moved to online submission exclusively in 2005. Unlike the FAFSA, which is free, students pay a fee to register for the CSS PROFILE and then a fee for each college to which the results are sent. In 2004–05, the registration fee was $5, with an additional charge of $18 per college. The PROFILE is available by early September, and colleges typically require students to submit the PROFILE within a few weeks of their application deadline.

Forms and More Forms

All applicants for need-based financial aid, regardless of where they live or where they are applying, must complete the FAFSA. Beyond that, the forms you'll need to submit will depend on the colleges to which you are applying and your home

Differences Between CSS PROFILE and FAFSA Calculations of Expected Family Contribution

- PROFILE includes home equity as a family asset. Life insurance, retirement plans, annuities, and so forth are also included in the calculation. FAFSA does not include any of these.

- PROFILE expects a student to make a minimum contribution, usually through summer work. FAFSA does not require a minimum contribution from the student.

- PROFILE requires information on income and assets of a noncustodial parent. FAFSA does not include this information.

- PROFILE collects information on private elementary and secondary school tuition, medical expenses, and so on and allows the campus-based financial aid officer considerable discretion in evaluating special financial circumstances. FAFSA does not.

state. Some students will have to complete the PROFILE, a supplementary form from their home state, or both. Students applying to certain colleges, mostly private ones, will also need to complete a third form in addition to the FAFSA and PROFILE, which the college itself prepares and administers. Thus, colleges vary from requiring one form, the FAFSA, to up to four forms (the FAFSA, a state form, the PROFILE, and a form of their own).

The good news is that the FAFSA, the PROFILE, and state forms are submitted only once; you indicate the list of colleges that should receive the information, and it is sent electronically by the processing agency. However, you will have to keep careful track of which forms your schools request. For example, the University of Virginia requires the FAFSA and a college-specific form. The University of North Carolina asks its applicants to submit the FAFSA and the PROFILE.

In all cases, it is also important for you to keep track of submission deadlines. If you plan to apply early action or early decision, colleges will typically ask you to submit the PROFILE and their own institutional form, if any, soon after the application deadline and then follow up with the FAFSA later. Getting your forms in as early as you can is always wise.

The Verification Process

Verification is a process to ensure the accuracy of the information that you submit to qualify for financial aid. The federal government selects about 30 percent of FAFSA applicants for verification, most of them randomly. A small percentage of verifications are targeted, however, because of inconsistencies or other anomalies reported on the form. The government asks one of the colleges that received your FAFSA results to take on the task of verification. If you are selected, you may be asked to submit a verification worksheet, federal tax returns, or other supporting documents directly to that college. It is a good idea to keep copies of all your financial aid application information in one place so you can get to it easily.

Although the FAFSA verification process affects less than a third of applicants, many private colleges require that all financial aid applicants submit supporting documentation. Be sure to check the financial aid application instructions carefully so that you will be aware of these requirements.

Why Do Need-Based Packages Differ from College to College?

You may be surprised to learn that your aid offers will differ, sometimes by a lot, even at colleges that offer only need-based aid and that promise to meet the full need of all admitted students. Although all colleges are required to use the FAFSA to compute the EFC (expected family contribution) for federal financial aid, they are also free to interpret the information as they deem appropriate and to use the PROFILE and their own forms to determine need for other sources of aid. Since different colleges may interpret your need differently, you can't know what your aid will look like, either in amount or type of aid, until you have your offer in hand.

This wasn't always the case. For over thirty years, a group of twenty-three high-profile, selective colleges known informally as the Overlap Group would meet each spring to agree on the need-based financial aid packages for students who were being admitted by two or more of them.[1] The goal of the Overlap Group was to meet student financial need without engaging in counterproductive "bidding wars" that would interfere with their ability to use their funding for the neediest students.

Things became more complicated when the federal government, having investigated the workings of the Overlap Group in 1989, called its practices a violation of antitrust laws that amounted to "price fixing." The meetings were permanently discontinued in 1991. With the demise of the Overlap Group, member colleges once again could make financial aid offers independently of the others. This "free market" approach to financial aid awards has led to a good deal of variability from college to college in the size of aid awards for the same student.

> "Increasingly, there is evidence that students and their parents are confused by the substantial disparities in the reports they receive from financial aid experts at different campuses of the costs of educational expenses that families will reasonably be expected to pay." [2]
>
> *Hunter Rawlings, former president of Cornell University and chair of the 568 Presidents' Working Group*

It is interesting that a number of colleges—some of which were part of the Overlap Group—are once again trying to bring greater coherence to financial aid. Known as the 568 Presidents' Working Group after a 1992 federal statute that permits colleges to collaborate on the qualifications for financial aid (as opposed to actual aid awards themselves), a group of twenty-eight college and university presidents have worked together since 1999 to develop a consensus on how need-based aid should be awarded. Formally known as the Consensus Approach to Need Analysis, their approach attempts to reduce the disparity among need-based awards. Their efforts may result in a more rational

---

Original Members of the 568 Presidents' Working Group

Amherst College	Haverford College	Rice University
Boston College	Macalester College	Stanford University
Bowdoin College	MIT	Swarthmore College
University of Chicago	Middlebury College	Vanderbilt University
Claremont McKenna	Northwestern	Wake Forest
Columbia University	University	University
Davidson College	University of	Wellesley College
Duke University	Notre Dame	Wesleyan University
Emory University	University of	Williams College
Georgetown	Pennsylvania	Yale University
University	Pomona College	

and consistent methodology for awarding institutional aid, at least for the colleges adopting the new guidelines. The participants recognize, however, that some variation will continue to exist. As stated in the preliminary report of the 568 Presidents' Working Group, "Although the Consensus Approach would standardize many policies now subject to professional judgment, it is important to recognize that no system will completely eliminate disparate results or the effects of individual institutional 'packaging' decisions."[3]

How Can You Estimate Your Financial Need?

It is a good idea to do a quick FAFSA analysis to get an idea of how much need-based aid you might qualify for under federal methodology. Although the FAFSA itself can't be filed before January 1, you can use online calculators at any time to get a ballpark idea of what your EFC would look like. The College Board Web site, www.collegeboard.com, has a very helpful and easy-to-use FAFSA calculator. You can access it through either the "For Students" or "For Parents" areas on the home page under "Paying for College."

You and your family may be pleasantly surprised to learn that your expected family contribution is lower than you thought it would be. Some families, however, may find that the government expects them to contribute more than they had planned. As a general rule, you should consider the estimated EFC using federal methodology to be the lowest estimate of your EFC and hence the most generous estimate of your financial need. The CSS PROFILE usually, but not always, calculates a higher EFC, meaning less need, because it includes many assets specifically excluded from the FAFSA. For example, a family with substantial home equity or a noncustodial parent with financial resources may find that its EFC is significantly higher using the institutional methodology. The College Board site also includes a calculator that lets you compute a basic EFC using the CSS PROFILE. If you are thinking about schools that require the PROFILE as well as the FAFSA, it is worth seeing how your EFC may differ based on the two calculations.

What Goes into a Financial Aid Package?

The financial aid that a student typically receives from a college is made up of different kinds of assistance from federal, state, and college-based resources. The particular combination that you will receive to meet your need is known as your financial aid *package.* Need-based financial aid packages usually have three parts. A typical package has grant funds, work-study funding, and loans. Grants are considered *gift aid,* while work-study funding and loans are often referred to as *self-help.*

Grants

Grants are awards you don't have to repay. They are tax-free when used to cover the cost of tuition, fees, books, and supplies. There are no special conditions to receiving a grant other than remaining in good academic standing. (Grants can also be awarded for reasons other than need, and we will discuss these in the section on merit aid.) Need-based grants come from three primary sources: the federal government, state governments, and college resources. Currently, there are two major need-based federal grant programs:

• **Pell Grants** range from $400 to $4,050 a year for 2004–05, depending on need. In recent years, about 90 percent of Pell Grant recipients have had family incomes below $40,000.

• **Federal Supplemental Educational Opportunity Grants (FSEOG),** currently ranging from $100 to $4,000 per year, are designed for students with exceptionally high need. Priority is given to Pell Grant recipients.

Work-Study

Work-study programs provide part-time jobs to students who can then apply their earnings to tuition or living expenses. Jobs are considered financial aid when they are arranged through the financial aid office, and the earnings are not included in the EFC calculation. Work-study jobs are usually on or near campus and vary in their time commitment. Most work-study programs are subsidized by the federal government, which provides matching funds to colleges to pay for them. The federal program encourages work that performs a community service and work related to a student's area of study, although not all jobs meet one of those criteria. Students are paid at least the minimum wage, and freshmen typically work about ten hours a week when classes are in session, a load that is quite manageable.

Loans

Loans are borrowed money that have to be repaid with interest. To qualify as financial aid, a loan must have an interest rate that is lower than the current commercial rate and have favorable repayment terms. Financial aid loans may be taken out by students or parents, and may be guaranteed and often subsidized by the federal or state government. When a loan is subsidized, interest charges and repayment do not begin until six months after you graduate, leave school, or drop below half-time enrollment. The repayment period, once it starts, is usually ten years. There are several federal loan programs:

- **Perkins Loans** (to students) are fixed-rate, low-interest loans offered by participating schools to students with the greatest need. The federal government subsidizes these loans by paying the interest on them while the student is still in school. When repayment begins, these loans are repaid directly to the college.
- **Stafford Loans** (to students) are variable rate loans that take two forms: subsidized and unsubsidized. Subsidized loans are made on the basis of financial need. Unsubsidized loans are available to students independent of need, but the government does not pay the interest while the student is in school. The student may arrange to defer payment of the interest, or pay it as it accrues.
- **PLUS Loans** (to parents) allow parents to borrow up to the total cost of education for each child, minus any student financial aid that is awarded. The interest rate is variable but capped. PLUS loans are made without regard to financial need, but parents must have a positive credit history to be eligible. PLUS stands for Parent Loans to Undergraduate Students.

Stafford Loans and PLUS loans are offered through two different sources of funding: either directly from the government through the Direct Loan Program, or through the Federal Family Education Loan Program (FFELP), which uses banks and other private lenders. Colleges choose to participate in one program or the other—the terms and conditions of the two are nearly identical except for some administrative details.

How Is Your Package Put Together?

Grants are clearly the most desirable source of funding, since no extra work is required and they do not need to be repaid. Virtually all colleges, however, include some form of self-help as part of their financial aid packages. What varies is the proportion of the aid package that is self-help. Colleges with large endowments can usually afford to award a larger portion of the package as grant aid. For example, in 2001 Princeton University announced that it would no longer include loans in any of its financial aid packages, a first among major institutions. Work-study and grant funding would be the only components. In 2004, President Larry Summers of Harvard University announced that his campus would no longer require families with incomes of $40,000 or less to take out loans.

Although Princeton University and Harvard University are notable exceptions to the general rule that colleges include loans in a financial aid package, even less well-endowed colleges can and do exercise discretion in awarding aid. Two students may have identical need and receive the same amount of aid, but it may be packaged very differently. If a college is particularly eager to recruit a student, it may offer a higher percentage of grant money in the total package, making it more desirable to the student receiving it. Colleges also have flexibility in determining

> "In general, when awarding money from programs they administer but do not fund (i.e., federal programs), colleges give priority to the neediest of the able. When awarding money from their own funds, colleges give priority to the ablest of the needy."[4]
>
> *Anna and Robert Leider, authors of Don't Miss Out: The Ambitious Student's Guide to Financial Aid*

the final EFC—much more with institutional methodology than with federal methodology—based on the professional judgment of the financial aid staff.

When you eventually compare packages from different colleges, you'll need to look at both the individual components of the package and the total package amount. Be sure to check the college's figure for the cost of attendance, including tuition and fees, room and board, books, incidentals, and travel home. An unrealistically low estimate of these costs is equivalent to less financial aid, even if the awards are the same size. When you receive your aid offer, all of the components of the package will be itemized and listed separately, and you will be asked to accept or reject each part if you choose to attend that college. If the package is inadequate or less than another one you have received, you or your parents can ask the financial aid office to review your case for possible adjustment. We'll talk more about how to approach this in a later section of this chapter.

Will Your Need for Financial Aid Affect Your Chances for Admission?

Only a small percentage of all private colleges have the financial resources to admit students without regard to need and then to meet the full demonstrated need of those admitted. They include all of the colleges that are part of the 568 Presidents'

Working Group, as well as the other members of the Ivy League, Reed College, and a few others. These colleges are referred to as *need blind* and *full need* in their admissions and financial aid policies. Most of them have chosen to direct all of their available financial aid, with the exception of athletic scholarships where offered, to students demonstrating financial need.

Still other colleges have policies that are *need aware* or *need sensitive* to some extent. These colleges have sufficient resources to make most, but not all, of their admissions decisions independent of financial aid considerations, so they reserve some spots in the freshman class for students whose families are able to meet the full cost of attendance.

> "The College also remains committed to admitting students without regard to their financial resources, though, in any given year, we may have to admit a small portion of a class with some concern for their financial need." [5]
>
> Paul Thiboutot, director of admission, Carleton College, explaining his need-aware policy

If you apply to a need-aware college and need little or no financial aid, you may enjoy a small admissions advantage over someone with a similar record who needs substantial aid. This is especially true if you are a borderline candidate. Colleges that cannot afford to offer support to 100 percent of their students will offer the support they do have to the students they most want to admit. But the admissions advantage associated with being able to pay the full cost of college is usually quite small—not anything to count on if you have it or fret about if you don't.

Carleton College, Washington University in St. Louis, Oberlin College, and Union College are among the many colleges that are presently need aware to some extent. Policies can change, however, based on a college's financial situation. Carleton College had been need blind for many years until it could no longer afford to be. Brown University, in contrast, moved from a need aware to need blind admissions policy for the first time for the class of 2007.

Read the information about a college's financial aid policies carefully. You can usually find it posted on the Web along with other admissions-related information and included with printed application materials. If a college states that it meets the full need of all admitted students but doesn't state that it has a need-blind policy, it probably admits some percentage of its freshman class on a need-aware basis. If a college says it is need blind in its admissions policy but doesn't commit itself to meeting the full need of those admitted, some students may find a gap between the college's financial aid award and what they actually need to attend.

What About Merit-Based Aid?

More and more colleges, especially those that seek to build their reputations, are offering aid that is not based on need. Known as *merit-based* aid, these awards are often given to students in recognition of particular abilities, talents, or other criteria. Recipients may also have financial need, but need is not the basis for the award. There are three major sources of funding for merit awards: states, the colleges themselves, and private individuals and groups. There are no federal merit awards for undergraduates. Merit grants are often referred to as scholarships.

Colleges have learned that merit aid in the form of a $5,000 or $10,000 scholarship can encourage students with little or no financial need to accept an offer of admission at an institution they might otherwise decline. This kind of "tuition discounting" can help a college increase its yield and the number of students eager to attend. And a merit scholarship, often full-ride, extended to a student with an outstanding record may result in a "catch" for the college—an academic superstar whose presence can help raise standards and contribute positively to intellectual life on campus.

Some less selective public research universities like the University of Oklahoma and Iowa State University have pursued this approach by aggressively targeting National Merit Finalists (see Chapter Six for more information about the National Merit Scholarship Program). These students may be offered a generous scholarship if they inform the National Merit Scholarship Corporation that the university is their first choice and if they subsequently apply and enroll. National Merit Finalists usually have much stronger academic profiles than the typical enrollee at such an institution and are thus seen as very desirable potential students.

> "I talked to several parents who had not considered private schools because they thought the cost was prohibitive. Well, that's not always true. The most selective schools don't give merit aid, but others do. We were really fortunate that our kids were high achievers and worked hard in high school. They got a lot of merit-based aid."
>
> *Mother of family not eligible for need-based aid with two children in private colleges*

> "We want kids who are good at dancing, who are good at collecting butterflies, who are good at basketball. At the point where we have the capacity to attract students with the magnetism Harvard does, we'll be happy to follow Harvard's [need-based] policies." [6]
>
> *Stephen Trachtenberg, president of George Washington University*

Non-need-based financial aid is a controversial topic in higher education. Some colleges, usually the most selective, argue that all of their aid should be need based to ensure that financial need is not a barrier for students. Other colleges want to be able to give scholarships to academically talented students who don't have financial need, while still awarding the majority of their aid to those with demonstrated need. The debate between the two approaches to aid is not likely to end soon, and in fact shows signs of intensifying as colleges compete for students with special qualities they seek.

Seeking Scholarships

Scholarships from non-college-based sources are an additional source of financial aid. They represent a very small percentage of the total amount of money available for financial aid overall, but they are worth pursuing. Awarded to students for a variety of reasons—academic achievement, talent, writing competitions—these scholarships are generally sponsored by organizations, foundations, and businesses. Local Rotary Clubs and Lions Clubs, for example, award scholarships to high school students in communities across the country, and some large businesses offer scholarships for their employees' children. These awards are typically paid directly to a college to offset the cost of attendance. They vary

> "We encouraged our kids to apply for community-based scholarships. They are easier to get because you're only competing against people from your own local area."
>
> *Parent of student who applied for local scholarships*

widely in amount, from a few hundred dollars to many thousands. Most are fairly small, maybe $1,000 or less, but even those can make an important difference.

A number of states have their own merit scholarship programs as well that vary in terms of their generosity and how they can be used. HOPE scholarships, for example, cover full tuition at any state-supported institution for all Georgia students meeting a certain minimum GPA. The Florida Bright Futures Scholarship Program has several options, one of which covers 100 percent of tuition and fees at public or private institutions for Florida high school graduates meeting certain academic and community service criteria and who choose to stay in-state for college. Although most state scholarships are applicable only to in-state institutions and sometimes to a particular campus, others are more flexible and can be applied anywhere a student chooses to attend.

"I'd be willing to bet that most students who are in a position to need financial aid could finance their entire undergraduate education if they had the time to do all of the research, applications, and so on. My high school counselor helped me with a lot of the research simply by pointing me in the right directions in terms of Internet resources and the occasional specific scholarship opportunity, but many students don't realize that there are so many options out there. Once I'd completed the 'find and prune' maze to find what applied to me, then it was time for balancing regular schoolwork, admissions applications, financial aid applications, scholarship applications, loan research, and my after school jobs and extracurricular activities. I ended up getting a separate calendar simply for the application deadlines. It was hard for me since I was also suffering from senioritis — perhaps a little immature — but I think a lot of students in the application process feel the same way."

College junior

Questions to Ask Colleges About Financial Aid

- What percentage of incoming freshmen receive financial aid from federal, state, or institutional resources?

- Does the college meet the full need of all admitted students?

- Does the college offer merit aid, or does it offer need-based aid only?

- Is this college need blind or need aware?

- How will an outside scholarship affect my financial aid package?

- Assuming my need remains the same after freshman year, will the composition of my financial aid package change?

- What are the academic requirements for continued financial aid?

If a student receives an outside scholarship in addition to a need-based package that contains federal aid, federal law requires that the aid package be reduced by the amount of the scholarship, since financial aid may not exceed demonstrated need whenever federal funds are involved. Colleges are usually willing to substitute the scholarship, dollar for dollar, for all or part of the self-help components of the aid package rather than the gift aid component. This means that although a scholarship will not increase the actual amount of your package, it can make your package more desirable. Colleges vary somewhat in their policies and flexibility with regard to the treatment of outside scholarships, so it is worth asking the financial aid office of each college that admits you how such a scholarship would be handled.

Should You Use a Scholarship Search Service?

College-bound high school seniors and their parents often receive letters from businesses offering to help the student find or apply for financial aid. These letters may look very official and suggest that the student and family must participate in a special program to find out about financial aid opportunities.

It is easy to see why businesses like this exist. There are so many different kinds of financial aid that many families feel overwhelmed by the process of seeking it. A service that promises to ferret out thousands of dollars in awards in return for a fee of a few hundred dollars may seem like a good investment. But is it?

The general consensus among financial aid experts is that no student or family needs to pay for help finding financial aid. At best, these services provide information about funding programs that families can readily find themselves. At worst, they may be shady businesses involving illegal scams that defraud students and families. The Federal Trade Commission cautions families to be aware of the following approaches that can signal a scam:

> "I'm not saying there aren't people out there who are legitimate private counselors (for aid), but we try to direct families to where they can get help without spending unnecessary dollars." [7]
>
> Dallas Martin, president of the National Association of Student Financial Aid Administrators

- "The scholarship is guaranteed or your money back."

- "You can't get this information anywhere else."

- "I just need your credit card or bank account number to hold this scholarship."

- "You've been selected by a 'national foundation' to receive this scholarship," or "You're a finalist" in a contest you've never entered.

It is important to remember that most financial aid, whether federal, state, or college funded, is awarded through college financial aid offices after you've applied, completed your FAFSA and any other need analysis forms, and been accepted. Information about private scholarships is readily available, for free, from many sources. The counseling office at your high school is the first place to look. It can be particularly helpful as a source of information about scholarships awarded by local businesses and community organizations, in addition to national programs. Several Web sites, which make their money through advertising rather than fees, also provide good information about scholarship opportunities. Two sites worth checking out are www.finaid.com and www.fastweb.com.

Financial Aid and Your Decisions

Parents and students need to talk openly and honestly about how much they, collectively, are willing to contribute to the cost of college through savings and borrowing. It does little good to have a college say that a family has the resources to contribute $10,000 a year to a student's education when the family is either unwilling or unable to contribute that amount.

Thinking About Financial Aid Before You Apply

The uncertainties of financial aid (both up and down) are such that you should not let aid considerations determine where you apply. But if you have concerns about your family's ability to handle the Expected Family Contribution computed through the FAFSA, it is wise to include at least a couple of colleges that would be affordable based on what your family can contribute (and, of course, where you have a good chance of admission). Think of them as financial good-bet colleges. Having at least one or two schools that you would be happy to attend and that you know you can afford can provide some much-needed security. In the end, you may find that a private school with high tuition may actually cost your family no more than a less expensive state school because of generous financial aid. But you can't know that in advance.

"It was clear early on that our kids would not qualify for need-based financial aid. So then we became pretty adept at looking through the Web sites to identify which institutions gave merit-based aid."

Parent of two college students who received significant merit aid

College-based merit aid is a bit of a wild card in the financial aid equation. If a college offers such aid, it can be hard to predict your chances of getting it. You should

What Does It Cost to Attend Berkeley or Harvard? Cost of Attendance for 2004-05			
	Harvard	UC Berkeley (CA residents)	UC Berkeley (out-of-state)
Tuition and fees	$30,620	$6,730	$23,686
Room and board	$9,260	$11,630	$11,630
Books/personal Expenses	$2,570	$2,538	$2,538
Travel	depends on distance from home		
TOTAL	$42,450 (plus transportation)	$20,898 (plus transportation)	$37,854 (plus transportation)

certainly not count on it. The College Board Web site, www.collegeboard.com, is just one of several that makes it easy to see whether a college offers merit aid and how much they offer. It is worth checking out the colleges you are interested in to see their practices. If a college offers merit awards and your record is strong compared to that of an average freshman, you're a good prospect. Factor this into your thinking when you build your college list, but don't let it dominate your decisions.

Evaluating Aid After You've Been Accepted

Comparing financial aid offers can be an important part of your decision-making process once you have your letters of admission in hand. As we noted earlier, financial aid packages can vary widely, not only in total amount but also in their components. Financial aid letters also differ in the way they present information, so you should "translate" them into a common format before you begin. The Financial Aid Comparison Worksheet in Appendix D will help you do this.

Be sure to take a careful look at the total cost of attendance for each school. Is it realistic, or does it omit or underestimate some key expenses such as travel home? Another worksheet, in Appendix E, lets you compare the way colleges estimate cost of attendance. Since the cost of books, room and board, incidentals, and travel is

"I just graduated from a highly selective private college last June. Although it was a great experience, I wish I had thought more carefully before I agreed to take so many loans. They hang over my head now, affecting my decisions much more than I want. For example, I turned down a couple of teaching jobs in the Philippines because although they would pay enough for me to be able to live pretty well there, they would never have covered my loan payments.

My college is quick to say that if you can get in, you can come no matter what your financial situation. Their message to students is not to worry about it, but students should worry. I know a lot of people who were pretty shocked when they got to the 'exit interview' with Financial Aid and realized just how long they'd be paying off their loans. I don't think attending a really expensive school is worth it to everyone, and they should know the facts before they make their decision."

Recent college graduate

a key factor in determining your financial need, a figure that is unrealistically low will mean that you will have additional expenses that are not covered by your financial aid package.

Carefully compare the total amount of your aid package and its components. The total amount of aid is important, but so is the composition of the package. When completed, Appendix D will show you the breakdown as well as the total amount of each aid package. Two schools may offer the same amount of total aid, yet one may offer a much higher percentage of the package as grants that do not have to be repaid. From a purely financial perspective, the package with a higher percentage of gift aid is more desirable. Your offer of financial aid will give you the opportunity to accept or reject each individual component. You can choose to accept some parts of the package but not others.

Be sure you know each college's policies on financial aid for subsequent years. Do you have to reapply? Even if the amount of aid will remain the same (assuming no change in your family's financial circumstances), will the package change? Will packages in subsequent years contain a higher percentage of self-help aid? These are all questions to consider as you review your financial aid offers.

Students and parents often ask if they can appeal a financial aid offer. Although most colleges are not interested in "negotiating" revised packages, they are usually open to reviewing their offer in light of new information. You may, in fact, be able to work out a more favorable package at a given college based on changes in your family's financial situation, a possible error in the way your financial information was interpreted, or an offer at another college. Appealing your financial aid offer should be done diplomatically and without any hint of arrogance or entitlement.

Adjustments to reflect new circumstances or clarification of previously submitted information are the easiest ones for colleges to accommodate. Perhaps your mother's self-employment income suddenly dropped, or the college did not adequately consider family expenses associated with caring for your elderly grandparents. You or your parent should respectfully ask the financial aid office to review your package, making clear the basis for your request and your sincere interest in attending the college. You'll be asked to put your request in writing.

> "Too many parents jump quickly into negotiation mode, trying to play one school's offer against another's. If they sense you are just trying to get a better deal and you are treating it like a car, even if there's flexibility on their end, they're not likely to show it." [8]
>
> *Stephen Pemberton, private college consultant*

> "A number of elite privates give substantially different packages depending on how much they want you." [9]
>
> *Morton Owen Shapiro, president of Williams College*

It's more difficult for colleges to make adjustments based on offers from other colleges, and some are unwilling to do so. As a general rule, though, a college is more likely to increase your offer based on one from another college if it routinely competes with that college (or aspires to compete with it) for students. A highly selective college, for example, will be more inclined to match a package offered by another highly selective college. Similarly, a college may be more likely to increase its financial aid offer if you have exceptional academic qualifications or other talents relative to its overall pool of admitted students. It is better for you to be a big fish in a small pond rather than a small fish in a big pond in these cases.

A Word About Early Decision

In Chapter Seven, we noted that one of the major criticisms of early decision programs is that they commit students to attending a college without giving them a chance to compare financial aid packages. Since packages can vary significantly, especially when merit awards are involved, this is a real concern if you hope to maximize your financial aid offer. Ironically, those with the greatest need may have the least to be concerned about when applying early, since colleges committed to meeting the full need of accepted students will provide packages to cover the total cost of tuition, room and board, and other expenses. Those with less need, however, must face the fact that colleges vary in how they define need and how they propose to meet it. It is precisely those students who will want to compare aid packages and for whom early decision may be unwise.

You do not lose all flexibility, however, if you apply early decision. You may still request that a college review your early decision financial aid package if the award amount is insufficient for you to be able to attend. Adjustments are often made, and if the package does not meet your need, you can exercise your right to decline the offer and choose from among colleges to which you have applied regular decision. But you cannot hold onto your early aid offer until April and then decide to attend if it turns out to be the best.

Planning Ahead When Your Child Is Young

This chapter has been devoted to discussing financial aid issues that face families in a student's senior year. At that point a family's income and assets are usually a given. But what if you are reading this book when your child is much younger? What can you do to prepare for the financial burdens of a college education? We want to mention briefly some important, but often overlooked, points about saving for college. More detailed advice on the topic can be found on financial aid Web sites and in books on financial planning. Laws and practices can change quickly, however, so it is important to be sure to seek the most current information at the time you are making your plans.

• **It may be advantageous to save money for college in a parent's name rather than in the student's name.** Currently, federal need analysis formulas "count" parent assets at a much lower rate than student assets. Saving money in the parent's name also has the advantage of keeping it under parental control until it is needed. But parental income is usually taxed at a higher rate than children's income, so you have to estimate the relative gains in this context.

• **529 College Savings Plans, available in each state, are worth a careful look.** Although contributions are after-tax, they grow tax-deferred in the parent's name. When used for postsecondary educational expenses, earnings are currently tax-free, both at federal and state levels.

- **Education IRAs are a good way for some families to save for college expenses.** Contributions are nondeductible, but earnings accumulate tax-free and remain tax-free if they are used for college. There are annual contribution limits, as well as limitations based on annual income.

Some people have observed that financial aid policies do not provide families with an incentive to save, since savings reduce the amount of aid for which a student is eligible. Although it is true that savings will reduce the amount of financial aid your child may receive, there are no guarantees about which colleges will accept your child or what their financial aid polices will be. The more money you can save toward a college education, the greater your flexibility in choosing colleges and in dealing with the vagaries of financial aid. Not all parents can save enough money for college, however, and aid policies are designed to help their children. But those who can and do save are, in a very real sense, making an investment in their children's future—one of the best long-term investments a parent can ever make.

Making *Your* Decision After the Colleges Make *Theirs*

Up to this point, *Admission Matters* has focused on the process of choosing colleges and preparing strong applications. We now want to shift attention to the end of the process and talk about how to approach the choices you and your family will have to make once the colleges' decisions come in. For students applying early action or early decision, closure may come quickly. Colleges usually notify students mid-December (or mid-February, for those taking advantage of early decision II rounds offered by some colleges). Many colleges with rolling admissions, most often state universities such as Purdue University, the University of Washington, and Pennsylvania State University, also provide fast turnaround in just a few weeks or less. But for students applying regular decision (including those deferred from an early cycle), it will be the middle or end of March before most decisions are available. Ivy League colleges are usually among the last to announce their decisions, observing a common notification date at the beginning of April.

How Will You Be Notified?

Regardless of whether applications were submitted early or during the regular cycle, anxiety for parents and students naturally rises as the date for notification nears. Increasingly, colleges are choosing to notify students electronically to speed up the process and reduce uncertainty about when decisions will be received, since regular mail can be unpredictable. Colleges that communicate their decisions online or post them online typically announce the precise date and time when this information will be available. At the appointed hour, thousands of students across the country can be found in front of their computers checking for the final outcome.

Students expecting to receive their decisions via regular mail have a tougher time predicting exactly when their notifications will arrive. For many families, the familiar sight of the mail carrier or FEDEX driver is filled with anticipation. The "fat" packet—the one containing an acceptance letter along with enrollment forms and other information—is the one that everyone hopes to see. The "thin" business size envelope is usually (but not always) the bearer of disappointing news.

The Special Case of Early Decision

The wait for an early answer is often an emotionally intense time. By the very nature of the process, the student has been asked to make a major investment in a college as his or her "top choice." A lot seems to be riding on the outcome. When the outcome is a happy one, students and families are elated. When the outcome is not favorable, they can be severely disappointed, even if they knew it was a long shot.

It is easy for students to get caught up in their own feelings and forget that others around them are dealing with their own concerns over the admissions process. We encourage everyone to save overt bursts of emotion, be they shrieks of joy or

> "Early action and early decision letters should arrive next week. We feel that it is very important for students to treat other members of the community, and themselves, well—no matter what the results. Students who are admitted should consider the feelings of those who may not have been admitted or who have not applied early. Intense displays of happiness in public are not the most advisable behavior. Conversely, no one expects a student who did not get admitted to be happy about that. But intense public displays of anguish also can be a burden to others. We recommend that students try very hard to receive the decisions off-campus."
>
> *Posting on private school Web site*
> *in early December*

"I applied early action to Harvard. That's where my sister goes, but I didn't get in. The letter came on Wednesday and I was pretty upset for a couple of days. By Friday I was OK. Then the weekend came, and I just kind of forgot about it. Just because I didn't get into Harvard doesn't mean that there's anything wrong with me. It also helped that my sister had been rejected by Princeton and Yale. That showed me how random things could be. The other thing that really helped was that those who did get in did not run around screaming 'Oh, I got in early. My life is great!' That would have made it much worse for those of us who didn't get good news. Everyone was really respectful of everyone else. There were a lot of terrific kids who got rejected or deferred. It was like 'Join the club.' We kind of shared the pain."

High school senior

tears of disappointment, for a private setting. Some schools prohibit students from using on-site computers to access admission results for just this reason.

We also urge parents to respect their children's privacy with regard to decisions received at home. Children should be allowed privacy when receiving decisions, whether they arrive via e-mail or regular mail or are posted on a college's Web site. Some students may want family members present. Faced with possible disappointment, however, some prefer to be alone to absorb the decision. Parents should take their cue from their child and be there, literally or figuratively, to support him or her regardless of the outcome. If the news is disappointing, parents should be sure not to add to their child's burden with displays of anguish or anger. This is good advice not only for the early acceptance cycle, but also for the regular cycle notifications that may come later.

Accepted!

If your early application is a binding one, a "fat" packet brings your college search to an early, happy conclusion. If your acceptance packet does not include financial aid information, it will follow shortly, and if the offer covers your need, you are expected to submit your intent to enroll form and deposit by the deadline indicated. You will also be expected to withdraw all other pending applications. Unmet financial need is the only grounds for not attending a college that admits you under binding early decision. If your financial aid package provides less money than you will need to attend, contact the financial aid office immediately to explain the situation in detail and respectfully request that your financial aid package be reviewed. Perhaps something can be worked out. Remember, though, that there may be a difference between what a college believes a family needs and what the family wants. The two may not be totally reconcilable. The family, however, makes the final decision about whether the early decision financial aid package is sufficient to allow the student to attend.

Financial aid issues aside, colleges rely primarily on an honor system with regard to binding enrollment, since there is no legal action a college can take to force you to attend against your will. Guidance counselors also serve as enforcers of the rules. Selective colleges using early decision usually share their acceptance lists as a way to encourage compliance with the binding policy. Students who are not released from their binding commitment and who choose not to enroll at their early decision college may find some other doors closed to them. For the vast majority of students, however, the idea of not attending their early decision college never comes up, or if it does, the "buyer's remorse" passes quickly.

An early action acceptance can also bring your college search to a happy ending. But under the terms of early action, you have until May 1 to formally decide whether you will attend. For many students, especially those applying to schools that now use single-choice early action, the early action school is clearly their first choice. In these cases, it is courteous (although certainly not mandatory) for a student to withdraw other applications from the regular decision process and to refrain from submitting any new ones (especially when financial aid is not involved or when the financial aid offer is an especially generous one). The reason is simple: the more applications in the college pipeline, the lower the percentage of applicants who can be accepted by any given college. If you know for sure where you will be going in September, share your good fortune by giving your fellow students (locally and nationally) a better chance for a regular decision admission at one of the colleges they would like to attend.

But an early action acceptance may not end your college search. You may be interested in other colleges as well and want more time to make a decision. You may also want to see what your other financial aid packages may look like when you receive other acceptances in the spring. In that case, you'll have to wait until the regular cycle decisions are made. You can do so, however, secure in the knowledge that you already have an acceptance from a school you would be happy to attend.

Denied or Deferred

Many early applications end happily, but a lot do not. As more and more students discover the benefits of an early application, either early decision or early action, colleges find themselves having to deny or defer more of them to leave room for regular cycle admits. Colleges differ in their approach to dealing with applicants they do not accept. Some, like Harvard University and Georgetown University, choose to defer most of them, denying only those who clearly don't meet the qualifications for admission. A deferred application is considered again along with the applications submitted during the regular cycle. Other colleges choose to make hard decisions sooner rather than later, denying many qualified candidates who would probably be denied in the regular cycle anyway, and deferring just a small percentage who look competitive for the final round. Northwestern University has traditionally deferred no one; Stanford University defers only a small number. Colleges that deny a student during an early cycle do not allow them to re-submit their application for the regular cycle for the same year.

The problem with an early application denial is that it usually occurs in isolation, and it happens at holiday time. Because of all the restrictions, students usually apply early to only one college, and if they are denied, there are no simultaneous acceptances to ease the blow. But a deny decision does not mean that you weren't a strong applicant or that you weren't qualified to attend. It simply means that the admissions staff decided not to admit you—nothing more and nothing less—and that your application will not be considered further. Given the vagaries of the college admission process, it is best to accept such a decision as the luck of the draw and move on. If you follow our advice, you will have other applications to a carefully selected list of good-bet, possible, and long-shot colleges ready to go or already submitted.

What You Can Do If You Are Deferred

Students who find themselves deferred still face uncertainty about the final outcome, and it is hard to predict the chances for admission during the regular cycle. The admissions office may provide information in your letter about the percentage of applicants who were deferred. If not, they may tell you if you call and ask. You can also see whether your high school counselor is willing to call the admissions office to see how close you came to admission. Some colleges will provide this information, and it can help you predict your chances in the regular cycle. But if you can't get this information, don't worry. Just knowing what your chances are isn't going to increase them.

What *can* you do to increase your chances of admission if you have been deferred? A letter from you reaffirming your strong interest in the college is a good idea. Asking your high school counselor to send a similar note with your midyear grades is also appropriate. If you have received any significant new honors or participated in any noteworthy activities since you first applied, this information should also be included in the letters you and your counselor send. Finally, finishing the fall semester strong is always wise. During the regular cycle, unlike the early review, colleges will have access to your fall semester grades. If those grades are good, it will help you. In the absence of information to the contrary, the best approach to dealing with deferral is to assume that your chances of being admitted during the regular cycle are the same as they would have been had you first applied regular decision. No more and no less. Major changes are fairly rare after December, and you should never count on a deferral turning into an offer of admission.

Be prepared whatever the outcome. Because most early application outcomes can't be predicted with certainty, it is critical for students applying early to have a well-developed list of additional schools "in the wings" with applications ready to go (or, in many cases, already sent out by the time a decision arrives on December 15). Depending on how good a chance you believed your early application had to begin with, it can be psychologically quite deflating to be denied or deferred. You want to avoid, if at all possible, having to complete new applications at a time when your confidence may be shaken.

Above all, don't get discouraged! Try to remember what goes on in an admissions review. The outcome depends not only on your submitting a strong application, but also on the applications of others that year. It also depends to a great extent on the factors that each college and its review team choose to emphasize. All of these are out of your hands. Focus on what you *can* control. If you have prepared your college list wisely, you will have good choices at the end, regardless of the outcome at any particular college.

When It Is Your Turn to Decide

What takes place in mid-December, as intense as it may be, is just a dress rehearsal for what takes place in the spring when the regular admission cycle results start dribbling in. This time, many more students are waiting for responses from even more schools—and everything is drawn out over a longer period. But now, after waiting for many months to hear from colleges about their admissions decisions, students and families once again have a chance to make decisions of their own.

Choices Can Be Tough to Make

The process of making a final decision about which college to attend will vary, not surprisingly, from student to student and from family to family. A lot depends not only on personality and decision-making style but also on the specifics of the choices. A student admitted to his top-choice school with sufficient financial aid or no need for aid has a pretty easy decision to make.

Other students may have several desirable choices, with financial aid sometimes weighing heavily in the final decision. Some highly selective colleges offer only need-based aid. As a result, less-selective colleges find that they can compete for strong students by offering attractive merit aid packages, sometimes full rides, which go above and beyond calculated need. It can be hard to turn down a good school that offers a free or almost free education in favor of one, no matter how attractive, that would cost your family much more. Many students, particularly those with little or no financial need as calculated through need analysis, find themselves making this choice.

Sometimes students facing a difficult decision may find it helpful to make a list of pros and cons for each college. We suggest revisiting the priorities that emerged when you completed the questionnaire at the end of Chapter Four. Thinking through what is really important to you is critical. Use your list as a basis for discussion with family and friends.

> " I've asked people ahead of me in school, 'How did you choose?' They all said, 'I walked on campus and I just knew.' Well, I need something more concrete. I don't ever just know about anything. I don't have gut instincts on major life decisions. "
>
> *Senior approaching decision time*

You may, however, be one of those students who prefer to bypass lists and who goes with gut instinct. Both approaches can work and, in fact, a combination of both may be best of all. Do what you think will work best for you. The selection priorities will be different for each person, but make sure they are sound. One young man we know likes to plan ahead. Characteristically, he took a long view in making his final decision to attend a particular Ivy League college. "Thirty-five percent of legacy applicants get in," he said. "If I say yes to Ivy U, I'm saying yes for my children, I'm saying yes for everyone down the line."

Had this been a major factor in his decision (it wasn't), he would have been on shaky ground. No one knows whether the practice of legacy admission will exist in twenty-five years, let alone whether his children would even want to attend Ivy U.

Colleges ask that students declare their intentions, one way or the other, by May 1, the widely observed candidate reply date. It is courteous to respond as soon as you have made your decision—not only to the college you plan to attend, but to the others as well. All colleges overadmit because they know some students will go elsewhere. As we'll see in a later section, your decision not to attend a college may open up a spot for a student on the wait-list. The earlier a college can determine it has space, the sooner it can send the happy news to such a student.

> "What I did was flip a coin and wherever it landed I tried to decide how I felt about that. Every time it landed on College X, I got a gut feeling that I wasn't going to feel comfortable on that campus."
>
> *Senior who decided to attend College Y*

Dealing with Disappointment

While many students find themselves excited by the task of choosing a college, many others find themselves disappointed. A student who is admitted to only one or two good-bet colleges, but denied or wait-listed by the others, may not be excited by any of the choices. It isn't fun to be told no by a school you're really enthusiastic about. When several say no, it is even harder. Remember, though, what we emphasized in Chapter Three. Many factors in the college admissions process are beyond your control and have no bearing whatsoever on your qualities as a student or as a person. Realizing how uncertain the outcome can be at highly selective colleges can make it easier to accept each outcome gracefully—whether it is an acceptance or a denial.

> "My parents knew I was nervous, so they sat me down and said, 'Look, you've done everything you can do.' But when the rejection letters came in, I still felt like every mistake I'd made in the last four years of high school was coming back to haunt me."[1]
>
> *High school senior*

Even students with several acceptances may find themselves unhappy as they second-guess whether they made the right choices to start with. Having become a

"I applied early decision to Elite University although I didn't really think I'd get in. It was a big stretch for me, but you never know. I was rejected, which made me unhappy, but then I got over it. What *was* hard was getting rejected later at less competitive schools. The schools I got into, I could have gotten into without working so hard. People who played a lot and weren't so serious about school got to go there, too. I really wanted to have that happy acceptance thing and I didn't. I'd always wanted that day when I would open the mail and jump up and down and call my mom telling her all the great news. I missed that. It didn't happen and that was sad. But I've learned that if you don't get in where you want to go, it's not the end of the world, and I really thought it was. I thought my life was over. I had worked so hard, and I thought nothing good would ever come beyond that point. I'm not a religious person, so when people say everything happens for a reason, I'm like, 'Yeah, well.' But I think in this case, everything did happen for a reason. I'm really happy here."

College freshman

reality, none of the colleges looks good, and some students start to wonder whether they should have aimed "higher."

These reactions and others like them are normal. The important thing is to move beyond them. Dwelling on the negative, as well as "what-ifs," does little to move you forward. All colleges, no matter how highly rated or well regarded, have faults. And all colleges, even the most humble by most measures, have good points. If you have done your research carefully at the outset, you can be confident that your choice will be a good one no matter what form it finally takes. One young woman we know was denied in a tough year by all colleges except her one good bet. Disappointed, she decided to approach things as positively as she could. Ten weeks into her freshman year, she enthusiastically reported that she was very happy with her choice. She loved her classes, her new friends, and the college itself. Each year thousands and thousands of students have similarly happy endings after a disappointing start.

Remember also that choosing a college is not an irrevocable act. Students can and do transfer after freshman or sophomore year. Some students end up transferring from their first-choice schools and some from their good bets. Doing well in your freshman year will keep your transfer options open, although some colleges may be as selective for transfer students as they are for freshmen.

Making the Final Choice

Teens know instinctively that you become your own person by making your own choices. And yet, when college admission letters arrive, many students find themselves just plain stuck.

A student who receives several acceptances suddenly faces a great big choice. It's better than uncertainty and waiting, but it's not an easy time.

In April, I interviewed students who were in the middle of the struggle to decide.

"Paul" stood out. He sighed fifty times in our ten-minute conversation. Trying to decide between a liberal arts college and a large university, he favored the small school — until the big one invited him to join an honors program.

No matter how carefully students have ranked their choices, they may be jolted by last-minute developments like this. And parents sometimes express opinions they carefully withheld before. Paul confided, "Dad's trying to be objective, but he's biased for the big school."

The big school was closer to home.

Indeed, distance from the "nest" looms large for both parents and students. One student explained, "In September, everyone was excited about the option of going away. But people got closer. They put away their grudges, who did what to whom in sixth grade. People lost the desire to escape."

Some students wonder if they analyzed themselves correctly when they prepared their college list. One talented young vocalist viewed her singing as just one of many extracurricular activities. And yet, when a top women's college accepted her, she asked plaintively, "Do I want to spend four years in a chorus with no male voices?"

New details attract students as they make their final selection ("One school will wash, dry, and fold my clothing!" exclaimed a young man) but students told me that in-person visits were the best way to decide.

In May, I called Paul back. He didn't sigh even once when he reported that he chose the larger school.

"There's still some hesitation," he explained. "Did I choose the right place? But I'm really looking forward to college." I could almost hear his smile.

"It's a great feeling," he said, "to have it decided."

M. F.

Spring Admits

Inundated with more good applicants than they can accept, some colleges have developed a creative solution that allows them to admit a few more students each year. The solution involves offering a group of students the opportunity to enroll as freshmen starting in the spring semester rather than in the fall. A college can do this because it knows that some students will not return for spring semester. Students withdraw due to health, adjustment, or family problems, and a few seniors choose to graduate early. The spots opened up by the departures create an opportunity for students willing to start midyear.

Colleges offering spring admission encourage students to put the fall semester to good use, either through coursework at another college or through other enriching activities. Middlebury College and UC Berkeley, two very different campuses, have offered the option of spring admission for several years. Brandeis University is one of the most recent additions to the list of schools offering spring starts. The disadvantage of a midyear start is obvious—you don't have the opportunity to experience the first exciting semester of college life with your future classmates. On the plus side, though, after just a few short months you will join them, when you would not otherwise have had a chance. You don't apply for spring admission; if a school can't accept you for the fall but knows it will have room in the spring, it will advise you of that in your admission letter.

Taking Another Look

Most colleges host special "admit" days or weekends in April before the May 1 common reply date. Even if you have visited a college before, going to an admit weekend can be fun and a good way to get a feel for the campus. It can be especially important, though, if you haven't had a chance to visit in person before.

Finally, the pressure is off and you can enjoy being courted. Everyone realizes that the parties and food might be better than usual on this special weekend, but you'll still get to know the campus as it really is because you'll meet so many students. You'll also meet other "pre-frosh" with whom you can keep in touch.

Normally, the cost of travel to admit weekends is borne by the student. In some cases, though, a campus may be particularly eager to recruit a student and will offer an all-expense paid trip. This is especially true for underrepresented minorities or students from

> "The scary thing is that no one in our family, adult or child, has the slightest clue which school would be best. They all have pros and cons. Sometimes I think it might be a relief to get rejections from all but one to avoid having to make these incredibly difficult decisions."
>
> *A parent at decision time*

low-income families. If you are not offered financial assistance but find that the cost of travel is a hardship, consider calling the admissions office to ask whether the campus can cover the travel for you. The answer may be "no" because of budget limitations, but it doesn't hurt to ask.

Admit days, especially those where you stay overnight, give you a good chance to talk to current students about what the college is really like, as well as get a sense of who might be joining you in the freshman class. It is worth rereading the section on college visits in Chapter Five to refresh everyone's memory of what to look for. Some colleges encourage parents to attend the admit days and even offer special programs for them (although no dorm housing!), and all colleges welcome them regardless of whether formal events are provided. If you plan to go with your child to an admit weekend, that's fine—just be sure you give him or her lots of space.

> "I want to look at the academics and which one really fits my academic goals the most. Visiting becomes more important. Getting a feel for the people that go there. Making sure that they're compatible. Do I want to live in New Jersey? In Southern California? How much of a stretch do I want from my current lifestyle?"
>
> *Senior trying to make a decision between two very different but excellent colleges*

Revisiting Financial Aid

Once all your acceptance and financial aid offers are in, you may also want to make your top-choice college aware of any offer that is significantly larger than theirs if the differences in the aid packages may affect your final choice. Be sure also to make them aware of any new changes in your financial situation that might increase your eligibility for aid. Courteously requesting that a college review your financial aid offer to see whether anything more can be done is not only appropriate, but also smart. Be prepared, of course, for the answer to be no. The easiest adjustments for a college to make are ones where new information or a new interpretation of existing information results in a calculation of greater financial need. Adjustments can sometimes be made in the absence of such new information, but they are less common, and they are usually made for the applicants the college is most eager to recruit. And don't expect a college that offers only need-based aid to adjust its package to offset a merit scholarship at another college. At the same time, don't let a "no" discourage you from continuing to consider the college as an option, if you are excited about the college and it is within financial reach.

How Wait-Lists Work

A wait-list consists of applicants who are not admitted outright but who are notified that they will be considered for admission if space becomes available later in the spring. What should you make of a letter that essentially puts you in limbo?

Being placed on a wait-list means that your file will be considered again if the college eventually finds it has more openings than it anticipated when they mailed acceptance letters. Because no college gets a "yes" from every admitted student, they all accept more than they can accommodate. Then they wait until after the May 1 deadline to see how many students send in their deposits. The process is very similar to the way airlines fill their planes. It is common to overbook a plane, since some passengers will be no-shows. And if the number of no-shows means that there are empty seats when the plane is ready to leave, those seats can be filled by standbys who know that they may or may not get a seat.

If more students accept admission than planned, the result can be anything from increasing the number of freshmen in each dorm room to converting student lounges into bedrooms to using trailers or motels for temporary housing. One enterprising campus we know purchased smaller dorm room furniture when

"Amherst put me on their wait-list. The dean sent me a very nice letter that said, 'After long and careful consideration, the admission committee has decided to place your name on the waiting list for Amherst's class of 2008. . . . I congratulate you on your fine record of accomplishments which deserve a much more fitting recognition than I can provide right now. I hope you will remain interested in Amherst and that you will choose to hold a place on our waiting list. I also hope that I may ultimately have a chance to offer you a place in the class of 2008.'

Accompanying the letter was an attachment stating that about 1,000 students were placed on the wait-list, that about 300 to 400 were expected to remain on it, and that over a ten-year period the average annual number of acceptances from the wait-list was twenty-eight. At least they were up-front about how tough it would be."

Wait-listed student

it found it had to house three students in rooms meant for two. And of course, if a college finds itself in an "oversold" situation, it does not add anyone from the wait-list.

Who Goes on the Wait-List?

There has been a noticeable trend over the last few years toward longer wait-lists. This reflects, for the most part, the increasing number of highly qualified candidates who apply to a large number of selective institutions. A wait-list decision can often be equivalent to acknowledging that a candidate was fully qualified to attend and would indeed have been admitted if only there were room. The wait-list can also be a gentle way for a college to say "no" to a weaker candidate it finds difficult to deny outright for other reasons, for example, a legacy applicant. And as we saw in Chapter One, a few colleges place exceptionally qualified candidates on the wait-list if they strongly believe the student will receive and accept an offer elsewhere.

> *"I didn't like being wait-listed. It felt like a consolation prize. Why would they wait-list so many people when clearly they're letting in very few? It seemed so pointless."*
>
> *Senior who was wait-listed by Harvard University and declined to remain on the list*

Because of a combination of all or some of these factors, many wait-lists are as big, or bigger, than the size of the entire freshman class. The "Principles of Good Practice" of the National Association for College Admission Counseling require each college to tell you how many applicants have been placed on the wait-list for your year and for each of several previous years, along with the number on the wait-list eventually offered admission. But you may have to ask. The number admitted from the wait-list can vary greatly, from zero to low single digits to several dozen or more. It all depends on the ability of a college to predict its yield accurately in the first place. The importance of predicting yield is one of the reasons colleges embraced early decision so readily, and why some colleges consider demonstrated interest in making their admissions decisions.

Single-choice early action, implemented by Stanford, Yale, and Harvard in Fall 2003, introduced a new wild card into the wait-list picture. Since single-choice early action no longer locked students into an early commitment, it was harder for these three colleges to predict their yield. As a group, they took greater numbers of students from their wait-lists for the class of 2008 than they had for other recent classes. As students moved off the wait-list at those schools, colleges that compete with them for students found themselves with empty spots that they, in turn, filled from *their* wait-lists. And so on.

The trickle-down effect can be sizable and widespread. Princeton, for example, admitted seventy-eight students from its wait-list for the class of 2008, compared to twenty-seven the previous year. As colleges get more experience with single-choice early action, however, wait-list activity may return to previous low levels. It is too early to predict what will happen in the next few years.

> *"*I tell my wait-listed kids to put their wait-list schools out of their mind and make plans to attend one where they have been accepted because chances are pretty good that this is where they will go. If they find out later that they've won the lottery, then that's great and they can deal with it then. But they need to start forming new attachments. I'd also encourage parents to foster that attitude.*"*
>
> *Independent counselor*

Steps to Increase Your Chances of Acceptance from the Wait-List

If you receive a letter notifying you that you have been placed on the wait-list, a postcard asking whether you wish to stay on the wait-list will accompany it. What should you do? No single answer fits everyone. Usually, less than half of those placed on a wait-list opt to remain. If your other college choices are more attractive to you, then it obviously makes little sense to remain wait-listed. But if the wait-list college is still an appealing option, you may want to respond positively, with the full knowledge that your chances for moving from the wait-list

> *"*When we accept from the wait-list we build areas of need. We will probably add a couple of top-ranked musicians, students interested in research science, and people with a strong theater background.*"* [2]
>
> *Dick Nesbitt, director of admission at Williams College, referring to a wait-list of about 450 students for the class of 2008*

are low. You should also inquire about a college's policy regarding financial aid for students admitted from the wait-list. Will aid be available if you have financial need? And be sure to remember that you still need to send a deposit to one of the colleges where you have been accepted outright by the May 1 reply deadline.

Although airline standby lists are ordered in some kind of priority so passengers can assess their chances of getting a seat, wait-lists are usually unranked. This means that openings are not filled from the list in any pre-arranged order. As openings occur, a college may examine its whole freshman class along geographic, gender, racial, and many other dimensions and fill any perceived gaps from the wait-list. The person who came closest, in some sense, to admission during the regular review cycle will not necessarily be chosen from the list when openings occur.

Usually, there is little movement from a wait-list until colleges have a clear indication of their yield from those already accepted, and that generally doesn't happen until after the reply deadline. Mid-May through June are the busiest times for wait-list notifications. Wait-listed students who are accepted are usually notified first by phone, followed by written confirmation with a two-week, or sometimes much shorter, deadline for reply. If you tell the caller you are no longer interested, the college will move on to another wait-listed student and repeat the process. Most

---

What Can You Do If You Are Wait-Listed at Your Top Choice?

❑ Be sure to return the reply postcard indicating you want to remain active on the wait-list.

❑ Write a letter to the dean of admissions and let him or her know that you are still very eager to attend. Include any significant new information since you last wrote: grades, awards, and so forth.

❑ Ask your counselor to call or write the admissions office conveying your enthusiasm and his or her support for you.

❑ Consider sending an additional recommendation or letter from a teacher or another person who knows you well.

❑ Carefully select a school from among those that have admitted you and send in your deposit.

❑ Recognize that most students placed on the wait-list at selective colleges are not ultimately admitted. Once you have taken the steps indicated above, put the wait-list out of your mind and focus on the college you will probably be attending in the fall.

selective colleges officially close their wait-lists by the end of June and notify those who have not been accepted. Many have very little activity from the wait-list after Memorial Day.

If you decide to remain on a wait-list, it is wise to discuss your continued interest in the college with your high school counselor. Tell your counselor whether the college is your first choice. Your counselor can help your cause by contacting the college and conveying support for you as well as your enthusiasm for the college. A letter from you expressing your interest as well as any new accomplishments will be necessary. Don't rely on your counselor to do this for you. But again, it is important to remember that movement from the wait-list at a selective college

> " Colleges are looking for a 100 percent yield from any students they take off the wait-list, so they are going to be looking for commitment. The key is for students to demonstrate as much honest interest as they can and indicate that if offered admission they will definitely enroll. They are the students the admissions office will most likely look at first."
>
> *Experienced high school counselor*

is a long shot at best. Don't let hope of admission, which could even come well into the summer, spoil your excitement about getting ready for college. Sometimes the need for closure, even if it means deciding to attend a college lower on your list, is far better than the emotional limbo that staying on a wait-list can create. You know yourself best—be sure to weigh the wait-list option carefully before deciding what to do.

And remember in any case to send your intent to register form, along with your deposit, to the college of your choice from among your acceptance options. If you subsequently decide to join the freshman class of a college that accepts you from the wait-list, you will need to send a deposit as well to that college. You will forfeit the deposit you made to the first school, but it can be worth it if you end up where you really wanted to go.

Deposit Ethics

Students are expected to send a deposit to hold a spot at only one college by May 1. Holding more than one spot, known as double depositing, deprives others of the potential opportunity to move from a wait-list. If you are offered a spot from a wait-list and accept, you'll have to inform the first college you accepted of your change in plans as quickly as possible. A phone call isn't enough—they will want something in writing. Your letter doesn't have to be long unless you want it to be; a simple note informing the college of your new plans is sufficient. This happens all the time, so don't be bashful or embarrassed about your change in plans. The important thing is to notify the college quickly. The place you release will then generate an opening for a student on that school's wait-list, continuing the cascading effect.

A Word About Senioritis

Senioritis is an affliction that typically strikes students right after they receive their college acceptances. For those applying early, it may occur in mid-December, but for most others it attacks in mid-April. (Wait-list status seems to confer immunity, however.) Teachers know to expect senioritis, but they dread it nonetheless. Students start skipping classes and performing significantly below their pre-infection levels. High school no longer seems to matter very much since the big hurdle is over.

We encourage you to avoid falling victim to this disease. We'll review several reasons—perhaps one or more will resonate with you. First, colleges accept you on the condition that your performance for the remainder of the

> "I hope this letter is the one you were expecting and that it brings you the exhilaration you deserve to feel. I also hope that you will take the night off to celebrate with your loved ones. But as a mother, I expect you to get right back to work and finish up the year with top grades since we don't admit slackers to MIT and this offer of admission is contingent upon your successful completion of the school year."
>
> Marilee Jones, dean of admissions at MIT, excerpt from 2004 MIT admission letter

year will remain at its prior level. The last official part of your college application process is having your final transcript sent to the college of your choice at the end of the school year. Colleges actually review these to identify any marked departures from previous performance.

Many schools will send letters to students whose grades have noticeably dropped, asking for an explanation. A serious decline may result in a more strongly worded letter indicating that the student's admission is in jeopardy. Colleges reserve the right to put conditions on your enrollment (requiring summer school classes, for example) or may even rescind your admission entirely if your performance dramatically deteriorates or if you drop demanding courses without good reason. True, the drop in grades has to be pretty striking and without mitigating conditions for an offer of admission to be withdrawn, but a college can and will do it given the appropriate circumstances.

Another reason to take school seriously after college admission is that your high school record will be with you forever. While your grades in high school may not matter much once you have graduated from college, you may find yourself among the large group of students who choose to transfer to a different college at some point. A record that deteriorated in the second half of senior year will not help your case. Finally, and maybe most important, continuing your best effort (or close to it) shows respect for your parents, your teachers, and your counselors. They helped you get into college. You can show your appreciation by continuing to be a contributor to class and a good student. Almost everyone will cut you a little bit of slack—just don't abuse it.

Celebrate and Enjoy!

With college choice now behind you, it is time to enjoy the remaining weeks of your high school career. You can look forward to the Senior Prom, graduation, and more and more commonly, an alcohol-free all night party or trip for the entire senior class. Make the most of this time to cement the bonds with your classmates. Some of them will no doubt be life-long friends. Others will be people you will see only at ten-year intervals at class reunions. With the passage of time, you will remember most of them fondly, even if they aren't close friends now. One of us recently attended her forty year high school reunion, having missed the others, and can personally attest that this is true.

What Matters Most: Advice to Parents and Students

We wrote *Admission Matters* to help both students and parents navigate the college admissions process. We wanted to show you how the role of the student and the role of the parent are complementary, yet different, and provide you with the information and practical advice you need to work together to achieve a good outcome.

In this final chapter, we offer some parting thoughts that summarize and capture the heart of what this book is about. It may be helpful to read this chapter more than once as you become immersed in the college admissions process. It is easy for both students and parents to get caught up in the whirlwind and lose perspective, but this chapter will remind you what matters most. The chapter is divided into two parts. The first part is for parents; the second part is for students. Like the rest of the book, you should read not only the part intended for you but the other part as well. We think everyone will benefit.

Some Parting Thoughts for Parents

• **What your child will remember long after the college admissions process is over is how you supported him or her.**

It can be hard to accept that your almost grown child has ideas and preferences that differ significantly from your own. This is especially true when it comes to college choice, when so much seems to be at stake. Your child may want to experience a different part of the country—you may want your child to be close to home (or vice versa). You may feel an education at a liberal arts college is best—your child may be looking forward to the excitement of a large research university (or the reverse). The list goes on and on. The bottom line is that although your child should be respectful of your views, and may ultimately embrace them, the final choices—where to apply, what to put in the application, and where to go after acceptance—should be the student's.

Ideally, you want to be able to look back after the final college choice is made and savor the knowledge of having provided emotional and practical support for your child that contributed to a successful outcome. Just be aware that it may take your child a long time to appreciate your good intentions and acknowledge your contribution.

• **The parent's role is to support, advise, and listen, except when it comes to money.**

You can support your child in the college admissions process in many ways. Sharing your own thoughts and experiences, encouraging research into colleges including visits where feasible, and providing useful feedback and organizational support are among the many ways in which you can help. But you need to realize that your child must "own" this process—it is the student, not the parent, who is applying to and ultimately attending, college.

It is critical, however, that you be up-front about financial considerations. Colleges use a complex formula to determine the "expected family contribution." Aid packages based on financial need will not include money to cover this amount. The expected parental contribution is the amount colleges believe a family should be able to pay to help support their child's education—it is not the amount that parents are necessarily willing to pay. Doing some early calculations and being frank about what you are prepared to contribute financially is important to avoid misunderstanding and disappointment later on.

• **This is not the time to live vicariously through your child, however tempting that may be. It is also important to avoid using college admission as validation of your parenting skills.**

Most parents of high school seniors are forty years old or older. Participating in the process with their child gives them a chance to reexperience, or perhaps experience for the first time, an exciting rite of passage in our society. However, if you catch yourself saying, "We're applying to college," you may be overly involved.

Be aware that even the most confident children may fear they will disappoint a parent if they do not get into their parent's alma mater or dream college(s), or if they do less "well" than a superstar older sibling. Wise parents make sure they don't inadvertently contribute to that fear by their words or actions.

Similarly, parents sometimes lapse into the belief that all of their parenting efforts over the last eighteen years will be held up to scrutiny during the admissions process. The student who is accepted by one or more prestigious colleges has parents who have "done a good job," while parents of students who apply to less prestigious institutions or who are denied by brand-name colleges didn't do their job quite as well. Put bluntly, these inferences are ludicrous, but they frequently reside just under the surface. The bumper stickers and T-shirts that proclaim "Proud Mom of a Yalie" put them into words. So does the seemingly endless supermarket check-out line and carpool chatter about where Suzie has applied early, or where Tommy got accepted. All of this sends subtle messages that put teens under great pressure and promote values that are at best superficial and at worst actually harmful. A wise parent learns to be upbeat even when the news is disappointing and modest when the news is good.

• **Be aware that there are many first-rate institutions with reasonable acceptance rates where your child can get a fine education and be happy.**

Most people know surprisingly little about the amazing array of institutions of higher education in the United States. They can name a few local colleges, most of the Ivy League institutions, and some schools whose football games are televised nationally, but that's about it. As part of the college admissions process you can support your child by learning about colleges you may not be familiar with, and helping your child realize that a successful college experience is the result of a good fit between a college and student—and that while there is no perfect fit, many good ones are possible. There are wonderful colleges that accept a much higher percentage of their applicants than those considered very selective. By all measures, these colleges offer an education that is every bit as good and maybe even better than some highly selective, brand-name institutions. Helping your child explore options and supporting his or her choices can be an immensely rewarding experience.

• **Help your child with organizational matters and be a good sounding board and editor during the application process—but don't do the work for your child.**

The actual process of applying to college can be daunting. There are forms galore, short and long essays to be written, score reports and transcripts to be sent, and so on, all by looming deadlines. When asked what they would do differently if they had a chance to start over, many high school seniors say that they would have started the whole process earlier and procrastinated less. As a parent, you can encourage your child to get off to an early start and to keep good records of what has been done and what remains to be done. Some teens resent this; they have always been able to complete their work by the deadlines, so they are convinced they can do the same now. The problem, though, is that college applications are probably much more complex than any task they have undertaken before—and more hangs in the balance.

Students should be encouraged to organize their materials and set deadlines for themselves. If your child decides to apply early action or early decision, he or she will have to get everything together by November 1 or November 15—a very early date indeed. What kind of help can you provide? Proofreading of applications and help with essay ideas and constructive criticism can be very helpful (just be aware your efforts may not be enthusiastically welcomed!). Resist the urge at all costs to rewrite the application yourself, however, even if your child seems willing or even eager for you to do that. Admissions readers get pretty good at telling an authentic student "voice" from one that has been doctored in a major way by adults.

You can also assist with organizational matters if you have those skills and your child welcomes the help. Volunteer, for example, to address and stamp the envelopes that your child's teachers will use to send in their letters of recommendation and volunteer to take the applications to the copy shop to be copied when they are finished. Make the organizational tasks easier and less time-consuming for your child so he or she can devote his or her energies to the hard part. Of course, some teens enjoy these organizational tasks because they're easy to do and yield a sense of accomplishment. Make the offer to help and let your child decide.

- **Model ethical behavior and integrity.**

Our children learn many lessons from us, not the least of which are those we never explicitly teach. Children learn by observing others, and the most powerful role models are parents. Students and parents can sometimes feel pressure to do everything possible to ensure "success" in college admissions, even if it means compromising their integrity along the way. Don't give in to this temptation. The college admissions process is one of the major opportunities parents have to model ethical behavior and integrity for their children.

Don't offer inappropriate help with the application itself ("editing" an essay to the point of essentially writing it yourself, for example) and don't permit your child to seek it elsewhere (paying someone to write the essay). Similarly, discourage any tendency toward exaggeration of activities or accomplishments. Admissions officers look for consistency between what students have written about themselves and what teachers and counselors say about them.

But getting caught in a fabrication is the least of the reasons to encourage honesty in the application process. Our society has too many people who believe shaving the truth is not only OK but also the smart thing to do. Young adults need to know that their integrity is their most precious asset. Parents can reinforce that lesson through their actions.

For both parents and children, there is no better feeling than being accepted for your own efforts and for who you really are. Don't deny that to your children. You don't want them to arrive freshman week and think, "I'm not the person who was on my application. This school doesn't really want *me*."

- **Accompany your child on college visits, but stay in the background.**

Probably the best way for a student to get the feel for a college is to visit it. Where possible, encourage your child to visit a number of campuses, perhaps in conjunction with vacation, and go along if you can. Going to some nearby colleges of different sizes can help give your child an idea of the kind of college she might be interested in. When it comes time to look seriously at colleges, you can help schedule tours and encourage your child to participate in an interview if one is available. But remember that the visits are for your child's benefit. Encourage, and perhaps even encourage strongly, but let your child make the final call about whether or not to visit a given campus.

- **Help your child make realistic choices.**

One of the major themes of this book is that admission to selective colleges can be quite unpredictable. Your child can have a wonderful record yet be denied at a given college, while another student with a weaker record receives a fat admissions packet. A good part of the uncertainty is because many highly qualified students seek admission to the same small pool of colleges. If you understand the difficulty and uncertainty of selective college admissions, you can help your child consider a good range of colleges.

If your child is interested in a super-selective college and would be a competitive applicant, he or she should certainly apply. But your child should understand that admission to colleges that select less than 20 percent of their applicants is a long shot for just about everyone, simply because of numbers. After the final decisions arrive, support your child by sharing the disappointment at the denials and the joy over the acceptances. If choices were made carefully at the outset, there should be a happy outcome regardless of the particulars.

- **Be supportive as your child makes his or her choice.**

When the decisions come in from the colleges, your child may be elated or disappointed, or somewhere in between. Give him or her the space needed to sort it out and make his or her own final decision. Offer your perspective where appropriate, but remember that within the boundaries of financial constraints and family responsibilities, the choice is your child's, not yours.

- **Rejoice with your child.**

Express your love and let your son or daughter know how proud you are of the young adult he or she has become. Try not to focus too much on the size of the bill you may be expected to pay. It is probably one of the best investments you will ever make.

Some Parting Thoughts for Students

- **Parents want the best for you and want to help. Let them, within boundaries.**

Although parents differ widely in their knowledge, abilities, and resources, almost all want to help a college-bound student in whatever ways they can. Be gracious and communicate with your parents so that they can help in ways that work for them and for you. The trick is to define boundaries for what is helpful, what is intrusive, and what is counterproductive. Each parent and each child is different—so you'll have to work this out together with help from this book.

Parents can sometimes be a great source of suggestions about colleges to consider. They can also be your companions on trips to see colleges in person, the best way to determine whether a college is a good fit. And they can sometimes be good editors, proofreaders, and clerical assistants, depending on their background, as you prepare your applications. The more you both know about the college admissions process, the easier it will be to agree on what form their help should take. Encourage them to be partners with you. If they see you taking charge in a mature manner, they will be much less likely to feel that they have to be constantly "on your case."

- **Recognize that "launching" a child to adulthood is emotionally difficult for many parents—help them get through it.**

Sending a child off to college is bittersweet for many parents. They share your delight at your prospects for a wonderful future, but at the same time there is a sense of loss. The child they have loved and nurtured for eighteen years is now a young adult, ready to leave home for a new life in which the parents will play a much less prominent role. Try on occasion to put yourself in your parents' place. Something as simple as an occasional, heartfelt "thank you" in response to help that is offered can make all the difference to a parent struggling with a changing role.

Share something about the high school scene with your parents. Most know surprisingly little about the pressures at school, and they are often unaware of the many discussions about college that go on between you and your friends. If you help your parents understand the environment you operate in every day, they will appreciate why your experience of the college admissions process may be very different from theirs.

• **The most important part of the college admissions process is choosing institutions that would be a good match. Be as honest as you can with yourself about your interests, preferences, strengths, and weaknesses as you consider colleges.**

A recurring theme throughout *Admission Matters* is that a successful college experience is all about fit—finding a college that is a good match for you. The most important, and probably hardest, part of the college admissions process is self-assessment—an honest self-evaluation of your interests, preferences, strengths, and weaknesses. The next toughest part is doing the research that is needed to find colleges that are a good match based on your self-assessment. And part of that match includes a determination of the likelihood of acceptance. You want to be sure to have a range of colleges on your list to ensure that you will maximize the likelihood of a good outcome.

• **Have eight first choices.**

Well, the number doesn't have to be eight and they don't really have to be absolutely your first choice. But the idea is to be sure that all of the colleges to which you apply are ones that you would be happy to attend. This includes the good-bet applications as well as the long-shot ones. Joyce Mitchell, a high school counselor who has written her own book on college admissions, has made the "eight first choices" rule a cornerstone of her advice to students. It is good advice. Because you cannot predict the response from elite colleges, having several first choices including at least one that is a good bet virtually guarantees a happy outcome. The "eight first choices" rule should be in effect even if you apply early decision. In that case, the other colleges on your list should all be ones you would be happy to attend in case early decision doesn't work out.

- **Don't procrastinate at any point in the process.**

When you ask college seniors what they would do differently if they had a chance to redo their college application experience, the most common response is, "I would start earlier and not procrastinate." Procrastination is a normal reaction to a stressful process. But it really does make things worse. Leaving applications to the last minute invariably means rushed decisions, mistakes, potentially missed opportunities, not to mention needless stress. Establish a reasonable time frame for your efforts, setting deadlines for yourself along the way. Having deadlines and working to meet them will also reduce stress on your parents. Do this for them, as well as for yourself.

- **Get and stay organized; keep everything together and make copies of everything you send in.**

The college application process generates an astonishing amount of paper, even with the trend to doing more online. Brochures and college catalogs arrive by the dozen early on. Later, multipart applications have to be completed, reference forms submitted to teachers and counselors, and transcripts requested. Making things worse, different colleges have different requirements and deadlines. Staying on top of it all can be a real challenge, but it is a challenge that is important to meet. A simple filing system in a cardboard box is all that you need, along with a record of each school's requirements and deadlines that you can check off as you meet them. And be sure to make a copy of everything you send in, even online applications. Colleges rarely lose materials, but you don't want to take any chances. Starting over when you thought you were done is not fun.

- **Talk to your friends, but remember that each person is different.**

Peers can be wonderful sources of information. For example, a friend may return from a trip to another part of the country excited about the colleges he saw and open your eyes to new possibilities. It is always important to remember, however, that a good choice for one person may not be a good choice for another. When someone offers an opinion of a college, whether good or bad, try to find out what's behind it. Get to the facts, then see how those facts fit with your own needs. And be respectful of the choices of others. A good-bet college for one person may be a possible or even a long shot for another.

- **Remember to enjoy your senior year. College applications are important, but they should not be allowed to take over your life.**

It is easy to make college admissions the focus of your senior year. There is so much to do and so much seems to be at stake. But the senior year in high school should also be special in other ways—sharing adventures with old friends, enjoying a fleeting year of being "top banana," and beginning to enjoy the freedoms that come with being an adult. Balance is key. A wise student takes the college application process seriously but doesn't let it overwhelm everything else. If you approach things calmly and rationally, and in a timely way, you can achieve the dual goals of having an array of fine college choices and a senior year filled with wonderful memories.

- **End the college admissions process on a high note.**

When the final decisions from colleges come in, it will be your turn to decide. Make your decision carefully. Your choice may or may not be the one you hoped or thought you would make when the process first began, but if you have followed our advice, it will be a good choice. Celebrate with your family and friends, and begin to plan for your new life as a college student (but remember you still have to successfully complete your senior year).

Thank your teachers and counselors again for writing letters for you, and let them know you are glad you got to know them. Visit them to say "hi" when you return home over winter break during your freshman year, or send them cards if you can't see them in person. Above all, thank your parents for all they have done and still do for you, and tell them that you love them. Do this along the way, but especially when the college admissions process is over.

We end our book with a wonderful letter to students that Fred Hargadon, now-retired dean of admission at Princeton University, had for many years included with Princeton's application packet. Dean Hargadon's long and distinguished career in college admissions spanned thirty-five years and three major institutions: Swarthmore, Stanford, and Princeton. We believe the letter contains important messages for all applicants to selective colleges, not just those who applied to Princeton, and Dean Hargadon kindly allowed us to reprint it here. We've taken the liberty, with his permission, to lightly edit it to omit Princeton-specific references so that it would be clear that it applies to everyone.

A Letter from the Dean of Admission to All Prospective Applicants for Admission to the Class of _____

In a favorite book of mine, *The Phantom Tollbooth*, one of the delightful characters the reader meets up with is the Dodecahedron (named after a mathematical shape with twelve sides). He introduces himself in the following manner: "My angles are many. My sides are not few." Those words have always struck me as a pretty good description of the admissions process not only at this university, but at many similar colleges and universities as well. In any event, as *you* approach the college admissions process, with its "many angles" and "not a few sides," I've been thinking about what sort of advice might be useful to share with you were we able to have a conversation about your applying to colleges. While a printed letter may be a poor substitute for a conversation, I've simply jotted down a few of the observations I'd most likely make if I had the opportunity to talk with you in person.

First of all, I'd tell you that I don't envy you the task of trying to determine to which colleges you should apply, or trying to estimate your chances of admission at any particular college, or, ultimately, having to make a choice about where to enroll from among those to which you are offered admission. I *can* tell you that I don't think there are any shortcuts (not even Harry Potter's "Sorting Hat"), to finding good answers to these questions, and that since this is one of the more significant decisions you will make in your life, it's worth as much time and effort and homework as you can put into it.

Following the old adage, "well-begun is half-done," I'd like to suggest that you begin your college search by taking some time to think hard about why it is you want to go to college in the first place and about what, once you get there, you hope to gain from those four years. The more thought you give now to what it is you think you want to learn and experience in college, the better informed will be your choice of colleges to which to apply. Otherwise, you're likely to find yourself in the situation akin to that of trying to decide whether to drive, fly, or take a train without first deciding where you want to get.

Set aside some quiet time in order to reflect frankly on your strengths and weaknesses: think about what it is that you now know, are especially interested in, do well, or just plain enjoy and therefore would like an opportunity to continue to pursue in college; and about what it is, on the other hand, that you don't know (but think you should) or don't do particularly well (but hope to learn to do better) and therefore also want to pursue in college.

I'd even go so far as to recommend that you sketch out a tentative plan of what it is you wish to accomplish in college (not a plan of what you want to do *after* college, but *in* college), keeping in mind that you're likely to alter it as you go along. You probably will find yourself making some changes in it even between now and next year. It just seems to me that the better the handle you try to get now on at least some of the ways in which you hope to change and grow as a result of your college experience, the better you will be able to identify those colleges that appear most likely to meet your needs. *(For example, whether your goal right now happens to be becoming a doctor, or an engineer, or a writer, you might decide that you also want to leave college having become bilingual, or having mastered a musical instrument, or having gained more than a superficial appreciation of art, or having taken up the sport of rowing. I regret, for instance, that I didn't spend some of my time in college learning to play the piano, however thankful my friends may be that I didn't. As someone once wisely pointed out, the person you will spend most of your life with is yourself, and therefore you owe it to yourself to become as interesting as possible.)*

While it's not unusual for students to talk of their "first choice" college, I think it's a rare individual for whom it can be said that there exists but a single, best college. Even if, as the result of the homework you do on colleges, you arrive at a point where you accord enough preference to one college to consider it your "first choice," your final list ought to include a number of colleges, any one of which you'd be happy to attend if admitted. Keep in mind that most students end up very much liking the college they attend, regardless of whether it had been their "first choice" when they applied.

It's also a good idea to focus at least as much attention on the *overall* quality of a college as on the quality of the particular department or academic area in which you may now be especially interested. Experience indicates that a fair number of students ultimately major in an academic area other than the one they had in mind when entering. This happens for any number of reasons. Some students simply find that the more they learn about what is involved in studying a particular subject, the less satisfying it becomes. Some find a different, but closely related, field more to their liking. More often, it happens that it is only after they get to college that students become familiar with one or another field of study, and subsequently find themselves more attracted by it than by their initial interests as freshmen. The point is that you will want to take into account the possibility of a change in your own interests while you are going through college, and therefore you ought to feel reasonably confident that the colleges to which you are applying are ones which will offer you an excellent education across the board. You should also try to imagine how well a given college will meet your needs and interests as a junior or senior, not just what it offers you as a freshman.

You need to be realistic, too. There are no absolutely perfect colleges. I've never met a student for whom *every* classroom experience, *every* faculty member, or *every* out-of-class experience turned out to be ideal. A good way to approach the colleges you are looking into is to think of each of them as a set of *probabilities.* And, depending upon your interests and the kinds of experiences you hope to have, you should try to get some sense of the probabilities of satisfying those interests or of having those experiences at one or another of them. For instance, what are the probabilities of being in classes of one size or another, or of getting to know at least some faculty members well, or of undertaking independent research, or of participating in one or another extracurricular activity? These are the sorts of questions you ought to be asking.

There isn't any quick or easy way that I know of in which to fully know what a particular college is like, despite the proliferation of commercial publications that purport to give you capsule summaries or the "inside" story. Colleges and universities are dynamic and complex institutions, if for no other reason than the fact that one-quarter of the student body is new each year. While some information is relatively easy to come by (size, costs, course offerings, and the like), many of the factors you may wish to weigh and compare are simply not so easily measured and assessed. For instance, I'd be surprised if on any given day, let alone over the course of four years, any two students at my university experience this place in quite the same way. There are many paths, both academic and nonacademic, through any *single* college, and almost every student travels more than one of those paths during the course of his or her four years.

In any event, try to avoid falling into the trap of thinking about one or another college solely in terms of a few descriptive adjectives or traits. And remember that any college is going to be at least slightly different than it now is simply by virtue of your enrolling there. If at all possible, you should visit the campuses of the colleges in which you are most interested, attend classes, and talk with some currently enrolled students. Rather than rely on any single source of information, seek out a number of different sources, always keeping in mind the fable about the seven blind philosophers, each of whom, upon touching a different part of an elephant, described the seven quite different animals they thought it to be. So, too, is the same university likely to be perceived, at least in part, quite differently by its various members.

Neither you nor your parents will be able to ignore the fact that some colleges (including mine) are more expensive than others. Even if I were not representing one of those institutions, I'd still be telling you that I don't think it wise to cross *any* college off your list just because it appears to cost a small fortune to attend. In the first place, while we all know that cost is not a perfect indicator of quality, it is also true that a first-rate college education does not come cheaply. Second, a number of colleges and universities make their admission decisions completely without regard to whether an applicant will need financial aid.

Keep in mind the following: first, you can always turn down a college's offer of admission should the amount of financial aid it awards you appear inadequate; second, the one sure way *not* to gain admission or *not* to receive financial aid is by deciding not to apply in the first place.

Now, about applying for admission. What you will quickly learn over the next few months is that with regard to many of the questions you are likely to have about various aspects of the admission process, there is no single set of answers that apply for all colleges. Do colleges require personal interviews? Some do and some don't. Do colleges treat your SAT results as a combined score or treat the component scores separately? Some do the former, some the latter.

You will find these differences frustrating in at least two respects. First, you will have to treat each institution (and therefore each application) individually. That's not so bad when you think of it, given that we assume you want the colleges to treat your application individually. Second, a particular college's practice with regard to how it treats your high school transcript or your test scores, and so forth, may not be in accord with your preference in such matters. After all, it's only human nature for an applicant to want colleges to place the greatest weight on those factors he or she shows up best on and the least amount of weight on those factors he or she shows up less well on. My advice is simply to roll with these differences, especially since there is not much you'll be able to do about them anyway. A good rule of thumb here is simply to make sure that you meet each college halfway in completing its application.

I think it helps to understand from the outset that the context within which a college views an applicant (say, as one of a large number of similarly qualified applicants from across the country) is bound to be different from the context within which that applicant is viewed locally. Moreover, the context within which an applicant is viewed by one college is also bound to be different from the context within which that same applicant is viewed by another college, given not only that applicant groups are not completely identical from one college to another but also that the sizes of their respective freshman classes may vary considerably. Lots of times this explains why an applicant is offered admission by one college and not another.

Nor is there a single scale (or at least none that makes sense to us) against which colleges are able to precisely rank-order applicants from one to whatever number of thousands it is who apply. There are simply too many variables. For instance, similar grade point averages may represent quite different levels of achievement across thousands of high schools or even across different departments within the same school. And think of the number of possible combinations of SAT scores as well as the various SAT Subject Test scores. That is why we treat each application individually, and why we make every effort to take into account the enormous variation in academic and extracurricular opportunities from one school to the next, from one community to the next, from one state to the next, and from one country to the next. Experience suggests that excellence does not always and everywhere come in uniform dimensions.

While it is true that, all other things being equal, the better one's aca-
demic credentials, the better one's chances for admission, it is not the case
that every student we admit will have higher test scores or a higher grade
point average or a higher rank-in-class than those who are not offered ad-
mission. Colleges like mine are "selective" in two ways: first, every year,
more well-qualified students apply than it is possible for us to admit
to a freshman class as relatively small as ours, and therefore we have to
make a lot of difficult choices; second, in setting out to enroll a freshman class that is characterized by a variety of academic and nonacademic interests, exceptional skills and talents, experiences, aspirations,
and backgrounds, we exercise judgments relating to factors other than
just quantitative ones. We are aware that an important part of a student's education here is derived from the mix of students he or she will
live with, study and play with, and come to know.

In other words, you should realize that in applying to a college with
more qualified applicants than there are places available in the freshman class, there will be some factors affecting the ultimate decision on
your application (primarily, the number and nature of all the *other*
applications) over which you have no control and for which you should
not feel responsible. Too often, applicants not offered admission automatically assume that there are specific deficiencies or faults in their applications when in fact that simply isn't the case. No college enjoys the
prospect of disappointing qualified applicants, but applicants who are
not in some measure prepared for the *possibility* of being disappointed
are being unrealistic. *(When all is said and done, I happen to believe that*
the saving grace of college admissions as a whole in this country is the fact
we don't all agree on precisely the same students to admit in a given year.)

Elsewhere in the application materials, I have suggested that in
completing your application, you should just be yourself, rather than
attempting to match some imagined ideal candidate you think we have
in mind. And I confess that every time I offer that advice, I remember
the comment Mark Twain made: *"Telling a person to be himself is the*
worst advice you can give to some people!" Still, that's my advice.

In thinking about what you hope to gain from college, you might
also want to consider the possibility of taking a break between school
and college—*deferring* your entrance to college, in other words. Every

year, about two dozen or so of the students to whom we offer admission choose to defer their entrance for a year, some just to work, some to travel abroad on an American Field Service or similar program, some to continue private music study, and so forth. I mention it here just so you are aware that it is an option.

Not one of us who annually reads and rereads the thousands of applications for admission believes either the process or our ultimate decisions to be perfect, whatever criteria for perfection are used. Ultimately, however, to the best of our limited abilities we make those decisions. While I can't guarantee you admission should you apply, what I can do is to assure you that we will evaluate your application with an open mind, respect for you as an individual, and no small measure of humility.

As you go through this year, try to retain a sense of perspective and even a sense of humor. I know how important where you attend college is to you, but I also know that students often see as critical those differences between attending one college and another which, in many cases, are very slight. Whatever you do, don't let the college application process so preoccupy you that you miss out on all that your school has to offer you during your senior year. OK, that's not all of the advice I'd like to give you, but it's about the limit of one letter and I hope that some of it is useful.

Happy trails.

Fred Hargadon
Dean of Admission

APPENDIXES

Appendix A

COLLEGE RESEARCH WORKSHEET

(Make copies of this form and complete one for each college
you are seriously considering.)

Name of School _____ Location _____

Admissions Phone and E-mail _____ Campus Web Site _____

Testing Requirements (circle all that apply):

Required: SAT   ACT   ACT Writing   SAT II _____

Recommended: SAT   ACT   ACT Writing   SAT II _____

Optional: SAT   ACT   ACT writing   SAT II _____

Freshman Class Profile:

GPA: % in the top 10% of class _____   % in the top 20% of class _____

% in the top 50% of class _____

applications _____   % admitted _____

early applications _____   % admitted _____   % of class filled early _____

SAT: mid-50% math _____   mid-50% critical reading _____   mid-50% writing _____

ACT: mid-50% composite _____

Total # undergraduates _____   Total # students on campus _____

COLLEGE RESEARCH WORKSHEET, Cont'd.

Academic Profile

Circle one: Research University   Liberal Arts College   Other _____

Majors of interest to you: _____
_____

Curriculum requirements (general education, senior thesis, etc.): _____
_____

Special programs of interest (honors program, arrangements with other colleges, etc.):
_____

Overall impression of academic pace and rigor: _____
_____

Other: _____
_____
_____

Campus Life

Campus Housing: Guaranteed for _____ years
Details (process for assignment, housing options, % living on campus): _____
_____
_____

Characteristics of Student Body (single sex, geographic and ethnic diversity, liberal/
conservative, etc.):_____
_____
_____

Social Life and Activities (% in sororities and fraternities, intramural and club sports,
recreational facilities, clubs of special interest, etc.):_____
_____
_____
_____

Other:_____
_____
_____

COLLEGE RESEARCH WORKSHEET, Cont'd.

Special Interests

Intercollegiate Athletics:

Your sport: _____   NCAA Division: _____

Coach's name and contact info: _____

_____

Arts, Music, or Special Academic Focus:

Area: _____   Contact: _____

Area: _____   Contact: _____

Other: _____

_____

_____

Financial Aid Policies

Circle all that apply: Guarantees to meet full demonstrated need   Offers merit aid

Need-blind admissions   Need-based aid only

Financial Aid Deadlines: FAFSA _____   CSS Profile _____   Other(s) _____

Application Process

Circle all that apply: College specific form   Pre-application

Common Application   Common Application Supplement

Application Deadlines: Early action_____   Early decision _____

Regular _____   Rolling _____   Fee _____

Interview: Required   Optional   Not offered

Details: _____

_____

_____

Other Notes

_____

_____

_____

Appendix B

Adelphi · Agnes Scott · Albertson · Albion · Albright · Alfred · Allegheny · American · Amherst · Antioch · Arcadia · Assumption · College of the Atlantic · Austin College · Babson · Baldwin-Wallace · Bard · Barnard · Bates · Beloit · Bennington · Bentley · Binghamton · Birmingham-Southern · Boston College · Boston U · Bowdoin · Bradley · Brandeis · Bryant · Bryn Mawr · Bucknell · Butler · California Lutheran · Carleton · Carnegie Mellon · Case Western Reserve · Catawba · Centenary (La.) · Centre · Chatham · Claremont McKenna · Clark U · Clarkson U · Coe · Colby · Colby-Sawyer · Colgate · Colorado College · Concordia College (N.Y.) · Connecticut College · Converse · Cornell College · Cornell U · U of Dallas · Dartmouth · Davidson · U of Delaware · Denison · U of Denver · DePauw · Dickinson · Dominican U (Calif.) · Drew · Duke · Earlham · Eckerd · Elizabethtown · Elmira · Embry-Riddle · Emmanuel College (Mass.) · Emory · Eugene Lang · Fairfield · Findlay · Fisk · Florida Southern · Fordham · Franklin & Marshall · Furman · George Fox · George Washington · Gettysburg · Gonzaga · Goucher · Grinnell · Guilford · Gustavus Adolphus · Hamilton · Hampden-Sydney · Hampshire · Hanover · Hartwick · Harvard · Harvey Mudd · Haverford · Hendrix · Hiram · Hobart & William Smith · Hofstra · Hollins · Holy Cross · Hood · Illinois Wesleyan · Iona · Ithaca · John Carroll · Johns Hopkins · Juniata · Kalamazoo · Kenyon · Knox · La Roche · La Salle · La Verne · Lafayette · Lake Forest · Lawrence · Le Moyne · Lehigh · Lesley · Lewis & Clark · Linfield · Loyola College · Loyola U (La.) · Luther · Macalester · U of Maine (Farmington) · U of Maine (Orono) · Manhattan · Manhattanville · Marietta · Marlboro · Marquette · Mary Washington · McDaniel · Merrimack · U of Miami (Fla.) · Miami U (Ohio) · Middlebury · Mills · Millsaps · Moravian · Morehouse · Mount St Vincent · Mt Holyoke · Muhlenberg · Nazareth · New College (Fla.) · New England College · U of New Hampshire · College of New Jersey · New York U · Northeastern U · Northland · Notre Dame (Md.) · Notre Dame de Namur · Oberlin · Occidental · Oglethorpe · Ohio Wesleyan · Pace · U of the Pacific · Pitzer · Pomona · U of Portland · Presbyterian · Prescott · Princeton · Providence · Puget Sound · Queens U (N.C.) · Randolph-Macon · Randolph-Macon Woman's · Redlands · Reed · Regis College · Regis U · Rensselaer · Rhodes · Rice · U of Richmond · Rider · Ripon · U of Rochester · Rochester Inst of Tech · Roger Williams · Rollins · St Anselm · St Benedict & St John's · St Joseph's College (Me.) · St Joseph's U · St Lawrence · St Leo · St Louis U · St Mary's College (Calif.) · St Mary's College (Ind.) · St Michael's · St Norbert · St Olaf · St Peter's · St Vincent · Salem (N.C.) · Salve Regina · U of San Diego · U of San Francisco · Santa Clara · College of Santa Fe · Sarah Lawrence · Scranton · Scripps · Seattle U · Seton Hill · Sewanee · Simmons · Skidmore · Smith · Southern Maine · Southern Methodist · Southern New Hampshire · Southwestern U · Spelman · Spring Hill · Stetson · Stevens Inst of Tech · Stonehill · Suffolk · Susquehanna · Swarthmore · Sweet Briar · Syracuse · U of Tampa · TCU · Texas Christian · Trinity College (Conn.) · Trinity U · Tufts · Tulane · Tulsa · Union College (N.Y.) · Ursinus · Utica · Valparaiso · Vanderbilt · Vassar · U of Vermont · Villanova · Wabash · Wagner · Wake Forest · Washington College · Washington U (Mo.) · Washington & Jefferson · Washington & Lee · Webster · Wellesley · Wells · Wesleyan · Westminster (Mo.) · Westminster (Pa.) · Wheaton (Mass.) · Wheelock · Whitman · Whittier · Widener · Willamette · William & Mary · William Jewell · Williams · Wilson · Wittenberg · Wofford · Wooster · WPI · Xavier (Ohio) · Yale

COMMON APPLICATION™
2005–2006

APPLICATION FOR UNDERGRADUATE ADMISSION

The member colleges and universities listed above fully support the use of this form. No distinction will be made between it and the college's own form. Please type or print in black ink. Be sure to follow the instructions on the cover page of the *Common Application* booklet to complete, copy, and file your application with any one or several of the member colleges and universities.

OPTIONAL DECLARATION OF EARLY DECISION/EARLY ACTION

Complete this section ONLY for the individual college to which you are applying ED or EA. It is your responsibility to follow that college's instructions regarding early admission, including obtaining and submitting any ED/EA form provided by that college. *Do NOT complete this ED/EA section on copies of your application submitted to colleges for Regular Decision or Rolling Admission.*

College Name _____ Deadline _____

☐ Early Decision ☐ Early Action ☐ EASC

PERSONAL DATA

Legal Name _____
Enter name exactly as it appears on passports or other official documents. Last/Family   First   Middle (complete)   Jr., etc.   Gender

Nickname (choose only one) _____ Former last name(s) if any _____

Are you applying as a ☐ freshman or ☐ transfer student? For the term beginning _____

Birthdate _____   E-mail Address _____
   mm/dd/yyyy

Permanent Home Address _____   Permanent Home Phone (_____) _____
   Number and Street   Area Code   Number

_____ _____ _____ _____
City or Town   State/Province   Country   Zip Code or Postal Code

If different from above, please give your mailing address for all admission correspondence.

Mailing Address (from _____ to _____) _____
   (mm/yyyy)   (mm/yyyy)   Number and Street

_____ _____ _____ _____
City or Town   State/Province   Country   Zip Code or Postal Code

Phone at mailing address (_____) _____   Cell phone (_____) _____
   Area Code   Number   Area Code   Number

Citizenship ☐ US citizen   ☐ Dual US citizen; please specify other country of citizenship _____

☐ US Permanent Resident visa; citizen of _____   Alien Registration Number _____

☐ Other Citizenship _____   _____
   Country(ies)   Visa type

If you are not a US citizen and live in the United States, how long have you been in the country? _____

Possible area(s) of academic concentration/major(s) _____ or undecided ☐

Special college or division if applicable _____

Possible career or professional plans _____ or undecided ☐
Will you be a candidate for financial aid? ☐ Yes ☐ No   If yes, the appropriate form(s) was/will be filed on _____

The following items are *optional*. No information you provide will be used in a discriminatory manner.

Place of birth _____   Social Security Number (if any) _____ ____ _____
   City   State/Province   Country

First language, if other than English _____   Language spoken at home _____

If you wish to be identified with a particular ethnic group, please check all that apply

☐ African American, Black   ☐ Mexican American, Chicano
☐ Native American, Alaska Native (tribal affiliation _____ enrolled _____)   ☐ Native Hawaiian, Pacific Islander
☐ Asian American (countries of family's origin _____)   ☐ Puerto Rican
☐ Asian, including Indian Subcontinent (countries _____)   ☐ White or Caucasian
☐ Hispanic, Latino (countries _____)   ☐ Other (specify _____)

2005–2006   AP-1

EDUCATIONAL DATA

Secondary school you now attend (or from which you graduated) _____ Date of entry _____

Address _____ CEEB/ACT code _____
     Number and Street

_____
     City or Town   *State/Province*   *Country*   *Zip Code or Postal Code*

Date of secondary graduation _____ Type of school ☐ public ☐ private ☐ parochial ☐ home school

Guidance Counselor's Name Mr./Mrs./Ms _____ Position _____

Counselor's E-mail _____ Phone (____) _____ Fax (____) _____
                           Area Code   *Number*   *Ext.*   *Area Code*   *Number*

List all other secondary schools, including summer schools and programs you have attended beginning with ninth grade.

Name of School	*Location (City, State/Province, Zip, Country)*	*Dates Attended*
_____	_____	_____
_____	_____	_____
_____	_____	_____

List all colleges/universities at which you have taken courses for credit; list names of courses taken and grades earned on a separate sheet. Please have an official transcript sent from each institution as soon as possible.

Name of College/University & CEEB/ACT Code	*Location (City, State/Province, Zip, Country)*	*Degree Candidate?*	*Dates Attended*
_____	_____	☐	_____
_____	_____	☐	_____
_____	_____	☐	_____

☐ Not currently attending school   ☐ Graduated from secondary school early.
    Describe in detail, here or on a separate sheet, your activities since last enrolled.

TEST INFORMATION

Be sure to note the tests required for each institution to which you are applying. The official scores from the appropriate testing agency must be submitted to each institution as soon as possible. Please list your test plans below.

ACT

Date taken/ to be taken	*English*	*Math*	*Science*	*Composite*	*Combination English/Writing*

SAT I or SAT Reasoning Tests

Date taken/ to be taken	*Verbal/Critical Reading*	*Math*	*Writing*	*Date taken/ to be taken*	*Verbal/Critical Reading*	*Math*	*Writing*	*Date taken/ to be taken*	*Verbal/Critical Reading*	*Math*	*Writing*

SAT II or Subject Tests

Date taken/ to be taken	*Subject*	*Score*	*Date taken/ to be taken*	*Subject*	*Score*	*Date taken/ to be taken*	*Subject*	*Score*

Test of English as a second language (TOEFL or other exam)

Test	*Date taken/ to be taken*	*Score*	*Test*	*Date taken/ to be taken*	*Score*

AP-2   2005–2006

FAMILY

Parent 1 _____
      Last/Family   *First*   *Middle*   *Gender*

Living?   ☐ Yes   ☐ No (Date deceased _____)

Home address if different from yours

_____

_____

Home phone _____ E-mail _____

Occupation _____

Name of employer _____

College (if any) _____

Degree _____ Year _____

Graduate school (if any) _____

Work phone _____ E-mail_____

Degree _____ Year _____

Parent 2 _____
      Last/Family   *First*   *Middle*   *Gender*

Living?   ☐ Yes   ☐ No (Date deceased _____)

Home address if different from yours

_____

_____

Home phone _____ E-mail _____

Occupation _____

Name of employer _____

College (if any) _____

Degree _____ Year _____

Graduate school (if any) _____

Work phone _____ E-mail_____

Degree _____ Year _____

Parents' marital status: ☐ married   ☐ separated   ☐ divorced (date _____)   ☐ never married   ☐ widowed

With whom do you make your permanent home?   ☐ Parent 1   ☐ Parent 2   ☐ Legal Guardian   ☐ Other relation

Legal guardian's name/address _____

Please give names and ages of your brothers or sisters. If they have attended college, give the names of the institutions attended, degrees, and

approximate dates. _____

EXTRACURRICULAR, PERSONAL, AND VOLUNTEER ACTIVITIES (including summer)

Please list your **principal** extracurricular, community, and family activities and hobbies **in the order of their interest to you.** Include specific events and/or major accomplishments such as musical instrument played, varsity letters earned, etc. Check (✓) in the right column those activities you hope to pursue in college. **To allow us to focus on the highlights of your activities, please complete this section even if you plan to attach a résumé.**

Activity	Grade level or post-secondary (PS) 9 10 11 12 PS	Approximate time spent Hours per week / Weeks per year	Positions held, honors won, or letters earned	Do you plan to participate in college?
_____			_____	☐
_____			_____	☐
_____			_____	☐
_____			_____	☐
_____			_____	☐
_____			_____	☐
_____			_____	☐
_____			_____	☐

ACADEMIC HONORS

Briefly list or describe any scholastic distinctions or honors you have won since the ninth grade (e.g., National Merit, Cum Laude Society).

_____

_____

_____

2005–2006

AP-3

WORK EXPERIENCE

List any job (including summer employment) you have held during the past three years.

Specific nature of work	Employer	Approximate dates of employment	Approximate no. of hours spent per week
_____	_____	_____	_____
_____	_____	_____	_____
_____	_____	_____	_____
_____	_____	_____	_____
_____	_____	_____	_____

SHORT ANSWER

Please describe which of your activities (extracurricular and personal activities or work experience) has been most meaningful and why (150 words or fewer).

_____

_____

_____

_____

_____

_____

_____

PERSONAL ESSAY

This personal statement helps us become acquainted with you in ways different from courses, grades, test scores, and other objective data. It will demonstrate your ability to organize thoughts and express yourself. We are looking for an essay that will help us know you better as a person and as a student. Please write an essay (250–500 words) on a topic of your choice or on one of the options listed below. *Please indicate your topic by checking the appropriate box below.*

☐ 1 Evaluate a significant experience, achievement, risk you have taken, or ethical dilemma you have faced and its impact on you.

☐ 2 Discuss some issue of personal, local, national, or international concern and its importance to you.

☐ 3 Indicate a person who has had a significant influence on you, and describe that influence.

☐ 4 Describe a character in fiction, an historical figure, or a creative work (as in art, music, science, etc.) that has had an influence on you, and explain that influence.

☐ 5 A range of academic interests, personal perspectives, and life experiences adds much to the educational mix. Given your personal background, describe an experience that illustrates what you would bring to the diversity in a college community, or an encounter that demonstrated the importance of diversity to you.

☐ 6 Topic of your choice.

☞ Attach your essay on a separate sheet(s) (same size please).
You <u>must</u> put your full name, date of birth, and name of secondary school <u>on each sheet</u>.

APPLICATION FEE PAYMENT   ☐ Check/money order attached   ☐ Counselor-approved Fee Waiver attached

REQUIRED SIGNATURE   Your signature is required whether you are an ED, EA, EASC, or regular decision candidate.
I certify that all information in my application, including my Personal Essay, is my own work, factually true, and honestly presented.

Signature _____   Date _____

IF APPLYING VIA EARLY DECISION OR EARLY ACTION   (1) Complete the Optional ED/EA/EASC Declaration for your early application *only*. (2) Submit the college's required ED/EA/EASC form, if any. (3) Understand that it is your responsibility to report any changes in your schedule to the colleges to which you are applying.

These colleges are committed to administer all educational policies and activities without discrimination on the basis of race, color, religion, national or ethnic origin, age, handicap, or gender.

AP-4   2005–2006

Adelphi · Agnes Scott · Albertson · Albion · Albright · Alfred · Allegheny · American · Amherst · Antioch · Arcadia · Assumption · College of the Atlantic · Austin College · Babson · Baldwin–Wallace · Bard · Barnard · Bates · Beloit · Bennington · Bentley · Binghamton · Birmingham–Southern · Boston College · Boston U · Bowdoin · Bradley
Brandeis · Bryant · Bryn Mawr · Bucknell · Butler · California Lutheran · Carleton · Carnegie Mellon · Case Western Reserve · Cazenovia · Centenary (La.) · Centre · Chatham · Claremont McKenna · Clark U · Clarkson U · Coe · Colby · Colby–Sawyer · Colgate · Colorado College · Concordia College (N.Y.) · Connecticut College · Converse
Cornell College · Cornell U · U of Dallas · Dartmouth · Davidson · U of Delaware · Denison · U of Denver · DePauw · Dickinson · Dominican U (Calif.) · Drew · Duke · Earlham · Eckerd · Elizabethtown · Elmira · Embry–Riddle · Emmanuel College (Mass.) · Emory · Eugene Lang · Fairfield · Findlay · Fisk · Florida Southern · Fordham
Franklin & Marshall · Furman · George Fox · George Washington · Gettysburg · Gonzaga · Goucher · Grinnell · Guilford · Gustavus Adolphus · Hamilton · Hampden–Sydney
Hampshire · Hanover · Hartwick · Harvard · Harvey Mudd · Haverford · Hendrix · Hiram · Hobart & William Smith · Hofstra · Hollins · Holy Cross · Hood · Illinois Wesleyan · Iona
Ithaca · John Carroll · Johns Hopkins · Juniata · Kalamazoo · Kenyon · Knox · La Roche · La Salle · La Verne · Lafayette · Lake Forest · Lawrence · Le Moyne · Lehigh · Lesley
Lewis & Clark · Linfield · Loyola College · Loyola U (La.) · Luther · Macalester · U of Maine (Farmington) · U of Maine (Orono) · Manhattan · Manhattanville · Marietta
Marlboro · Marquette · Mary Washington · McDaniel · Merrimack · U of Miami (Fla.) · Miami U (Ohio) · Middlebury · Mills · Millsaps · Moravian · Morehouse · Mount St Vincent
Mt Holyoke · Muhlenberg · Nazareth · New College (Fla.) · New England College · U of New Hampshire · College of New Jersey · New York U · Northeastern U · Northland
Notre Dame (Md.) · Notre Dame de Namur · Oberlin · Occidental · Oglethorpe · Ohio Wesleyan · Pace · U of the Pacific · Pitzer · Pomona · U of Portland · Presbyterian
Prescott · Princeton · Providence · Puget Sound · Queens U (N.C.) · Randolph–Macon · Randolph–Macon Woman's · Redlands · Reed · Regis College · Regis U · Rensselaer · Rhodes
Rice · U of Richmond · Rider · Ripon · U of Rochester · Rochester Inst of Tech · Roger Williams · Rollins · St Anselm · St Benedict & St John's · St Joseph's College (Me.) · St Joseph's U · St Lawrence · St Leo · St Louis U · St Mary's College (Calif.) · St Mary's College (Ind.) · St Michael's · St Norbert · St Olaf · St Peter's · St Vincent · Salem (N.C.)
Salve Regina · U of San Diego · U of San Francisco · Santa Clara · College of Santa Fe · Sarah Lawrence · Scranton · Scripps · Seattle U · Seton Hill · Sewanee · Simmons · Skidmore · Smith · Southern Maine · Southern Methodist · Southern New Hampshire · Southwestern U · Spelman · Spring Hill · Stetson · Stevens Inst of Tech
Stonehill · Suffolk · Susquehanna · Swarthmore · Sweet Briar · Syracuse · U of Tampa · TCU · Transylvania · Trinity College (Conn.) · Trinity U · Tufts · Tulane · Tulsa · Union College (N.Y.) · Ursinus · Utica · Valparaiso · Vanderbilt · Vassar · U of Vermont · Villanova · Wabash · Wagner · Wake Forest · Washington College · Washington U (Mo.)
Washington & Jefferson · Washington & Lee · Webster · Wellesley · Wells · Wesleyan · Westminster (Mo.) · Westminster (Pa.) · Wheaton (Mass.) · Wheelock · Whitman · Whittier · Widener · Willamette · William & Mary · William Jewell · Williams · Wilson · Wittenberg · Wofford · Wooster · WPI · Xavier (Ohio) · Yale

TEACHER EVALUATION

**The member colleges and universities listed above fully support the use of this form. No distinction will be made between it and the college's own form.
Please type or print in black ink.**

TO THE APPLICANT

Fill in the information below and give this form and a stamped envelope, addressed to each college to which you are applying that requests a Teacher Evaluation, to a teacher who has taught you an **academic** subject.

Birthdate _____ Gender _____ Social Security No. _____

mm/dd/yyyy *(Optional)*

Student Name _____

Last/Family *First* *Middle (complete)* *Jr., etc.*

Address _____

Number and Street *City or Town* *State/Province* *Country* *Zip Code or Postal Code*

School you now attend _____ CEEB/ACT code __ __ __ __ __ __

TO THE TEACHER

The Common Application group of colleges finds candid evaluations helpful in choosing from among highly qualified candidates. We are primarily interested in whatever you think is important about the applicant's academic and personal qualifications for college.

Please submit your references promptly. A photocopy of this reference form, or another reference you may have prepared on behalf of this student, is acceptable. You are encouraged to keep the original of this form in your private files for use should the student need additional recommendations. Please return it to the appropriate admission office(s) in the envelope(s) provided you by this student. We are grateful for your assistance. *Be sure to sign below.*

Teacher's Name Mr./Mrs./Ms _____ Position _____

Please print or type

Secondary School _____

School Address _____

Teacher's Phone (_____) _____ Ext. _____ Teacher's E-mail _____

Area Code *Number*

Signature _____ *Date* _____

BACKGROUND INFORMATION

How long have you known this student and in what context? _____

_____

What are the first words that come to your mind to describe this student? _____

_____

List the courses you have taught this student, noting for each the student's year in school (10th, 11th, 12th; first-year, sophomore; etc.) and the level of course difficulty (AP, accelerated, honors, IB, elective; 100-level, 200-level, etc.).

_____

_____

_____

_____

_____

Please detach along perforation

EVALUATION Please write whatever you think is important about this student, including a description of academic and personal characteristics. We are particularly interested in the candidate's intellectual promise, motivation, maturity, integrity, independence, originality, initiative, leadership potential, capacity for growth, special talents, enthusiasm, concern for others, respect accorded by faculty, and reaction to setbacks. We welcome information that will help us to differentiate this student from others.

RATINGS

Compared to other students in his or her class year, how do you rate this student in terms of:

No basis		Below Average	Average	Good (above average)	Very Good (well above average)	Excellent (top 10%)	Outstanding (top 5%)	One of the top few encountered in my career
	Creative, original thought							
	Motivation							
	Self-confidence							
	Independence, initiative							
	Intellectual ability							
	Academic achievement							
	Written expression of ideas							
	Effective class discussion							
	Disciplined work habits							
	Potential for growth							

CONFIDENTIALITY We value your comments highly and ask that you complete this form in the knowledge that it may be retained in the student's file should the applicant matriculate at a member college. In accordance with the Family Educational Rights and Privacy Act of 1974, matriculating students *do* have access to their permanent files, which may include forms such as this one. Unless required by state law, colleges may not provide access to admission records to applicants, those students who are denied admission, or those students who decline an offer of admission. Again, your comments are important to us and we thank you for your cooperation. These colleges are committed to administer all educational policies and activities without discrimination on the basis of race, color, religion, national or ethnic origin, age, handicap, or gender.

TE-2 TEACHER EVALUATION I COMMON APPLICATION ™ 2005–2006

Adelphi · Agnes Scott · Albertson · Albion · Albright · Alfred · Allegheny · American · Amherst · Antioch · Arcadia · Assumption · College of the Atlantic · Austin College · Babson · Baldwin—Wallace · Bard · Barnard · Bates · Beloit · Bennington · Bentley · Binghamton · Birmingham—Southern · Boston College · Boston U · Bowdoin · Bradley · Brandeis · Bryant · Bryn Mawr · Bucknell · Butler · California Lutheran · Carleton · Carnegie Mellon · Case Western Reserve · Cazenovia · Centenary (La.) · Centre · Chatham · Claremont McKenna · Clark U · Clarkson U · Coe · Colby · Colby—Sawyer · Colgate · Colorado College · Concordia College (N.Y.) · Connecticut College · Converse · Cornell College · Cornell U · U of Dallas · Dartmouth · Davidson · U of Delaware · Denison · U of Denver · DePauw · Dickinson · Dominican U (Calif.) · Drew · Duke · Earlham · Eckerd · Elizabethtown · Elmira · Embry—Riddle · Emmanuel College (Mass.) · Emory · Eugene Lang · Fairfield · Findlay · Fisk · Florida Southern · Fordham · Franklin & Marshall · Furman · George Fox · George Washington · Gettysburg · Gonzaga · Goucher · Grinnell · Guilford · Gustavus Adolphus · Hamilton · Hampden—Sydney · Hampshire · Hanover · Hartwick · Harvard · Harvey Mudd · Haverford · Hendrix · Hiram · Hobart & William Smith · Hofstra · Hollins · Holy Cross · Hood · Illinois Wesleyan · Iona · Ithaca · John Carroll · Johns Hopkins · Juniata · Kalamazoo · Kenyon · Knox · La Roche · La Salle · La Verne · Lafayette · Lake Forest · Lawrence · Le Moyne · Lehigh · Lesley · Lewis & Clark · Linfield · Loyola College · Loyola U (La.) · Luther · Macalester · U of Maine (Farmington) · U of Maine (Orono) · Manhattan · Manhattanville · Marietta · Marlboro · Marquette · Mary Washington · McDaniel · Merrimack · U of Miami (Fla.) · Miami U (Ohio) · Middlebury · Mills · Millsaps · Moravian · Morehouse · Mount St Vincent · Mt Holyoke · Muhlenberg · Nazareth · New College (Fla.) · New England College · U of New Hampshire · College of New Jersey · New York U · Northeastern U · Northland · Notre Dame (Md.) · Notre Dame de Namur · Oberlin · Occidental · Oglethorpe · Ohio Wesleyan · Pace · U of the Pacific · Pitzer · Pomona · U of Portland · Presbyterian · Prescott · Princeton · Providence · Puget Sound · Queens U (N.C.) · Randolph—Macon · Randolph—Macon Woman's · Redlands · Reed · Regis College · Regis U · Rensselaer · Rhodes · Rice · U of Richmond · Rider · Ripon · U of Rochester · Rochester Inst of Tech · Roger Williams · Rollins · St Anselm · St Benedict & St John's · St Joseph College (Me.) · St Joseph's U · St Lawrence · St Leo · St Louis U · St Mary's College (Calif.) · St Mary's College (Ind.) · St Michael's · St Norbert · St Olaf · St Peter's · St Vincent · Salem (N.C.) · Salve Regina · U of San Diego · U of San Francisco · Santa Clara · College of Santa Fe · Sarah Lawrence · Scranton · Scripps · Seattle U · Seton Hill · Sewanee · Simmons · Skidmore · Smith · Southern Maine · Southern Methodist · Southern New Hampshire · Southwestern U · Spelman · Spring Hill · Stetson · Stevens Inst of Tech · Stonehill · Suffolk · Susquehanna · Swarthmore · Sweet Briar · Syracuse · U of Tampa · TCU · Transylvania · Trinity College (Conn.) · Trinity U · Tufts · Tulane · Tulsa · Union College (N.Y.) · Ursinus · Utica · Valparaiso · Vanderbilt · Vassar · U of Vermont · Villanova · Wabash · Wagner · Wake Forest · Washington College · Washington U (Mo.) · Washington & Jefferson · Washington & Lee · Webster · Wellesley · Wells · Wesleyan · Westminster (Mo.) · Westminster (Pa.) · Wheaton (Mass.) · Wheelock · Whitman · Whittier · Widener · Willamette · William & Mary · William Jewell · Williams · Wilson · Wittenberg · Wofford · Wooster · WPI · Xavier (Ohio) · Yale

SCHOOL REPORT

The member colleges and universities listed above fully support the use of this form. No distinction will be made between it and the college's own form. Please type or print in black ink.

TO THE APPLICANT

After filling in the information below, give this form to your guidance counselor.

Birthdate _____   Gender _____   Social Security No. _____
    mm/dd/yyyy   *(Optional)*

Student Name _____
    Last/Family   *First*   *Middle (complete)*   *Jr., etc.*

Address _____
    Number and Street   *City or Town*   *State/Province*   *Country*   *Zip Code or Postal Code*

Current year courses—please indicate title, level (AP, IB, advanced honors, etc.) and credit value of all courses you are taking this year.

First Semester/Trimester   *Second Semester/Trimester*   *Third Trimester*

_____   _____   _____
_____   _____   _____
_____   _____   _____
_____   _____   _____
_____   _____   _____
_____   _____   _____
_____   _____   _____
_____   _____   _____

Please detach along perforation

TO THE SECONDARY SCHOOL GUIDANCE COUNSELOR

Attach applicant's official transcript, including courses in progress, a school profile, and transcript legend. (Please check transcript copies for readability.) After filling in the blanks below, use both sides of this form to describe the applicant. Please provide all available information for this candidate. *Be sure to sign below.*

Class rank _____ in a class of _____ , covering a period from _____ to _____   **S.S. graduation date** _____
    (mm/yyyy)   *(mm/yyyy)*

  The rank is ☐ weighted ☐ unweighted. How many students share this rank? _____

Are classes taken on a block schedule?
☐ yes ☐ no

  If a precise rank is not available, please indicate rank to the nearest tenth from the top _____

Cumulative GPA _____ on a _____ scale, covering a period from _____ to _____
    (mm/yyyy)   *(mm/yyyy)*

If yes, in what year did _____
block scheduling begin?

  This GPA is ☐ weighted ☐ unweighted. The school's passing mark is _____

  Percentage of graduating class attending: _____ four-year _____ two-year institutions   Highest grade/GPA in class _____

In comparison with other college preparatory students *at our school,* the applicant's course selection is
☐ most demanding ☐ very demanding ☐ demanding ☐ average ☐ less than demanding

Counselor's Name Mr./Mrs./Ms _____
    Please print or type

Signature _____   **Date** _____

Position _____   School _____

Counselor's Address _____

Counselor's Phone (_____) _____   Counselor's Fax (_____) _____
    Area Code   *Number*   *Ext.*   *Area Code*   *Number*

Secondary School CEEB/ACT Code __ __ __ __ __ __   Counselor's E-mail _____

SR-1

EVALUATION Please write whatever you think is important about this student, including a description of academic and personal characteristics. We are particularly interested in the candidate's intellectual promise, motivation, maturity, integrity, independence, originality, initiative, leadership potential, capacity for growth, special talents, enthusiasm, concern for others, respect accorded by faculty, and reaction to setbacks. We welcome information that will help us to differentiate this student from others.

How long have you known this student and in what context? _____

_____

What are the first words that come to your mind to describe this student? _____

_____

RATINGS

Compared to other students in his or her class year, how do you rate this student in terms of:

No basis		Below Average	Average	Good (above average)	Very Good (well above average)	Excellent (top 10%)	Outstanding (top 5%)	One of the top few encountered in my career
	Academic achievement							
	Extracurricular accomplishments							
	Personal qualities and character							
	Creativity							

I recommend this student: ☐ With reservation ☐ Fairly strongly ☐ Strongly ☐ Enthusiastically

CONFIDENTIALITY We value your comments highly and ask that you complete this form in the knowledge that it may be retained in the student's file should the applicant matriculate at a member college. In accordance with the Family Educational Rights and Privacy Act of 1974, matriculating students *do* have access to their permanent files, which may include forms such as this one. Unless required by state law, colleges may not provide access to admission records to applicants, those students who are denied admission, or those students who decline an offer of admission. Again, your comments are important to us and we thank you for your cooperation. These colleges are committed to administer all educational policies and activities without discrimination on the basis of race, color, religion, national or ethnic origin, age, handicap, or gender.

SR-2   COMMON APPLICATION ™ 2005–2006

Adelphi · Agnes Scott · Albertson · Albion · Albright · Alfred · Allegheny · American · Amherst · Antioch · Arcadia · Assumption · College of the Atlantic · Austin College · Babson · Baldwin–Wallace · Bard · Barnard · Bates · Beloit · Bennington · Bentley · Binghamton · Birmingham–Southern · Boston College · Boston U · Bowdoin · Bradley · Brandeis · Bryant · Bryn Mawr · Bucknell · Butler · California Lutheran · Carleton · Carnegie Mellon · Case Western Reserve · Cazenovia · Centenary (La.) · Centre · Chatham · Claremont McKenna · Clark U · Clarkson U · Coe · Colby · Colby–Sawyer · Colgate · Colorado College · Concordia College (N.Y.) · Connecticut College · Converse · Cornell College · Cornell U · U of Dallas · Dartmouth · Davidson · U of Delaware · Denison · U of Denver · DePauw · Dickinson · Dominican U (Calif.) · Drew · Duke · Earlham · Eckerd · Elizabethtown · Elmira · Embry–Riddle · Emmanuel College (Mass.) · Emory · Eugene Lang · Fairfield · Findlay · Fisk · Florida Southern · Fordham · Franklin & Marshall · Furman · George Fox · George Washington · Gettysburg · Gonzaga · Goucher · Grinnell · Guilford · Gustavus Adolphus · Hamilton · Hampden–Sydney · Hampshire · Hanover · Hartwick · Harvard · Harvey Mudd · Haverford · Hendrix · Hiram · Hobart & William Smith · Hofstra · Hollins · Holy Cross · Hood · Wesleyan · Iona · Ithaca · John Carroll · Johns Hopkins · Juniata · Kalamazoo · Kenyon · Knox · La Roche · La Salle · La Verne · Lafayette · Lake Forest · Lawrence · Le Moyne · Lehigh · Lesley · Lewis & Clark · Linfield · Loyola College · Loyola U (La.) · Luther · Macalester · U of Maine (Farmington) · U of Maine (Orono) · Manhattan · Marlboro · Marquette · Mary Washington · McDaniel · Merrimack · U of Miami (Fla.) · Miami U (Ohio) · Middlebury · Mills · Millsaps · Moravian · Morehouse · Mount St Vincent · Mt Holyoke · Muhlenberg · Nazareth · New College (Fla.) · New England College · U of New Hampshire · College of New Jersey · New York U · Northeastern U · Northland · Notre Dame (Md.) · Notre Dame de Namur · Oberlin · Occidental · Oglethorpe · Ohio Wesleyan · Pace · U of the Pacific · Pitzer · Pomona · U of Portland · Presbyterian · Prescott · Princeton · Providence · Puget Sound · Queens U (N.C.) · Randolph–Macon · Randolph–Macon Woman's · Redlands · Reed · Regis College · Regis U · Rensselaer · Rhodes · Rice · U of Richmond · Rider · Ripon · U of Rochester · Rochester Inst of Tech · Roger Williams · Rollins · St Anselm · St Benedict & St John's · St Joseph's College (Me.) · St Joseph's U · St Lawrence · St Leo · St Louis U · St Mary's College (Calif.) · St Mary's College (Ind.) · St Michael's · St Norbert · St Olaf · St Peter's · St Vincent · Salem (N.C.) · Salve Regina · U of San Diego · U of San Francisco · Santa Clara · College of Santa Fe · Sarah Lawrence · Scranton · Scripps · Seattle U · Seton Hill · Sewanee · Simmons · Skidmore · Smith · Southern Maine · Southern Methodist · Southern New Hampshire · Southwestern U · Spelman · Spring Hill · Stetson · Stevens Inst of Tech · Stonehill · Suffolk · Susquehanna · Swarthmore · Sweet Briar · Syracuse · U of Tampa · TCU · Transylvania · Trinity College (Conn.) · Trinity U · Tufts · Tulane · Tulsa · Union College (N.Y.) · Ursinus · Utica · Valparaiso · Vanderbilt · Vassar · U of Vermont · Villanova · Wabash · Wagner · Wake Forest · Washington College · Washington U (Mo.) · Washington & Jefferson · Washington & Lee · Webster · Wellesley · Wells · Wesleyan · Westminster (Mo.) · Westminster (Pa.) · Wheaton (Mass.) · Wheelock · Whitman · Whittier · Widener · Willamette · William & Mary · William Jewell · Williams · Wilson · Wittenberg · Wofford · Wooster · WPI · Xavier (Ohio) · Yale

MIDYEAR REPORT

The member colleges and universities listed above fully support the use of this form. No distinction will be made between it and the college's own form. Please type or print in black ink.

TO THE APPLICANT

Check institutional instructions to see if your selected colleges require this form. After filling in the information below, give this form to your guidance counselor.

Birthdate _____ Gender _____ Social Security No. _____
mm/dd/yyyy *(Optional)*

Student Name _____
Last/Family *First* *Middle (complete)* *Jr., etc.*

Address _____
Number and Street *City or Town* *State/Province* *Country* *Zip Code or Postal Code*

TO THE SECONDARY SCHOOL GUIDANCE COUNSELOR

Please submit this form when midyear senior grades are available (end of first semester or second trimester). Please complete the grid below or, if you prefer, attach your own grade report form or a copy of the secondary school transcript. Feel free to provide additional comments about the candidate on the reverse of this form or on a separate sheet of paper. *Be sure to sign below.*

Where possible, please provide IB and A-level predictions, as well as the grades for the trimester or semester.

Indicate if marking period is ☐ first semester ☐ second trimester S.S. graduation date _____
Course (include title and level) Grade Remarks

_____

_____

_____

_____

_____

_____

_____

_____

If available, please provide updated class rank or cumulative GPA through the senior fall semester/trimester.

Class rank _____ in a class of _____ , covering a period from _____ to _____
(mm/yyyy) *(mm/yyyy)*

The rank is ☐ weighted ☐ unweighted. How many students share this rank? _____
If a precise rank is not available, please indicate rank to the nearest tenth from the top _____

Cumulative GPA _____ on a _____ scale, covering a period from _____ to _____
(mm/yyyy) *(mm/yyyy)*

This GPA is ☐ weighted ☐ unweighted. The school's passing mark is _____

Have there been any substantial additions to or changes in this candidate's academic or extracurricular record since your previous report? ☐ yes ☐ no

If yes, or if your recommendation for this student has changed since the School Report was submitted, please comment on reverse.

Counselor's Name Mr./Mrs./Ms _____
Please print or type

Signature _____ *Date* _____

Position _____ School _____

Secondary School CEEB/ACT Code __ __ __ __ __ __

Please detach along perforation

Please use the space below, or a separate sheet of paper, for additional comments.

CONFIDENTIALITY We value your comments highly and ask that you complete this form in the knowledge that it may be retained in the student's file should the applicant matriculate at a member college. In accordance with the Family Educational Rights and Privacy Act of 1974, matriculating students *do* have access to their permanent files, which may include forms such as this one. Unless required by state law, colleges may not provide access to admission records to applicants, those students who are denied admission, or those students who decline an offer of admission. Again, your comments are important to us and we thank you for your cooperation. These colleges are committed to administer all educational policies and activities without discrimination on the basis of race, color, religion, national or ethnic origin, age, handicap, or gender.

Appendix C

SAMPLE STUDENT INFORMATION SHEET FOR LETTERS OF RECOMMENDATION

In order to write a recommendation letter for you, counselors and teachers need information that will be used solely and confidentially for that purpose. You benefit when they are able to provide a comprehensive academic and personal report. Read this entire form before you begin to fill it out to prevent yourself from entering duplicate information. Take your time and answer each question thoughtfully. You'll need to have this same information for your college applications, so it will help you later as well. When you have completed the form, prepare a packet for each person from whom you have requested a letter that contains the following: the copy of the form and all attachments; the recommendation forms from your colleges; a stamped and pre-addressed envelope for each college; and a listing of due dates. Packets should be submitted to your recommendation writers at least four weeks before the first due date.

Please print neatly or type your responses. You may attach separate sheets as needed.

Student Name _____   Nickname (if any) _____

Phone _____   E-mail _____

1. Test Score Information

ACT

Date _____ Verbal ____ Math ____ Sci ____ Read ____ Writing ____ Comp ____

Date _____ Verbal ____ Math ____ Sci ____ Read ____ Writing ____ Comp ____

Date _____ Verbal ____ Math ____ Sci ____ Read ____ Writing ____ Comp ____

SAT

Date _____ Critical Reading _____   Math _____   Writing _____

Date _____ Critical Reading _____   Math _____   Writing _____

Date _____ Critical Reading _____   Math _____   Writing _____

SAT Subject Test   Date_____   Subject _____   Score _____

SAT Subject Test   Date_____   Subject _____   Score _____

SAT Subject Test   Date_____   Subject _____   Score _____

SAT Subject Test   Date_____   Subject _____   Score _____

Future Test Dates for SAT _____ SAT Subject Test _____ ACT _____

SAMPLE STUDENT INFORMATION SHEET FOR LETTERS OF RECOMMENDATION, Cont'd.

AP or IB Test   Date: _____   Subject _____   Score _____

AP or IB Test   Date: _____   Subject _____   Score _____

AP or IB Test   Date: _____   Subject _____   Score _____

AP or IB Test   Date: _____   Subject _____   Score _____

AP or IB Test   Date: _____   Subject _____   Score _____

2. Do your test scores and grades accurately reflect your academic potential? _____
If not, explain why. _____
_____
_____
_____

3. Attach a copy of your transcript (for teacher recommendations only—your counselor already has your transcript). List any college courses taken during high school that are not included on your transcript.

Course _____   Where taken _____   Year _____

Course _____   Where taken _____   Year _____

Course _____   Where taken _____   Year _____

4. Attach a brief résumé (for grades 9–12) listing your extracurricular activities and achievements; academic honors and awards; hobbies, special interests, or talents; community service activities; and work experience.

5. Attach a copy of your college personal essay if it is completed or, on a separate sheet of paper, answer "What sets you apart as an individual?"

6. Ask your parent/guardian or a friend to write an anecdote that describes your character and attach it to this form. This should be about one paragraph long.

7. Where were you born? If not in the U.S., at what age did you move to the U.S? _____
_____

8. Do you speak more than one language? If so, list and indicate fluency. _____
_____

9. With whom are you living? Circle: Mother Father Both parents Other _____

10. Will you be the first person in your immediate family to attend college? _____

SAMPLE STUDENT INFORMATION SHEET FOR LETTERS OF RECOMMENDATION, Cont'd.

11. Please tell us about your family. List your siblings, providing name, age, current school and grade level, degrees, and/or occupation. _____

_____

_____

12. Parents' or guardians' occupations and highest level of education completed

Father/Guardian Occupation _____ Educ level/degree _____

Mother/Guardian Occupation _____ Educ level/degree _____

13. Do you have any significant travel experience? Describe, including dates. _____

_____

_____

_____

14. Have you ever been suspended from school during 9–12 grades? _____ If yes, when and for what reason? _____

_____

_____

_____

15. Is there any significant, unique, or unusual experience, situation, or involvement that you want to share? _____

_____

_____

_____

16. List three adjectives that you feel best describe you and explain why. _____

_____

_____

_____

_____

_____

SAMPLE STUDENT INFORMATION SHEET FOR LETTERS OF RECOMMENDATION, Cont'd.

17. List the colleges to which you are applying and the reason why you are interested in attending. If you plan to apply Early Decision (ED) or Early Action (EA) please indicate that next to the name of the college.

College _____ Reason_____

College _____ Reason_____

College _____ Reason_____

College _____ Reason_____

College _____ Reason_____

College _____ Reason_____

College _____ Reason_____

College _____ Reason_____

Please feel free to attach any other information that you believe would be helpful to those writing on your behalf.

Before submitting this form, please check that you completed all parts and have attached:

1. A copy of your transcript (see #3 above)

2. A copy of your activity resume (see #4 above)

3. A copy of a college essay or "What sets you apart?" essay (see #5 above)

4. Parent/guardian/friend anecdote (see #6 above)

Appendix D

FINANCIAL AID COMPARISON WORKSHEET

Name of College _____ _____ _____ _____

Cost of Attendance _____ _____ _____ _____

Financial Aid Package

Grants/Scholarships _____ _____ _____ _____

Loans _____ _____ _____ _____

Work-Study _____ _____ _____ _____

Total _____ _____ _____ _____

Expected Family Contribution (EFC)

Student Contribution _____ _____ _____ _____

Parent Contribution _____ _____ _____ _____

Total _____ _____ _____ _____

Unmet Need (If Any) _____ _____ _____ _____

Appendix E

COST OF ATTENDANCE WORKSHEET

Name of College	_____	_____	_____	_____
Tuition and Fees	_____	_____	_____	_____
Room and Board	_____	_____	_____	_____
Books and Supplies	_____	_____	_____	_____
Personal Expenses	_____	_____	_____	_____
Travel	_____	_____	_____	_____
Total	_____	_____	_____	_____

This college preparation time line covers key points in the college preparation process. The specifics will vary depending on both you and the counseling program at your high school. Use this time line as a preview of what is to come and as a general guide, but be sure to supplement and refine it with information provided by your counseling office and the colleges to which you will be applying.

In preparing the time line we have assumed that you will begin thinking seriously about college admissions by your junior year. If you are one of the many students who waits until senior year, we have a special Senior Year, Fall Semester time line designed especially for you. You'll find it at the end.

Freshman Year

Although no special focus on the college application process is needed during freshman year, the following steps are good preparation for success in general:

- Take challenging courses in "academic solids": English, foreign language, mathematics, science, social studies.
- Study hard.
- Explore extracurricular activities both inside and outside of school to find those that interest and excite you.

- Read as much as you can.

- Plan summer activities that will enrich you in some way: summer school, work experience, family travel, and so forth. Don't be a couch potato.

- At the end of the year, begin a permanent record of your extracurricular and volunteer activities, academic honors and awards, and so on.

Sophomore Year

In your sophomore year you'll want to continue taking challenging courses and developing your extracurricular interests and talents. It is also a time when students take on part-time jobs. Families may begin thinking about college in more concrete terms. Some high schools begin a formal program of college orientation in the sophomore year, but most do not.

All Year

- Study hard in a challenging curriculum.

- Continue involvement in extracurricular activities; look for opportunities to assume leadership roles.

- Consider volunteer activities.

- If you work part-time, be sure you keep on top of your academics.

- Save samples of your best papers and work in the arts (if applicable) for potential later use.

Fall

- Consider taking the PSAT or PLAN (or both) for practice.

- Seek help from your teachers early if you experience academic difficulties.

Winter

- PSAT and PLAN results arrive in December. After reading the information that comes with your scores, consider meeting with your counselor to discuss steps you might take to address your weaker areas.

- Plan a challenging program of classes for your junior year.

- Begin to make plans for summer activities that will be enriching (paid or volunteer work, classes, travel, for example).
- Register at school for May Advanced Placement tests, if appropriate.

Spring

- If your family will be traveling over spring break, consider including a trip or two to colleges that may be of interest to you.
- Consult your counselor and register for SAT Subject Tests, if appropriate.
- Update your record of extracurricular activities, awards, and so on that you began at the end of freshman year.

Summer

- Reap the benefits of your earlier planning for a productive summer. Continue to read.
- Some students who are interested in qualifying for the National Merit Scholarship Program prepare for the PSAT that they will take in October.

Junior Year

Junior year typically marks the start of the college selection process. Junior year grades play an especially important role in college admission, so a focus on academics is very important. By junior year, most students have identified the extracurricular areas in which they have the greatest talent and passion, although new interests can develop.

All Year

- Study hard in a challenging curriculum.
- Continue involvement in extracurricular and volunteer activities and seek leadership roles as appropriate.
- If you work part-time during the school year, make sure to continue a strong focus on your academics.
- Continue to save samples of your best papers and work in the arts (if appropriate) for potential later use.

- Students interested in athletics at the Division I and Division II level should talk to their coaches and explore eligibility requirements on the NCAA Web site, www.ncaa.org.

Fall

- Buy a copy of a "big book" college guide such as the *Fiske Guide to Colleges*. It will be a useful resource to you over the next eighteen months.
- Take the PSAT in October.
- Study hard in your classes. If you experience academic difficulty, seek help early.
- Complete the "Determining Your Priorities" questionnaire at the end of Chapter Four to help you decide what to look for in a college.
- Many colleges send representatives to high schools in the fall. If your school allows juniors to participate, consider attending those sessions that are of interest to you.

Winter

- PSAT results arrive. After reading your score report, talk to your counselor about steps you can take to improve your performance on the upcoming SAT or ACT as appropriate.
- Become familiar with the differences between the ACT and SAT and decide which one(s) you will take. Register for winter or spring SAT or ACT tests or both. February is a good month to take the ACT for the first time; March is a good month for the SAT.
- Winter is a good time to prepare (via book, software, or courses) for standardized tests.
- If you have not already met with your counselor to begin discussing college selection, do so now.
- Register at your school for May Advanced Placement tests.
- Choose challenging courses for your senior year.
- Make plans for an enriching summer. Once again, consider travel, coursework, volunteer or paid employment, workshops, or clinics that match your interests.

Spring

- Continue to develop your college list, ideally in consultation with your counselor.

- Start a filing system to help you keep all your college materials organized.

- Consider using the spring break to visit colleges.

- Register for and take spring SAT Subject Tests, as appropriate, depending on the requirements of the colleges that are of interest to you. Register and take the SAT or ACT (or both) as appropriate.

- Request materials from colleges that interest you.

- Attend a college fair if one is nearby.

- If you want to be a varsity athlete in college, contact the coaches at the schools that interest you if you have not already been contacted by them.

- Consider visiting colleges over the summer and plan these visits early.

- Continue to meet with your counselor as you develop your short list.

- Update your record of extracurricular activities, awards, and so forth.

Summer

- Reap the benefits of your planning for an enriching summer experience, whether it involves work, travel, study, or other activity.

- Visit colleges as appropriate to help further refine your college list.

- Consider getting a head start on the college application process by brainstorming about or actually drafting a personal essay.

- If your applications will require a portfolio or audition tape, get started on it now.

Senior Year

The senior year is the busiest in the college selection process. Some students will choose to apply "early" and will need to have a completed application ready to go by November 1 or 15. In general, students should have their college list identified by mid-November so that they can submit their rolling admissions and regular decision applications by the deadlines without being rushed.

All Year

- Study hard in a challenging curriculum. Colleges will receive your fall grades if you apply regular decision.

- Part-time work is often a part of senior year. Again, be sure to maintain appropriate focus on academics.

- Continue involvement in extracurricular and volunteer activities and leadership roles as appropriate.

Fall

- Visit additional colleges if time and circumstances permit. Arrange overnights and on-campus interviews where feasible and available.

- Meet with college representatives who are visiting your high school, and attend a fall college fair and college nights to get more information.

- Finalize your college list in consultation with your counselor. Decide if an early application is right for you.

- Be sure to check and make note of all deadlines for each of the colleges on your list.

- Register and take fall SAT or ACT tests, if necessary. Be aware of deadlines if you are submitting an early application and want a fall test administration to be part of your application.

- Ask teachers for letters of recommendation at least one month before the first letter is due.

- Finalize your essays, having carefully edited them with the benefit of appropriate input from teachers and parents.

- Submit applications by the required deadlines, double-checking that all parts are complete.

- Arrange to have standardized test scores and high school transcripts sent to colleges by their deadlines.

- Participate in alumni interviews as appropriate if applying early.

- If applying early, receive your decision by December 15. If admitted, congratulations! If not, move on. If you haven't yet submitted your regular decision applications, do so right now. Consider an early decision II application, if appropriate, to another school that is very high on your list.

- If you will be applying for financial aid, begin the process of learning about the FAFSA and CSS PROFILE, as appropriate, and ask your parents to gather the information needed to complete them. Start your scholarship search.

Winter

- If deferred when applying early, write to the college and express your continued interest in attending.

- Submit any remaining applications.

- For both deferred and regular applications, send significant new information regarding accomplishments and awards, if any, to colleges.

- Ask your counselor to send midyear report to colleges.

- Participate in alumni interviews as appropriate.

- Keep focused on your academic work.

Spring

- Decisions may arrive as early as February or as late as early April.

- Take advantage of "admit" weekend events in April, if possible, to learn more about the colleges that have admitted you.

- Carefully consider and compare your financial aid packages and consider requesting a review if a package is not adequate for your needs.

- Make your final decision about where you want to go and submit your deposit by May 1. Notify the other schools that you will not be attending.

- If you are wait-listed, decide whether or not to remain on the wait-list. Be sure to make a deposit by May 1 at a school where you have a firm acceptance. If you decide to remain on a wait-list, write to the admissions office conveying your enthusiasm as well as any new information. Ask your counselor to do the same.

- Enjoy the remainder of your senior year!

What If You Are Beginning Your Search in Senior Year?

A lot of students put off serious thinking about college until the fall of their senior year. Maybe you are one of them. While we don't recommend that approach, don't worry—you can make up for lost time if you use the time you do have wisely and to your best advantage. Once you get to January of your senior year, you'll be in sync with your classmates who started their college search much earlier. The following special fall senior year time line will help you get going.

- Buy the most recent edition of a "big book" such as the *Fiske Guide to Colleges*. You may also want to buy the most recent College Board *College Handbook* or consult it in the library. This book gives detailed information on requirements at thousands of colleges, and contains useful summary tables in the back with information about acceptance rates, college size, colleges that require or recommend SAT Subject Tests, and so on.

- Make sure you have already taken (or are registered to take) the SAT or ACT and SAT Subject Tests if they are likely to be recommended or required by the colleges to which you may be applying. If you can't complete certain tests in time, you will need to focus on the many colleges that do not require them.

- Read Chapters Four and Five of this book carefully and fill out the "Determining Your Priorities" questionnaire to help you identify your preferences. Meet with your counselor as soon as possible to discuss colleges that will meet your needs.

- Talk to friends, family members, and classmates about colleges they may recommend. Try a couple of online college search Web sites.

- Do careful research on the colleges that emerge from your data-gathering efforts. Read your big book and study college Web sites.

- Watch for visits by college representatives, evening programs, and nearby college fairs. Use them to gather additional information.

- Visit colleges on your list if you have a chance, taking advantage of high school holidays. But don't worry—you'll have another chance to visit in the spring after you are accepted but before you must make a decision.

- A good application takes time to prepare, especially if it requires a special essay or other custom responses. Keep this in mind as you decide where to apply.

- Make sure that your college list has an appropriate range of colleges: good bet, possible, and long shot. Check back with your counselor before you finalize it.

- Ask two teachers whether they would be willing to write letters of recommendation on your behalf. Talk to them as early as you can in the fall quarter once you determine that your probable colleges require such letters. Tell them that you will give background information about yourself once you have your final college list and application forms. Make sure they have at least three weeks to write their letters.

- Be aware that early action and early decision applications are generally due by November 1 or November 15. You may not have enough time to do a careful job of selecting a college and preparing a strong application by that date. If rushed, don't do it. Some colleges have a second early decision due date in mid-December or early January. This works better for late starters.

- Make sure you know all of the deadlines (pre-applications, applications, financial aid, test scores) for the schools you choose. Be sure to release your SAT or ACT scores to colleges on your list.

- Prepare your applications carefully and thoughtfully, and don't forget to proofread everything well. Have someone else help you proofread as well.

- Ask your parents to begin gathering necessary information for financial aid applications.

- Use the Common Application whenever possible to save time and effort, even if there is a supplementary form and essay required. Applying online can also make things easier for you.

Academic Index   A calculation based on standardized test scores and class rank (or equivalent) that is used by Ivy League colleges to ensure that athletic recruits have academic records that exceed a minimum threshold.

ACT   Short for ACT Assessment. A standardized college admissions test that is an alternative to the SAT.

Advanced Placement (AP)   A program coordinated by the College Board whereby high schools offer college-level courses with specific curricula in a large number of academic fields. Participating students have the option of taking an AP exam at the end of the course to demonstrate knowledge and potentially earn college credit.

Award letter   Financial aid terminology for the document sent to a financial aid recipient that indicates the amount and type of financial aid.

Candidate reply date   Postmark date by which a student must notify a college about his or her intention to enroll. May 1 is the standard date for students admitted regular decision.

Class rank   The student's place in his or her class based on a rank ordering of students by grade point average (GPA).

Common Application   A standardized application form accepted by over 250 colleges. Some colleges also require a school-specific supplementary form.

Consortium   Several colleges that join together in a cooperative arrangement that allows students to take courses and use library facilities on each campus.

Core curriculum	A group of specially designed courses in the humanities, arts, social sciences, and sciences designed to give students a strong foundation in general education.
Cost of education	Financial aid terminology for total educational costs, including tuition, fees, books, supplies, room and board, incidentals, and travel home.
CSS PROFILE	Abbreviation for College Scholarship Service PROFILE. A need assessment form administered by the College Board that is used by some schools to determine eligibility for institutionally based financial aid.
Deferral	A decision by a college to delay a final response to an early action or early decision application until the regular decision cycle.
Deferred admission	A decision on the part of an admitted student to wait until the following academic year to enroll.
Demonstrated need	Financial aid terminology for the difference between the total cost of education and the expected family contribution to the student's education.
Double deposit	Unethical practice of sending deposits to hold places at two or more colleges while deciding between them.
Division I, II, and III	National Collegiate Athletic Association (NCAA) groupings of colleges for purposes of athletic competition.
Early action (EA)	An application typically submitted by November 1 or November 15 in exchange for a decision by December 15 that does not bind the student to attend if admitted.
Early decision (ED)	An application typically submitted by November 1 or November 15 in exchange for a decision by December 15 that commits the student to attend if admitted.
ETS	Abbreviation for Educational Testing Service, the organization affiliated with the College Board that prepares, administers, and scores the PSAT, SAT, and AP tests.
Expected family contribution	Financial aid terminology for the amount of money a family is expected to contribute to a student's education based on methodology that considers income, assets, and other expenses.

FAFSA	Abbreviation for Free Application for Federal Student Aid. Used to determine eligibility for federal financial aid.
Federal methodology	The calculation of expected family contribution to the cost of college using the FAFSA.
Financial aid package	Total amount and types of aid a student receives from federal and nonfederal sources.
Gift aid	Financial aid terminology for the grant portion of the financial aid package that does not have to be repaid or earned through work.
GPA	Abbreviation for grade point average. An overall average of a student's grades.
Hook	A special quality that gives a student an edge in the admissions process over others with similar academic qualifications. Hooks may include athletic ability, legacy status, exceptional talent, having a parent with the ability to make significant donations, or being part of an underrepresented minority group.
IB	Abbreviation for International Baccalaureate. A special high school diploma awarded to students who complete a rigorous academic curriculum of special courses and who perform satisfactorily on a battery of nationally normed tests corresponding to that curriculum.
Institutional methodology	Expected family contribution to the total cost of education as calculated through the CSS PROFILE or other form that is institution-specific.
Liberal arts	An academic program that includes the sciences, social sciences, languages, arts, mathematics, and so forth as distinguished from professional programs that are focused on specific careers such as engineering, business, and nursing.
Need analysis	Financial aid terminology for the determination of the expected family contribution to college expenses based on the family's financial situation.
Need-aware (or need-sensitive) admissions	Admissions process that considers a student's ability to pay in the final admissions decision.

Need-blind admissions	Practice of reviewing an applicant's file and reaching a decision on admission without regard to the student's ability to pay.
Pell Grant	Federal grant to students from low-income families.
PLUS Loans	Abbreviation for Parent Loan to Undergraduate Students. A loan taken out by a parent that is not subsidized by the federal government.
Regular decision	Application process that involves applying by a late fall or early winter deadline in exchange for an admissions decision the following spring.
Rolling admission	A process by which colleges review and make decisions about applications as they are received. The application cycle usually opens in the early fall and may extend into the spring or until the freshman class is filled.
PSAT	Abbreviation for Preliminary SAT. A short version of the SAT that is typically taken in the fall by high school juniors as practice for the SAT and as a qualifying test for the National Merit Scholarship Program.
SAT	The most widely taken standardized test for college admission. SAT is the full name—it is not an acronym. Revised effective March 2005, the test contains three parts: writing, critical reading, and math.
Self-help	In financial aid terminology, the loan and work-study portions of a financial aid package.
Single-choice early action	A type of early action plan that places restrictions on the student's ability to apply early action or early decision to other schools.
Stafford Loan	Low interest loans to students.
Student Aid Report (SAR)	Official notification from the processing center that gives the results of the need analysis calculated from the FAFSA.
Student search	Mechanism for colleges to receive the names of potential applicants based on interests, grades, and so forth. Students taking the SAT and ACT are invited to participate when they take those tests. Colleges purchase the names and addresses of students meeting certain criteria and use them for targeted mailings.

Subsidized loan	A loan for which the United States government pays the interest while the student is enrolled in school.
Transcript	Official record of a student's courses and grades. Colleges usually require an official transcript, sent directly from the high school, as part of the application.
Wait-list	A group of students held in reserve through the late spring after a college makes its admissions decisions. If openings occur, students on the wait-list may be offered admission.
Work-study	A component of need-based financial aid in which the student works part-time in a campus or other job that is supported by government or institutional funding.
Yield	The percentage of students offered admission to a college who subsequently enroll.

RESOURCES

The resources below provide additional information on selected topics covered in *Admission Matters*. We've chosen some Web resources and a few books that we think do the job well, although we have not attempted to provide an exhaustive list, since there is a lot of duplication of information.

This list is a dynamic one as new materials appear and others become outdated or unavailable. Check our Web site at www.admissionmatters.com for changes.

General Admissions Information

Web

www.collegeboard.com	College Board site that contains useful information about all aspects of college search and selection. The site has separate sections for students and parents.
www.nacac.com	Site of the National Association for College Admission Counseling geared primarily for high school and college counselors but contains a section for students with helpful information.

www.princetonreview.com	Princeton Review site contains a lot of free information about the college admissions process, including test preparation. The site also sells test preparation courses and materials.
www.collegeconfidential.com	Site of College Confidential, a fee-based online college counseling service. The site has a lot of very useful free information about all aspects of college admission.

Reference Guides to Colleges

Web

See the College Board and Princeton Review sites above. Each contains detailed profiles of individual colleges as well as a search feature that identifies colleges meeting criteria entered by the user.

http://nces.ed.gov/ipeds/cool	College Opportunities Online sponsored by the Department of Education. The site contains a database of thousands of schools that allows search by location, program, and degree offerings.
www.usnews.com	Site provides free, limited access to the *U.S. News and World Report* database used to generate college rankings. Although we do not favor the use of these rankings, the data used to generate them can be helpful. The full database can be accessed for an annual fee.
www.utexas.edu/world/univ/state/	Site provides links to the home pages of four-year colleges and universities throughout the United States. The links are arranged by state, but they can also be sorted alphabetically.

Books

Barron's Profile of American Colleges 2005 by Barron's Educational Series. 26th edition published July 2004 by Barron's Educational Series.	Updated periodically but not annually. Contains profiles of over 1,650 four-year colleges that are rated according to degree of competitiveness. Includes CD-ROM.

2005 College Handbook by
the College Board. 42nd edition
published August 2004 by the
College Board.

Updated annually. Contains profiles of
all 3,600 four-year and two-year colleges
in the United States. Special tables show
policies and outcomes for early decision,
early action, and wait-list applicants at
many colleges.

*Rugg's Recommendations
on the Colleges* by Frederick
Rugg, 21st edition published
June 2004 by Rugg's
Recommendations.

Provides lists of recommended
academic programs in 660 colleges
arranged by type of program.

Narrative Guides to Colleges

Web

www.collegesofdistinction.com

Site that originated with *Colleges That
Change Lives* by Loren Pope but that
now has expanded to include other
institutions as well. This site contains
lots of good information about college
selection.

Books

*Colleges That Change Lives: 40 Schools
You Should Know About Even If
You're Not a Straight-A Student*
by Loren Pope. Published 2000 by
Penguin Books.

Descriptions of forty colleges that may
not be among the most selective but
that provide an outstanding education.

Fiske Guide to Colleges 2005 by
Edward Fiske. 21st edition published
July 2004 by Sourcebooks.

Updated annually. Contains profiles and
personal descriptions of more than 330
popular colleges and universities.

Insider's Guide to the Colleges, 2005
by *Yale Daily News*. 31st edition
published July 2004 by
St. Martin's Griffin.

Updated annually. Contains profiles and
narrative descriptions of over 300
schools. "Written and researched by
students for students."

*Looking Beyond the Ivy League:
Finding the College That's Right
for You* by Loren Pope. Published
1996 by Penguin Books.

Contains sound advice about the
importance of fit and provides valuable
information about some lesser known
colleges that have strong programs.

Best 357 Colleges by Robert Franek et al. 2005 edition published August 2004 by Princeton Review.

Updated annually. Contains profiles and insights from students on over 350 colleges.

"Insider" Accounts

These are best viewed as a window into the admissions process at highly selective institutions rather than as a "how to" guide to gain admission to them.

The Gatekeepers: Inside the Admissions Process of a Premier College by Jacques Steinberg. Published 2002 by Viking.

Describes the author's experience observing an admissions cycle at Wesleyan University. As riveting as a novel, it provides valuable insights into the admissions process at a selective liberal arts college.

Questions and Admissions: Reflections on 100,000 Admissions Decisions at Stanford University by Jean Fetter. Published 1995 by Stanford University Press.

Based on the author's long experience as dean of admission at Stanford. Excellent discussion of the factors taken into consideration at a highly selective institution.

A is for Admission by Michele Hernández, published 1997 by Warner Books.

Based on the author's experience as an assistant director of admissions at Dartmouth College. The book focuses on Dartmouth and the Ivy League.

Special Interest Guides

Web

www.ajcunet.edu

Site sponsored by Jesuit colleges.

www.hillel.org

Site of Hillel, the Foundation for Jewish Campus Life.

www.womenscolleges.org

Official site of the Women's Colleges Coalition.

www.blackexcel.org

"The College Help Network" for African American students.

| www.npda.edu | Site of the National Portfolio Day Association, a group of accredited arts colleges and university art departments that are members of the National Association of Schools of Art and Design. |

Books

K&W Guide to Colleges for Students with Learning Disabilities or Attention Deficit Disorder by Marybeth Kravets and Imy Wax. 8th edition published 2005 by Princeton Review.	Profiles the services for learning disabled students at over 300 colleges.
Black Excel African American Student's College Guide by Isaac Black. Published 2000 by Wiley.	Advice for African American students.
Professional Degree Programs in the Visual and Performing Arts by Peterson's. 10th edition published 2004 by Peterson's.	Guide to programs in music, arts, theater, and dance.

Financial Aid

Web

| www.collegeboard.com | Site (click on Paying for College) for information on the CSS PROFILE. Many private schools require the PROFILE for institutional aid, which is submitted online. This site also has expected financial contribution calculators for both federal aid and institutional aid, as well as a tool to compare financial aid packages. |
| www.fafsa.ed.gov | Federal site for Free Application for Federal Student Aid. If you are applying for need-based aid, visit this site. You can complete the FAFSA online. |

Resources

www.fastweb.com	General site with terrific scholarship search as well as expected family contribution calculator.
www.finaid.org	General site with lots of information about all aspects of financial aid.
http://studentaid.ed.gov	Comprehensive government site with information in both English and Spanish.

Books

College Cost and Financial Aid Handbook 2005 by the College Board. 25th edition published 2004 by the College Board.	Provides information on costs and financial aid at over 3,000 colleges.

Athletics

Web

www.ncaa.org	Web site of the National Collegiate Athletics Association. A must-read for those interested in varsity athletics at colleges and universities that belong to the NCAA.
www.varsityedge.com	Information about the recruiting process, applications, and so forth.

Books

Reclaiming the Game: College Sports and Educational Values by William Bowen and Sarah Levin. Published 2003 by Princeton University Press.	Analysis of the role of athletics in the admissions processes at Ivy League and selective liberal arts colleges.
The Student Athlete's Handbook: The Complete Guide for Success by Perry Bromwell and Howard Gensler. Published 1997 by Wiley.	Guidance on choosing an NCAA division and handling the recruitment process.

Test Preparation

Web

www.collegeboard.com	Information and preparation for the PSAT and SAT. The site can be used for online test registration for the SAT.
www.ACT.org	Information and preparation for the PLAN and ACT. The site can be used for online test registration for the ACT.

Books

The Official SAT Study Guide: For the New SAT by the College Board. Published 2004 by the College Board.	"Official" test preparation guide to the SAT published by the College Board.
The Real ACT Prep Guide by the ACT. Published 2005 by Peterson's.	"Official" test preparation guide to the ACT prepared by the organization that administers the test.

Essay Writing

On Writing the College Application Essay by Henry Bauld. Published 1987 by HarperResource.	A former Ivy League admissions officer provides tough and funny advice on coming up with the best essay possible.
The College Application Essay, Revised Edition by Sarah Miles McGinty. Published 2004 by the College Board.	Contains excellent, easy-to-follow advice on writing effective college application essays.

Miscellaneous

www.campustours.com/	Site with links to virtual campus tours at hundreds of campuses.
www.collegiatechoice.com/	Source to purchase sixty-minute videos of actual student-guided campus tours of more than 300 colleges at $15 each. Tapings are "home movie" quality.

www.nacac.com/fairs.html	Site contains schedules of college fairs nationwide.
www.fairtest.org/univ/optional.htm	List of more than 700 colleges and universities nationwide that admit a substantial number of students without regard to test scores.
www.usafa.af.mil	Site of United States Air Force Academy.
www.usma.edu	Site of United States Military Academy (West Point).
www.usna.edu	Site of United States Naval Academy.
www.usmma.edu	Site of United States Merchant Marine Academy.
www.cga.edu	Site of United States Coast Guard Academy.

Chapter One

1. *San Diego Tribune,* April 15, 2003, p. A1.
2. *www.wsj.com,* May 29, 2002.
3. *www.washingtonpost.com,* June 17, 2003.
4. *Boston Globe,* November 20, 2002, p. A1.
5. *Sacramento Bee,* April 28, 2003, p. A1.
6. *USA Today,* April 30, 2003, p. 8D.
7. *Knocking at the College Door: Projections of High School Graduates by State, Income, and Race/Ethnicity.* Boulder, CO: Western Interstate Commission for Higher Education, 2003.
8. Mayher, B. *The College Admissions Mystique.* New York: Farrar, Straus and Giroux, 1998, p. 28.
9. Fallows, J. "The New College Chaos." *The Atlantic,* 2003, *292*(4), pp. 106–114.
10. Casper, G. Letter to James Fallows, Editor of *U.S. News and World Report,* September 23, 1996 [www.stanford.edu/dept/pres-provost/president/speeches/961206gcfallows.html]. January 8, 2005.
11. ibid.
12. Graduation rate performance measures the difference between a school's six-year graduation rate for a given class and the predicted rate for that class based on characteristics of the students as entering freshmen and the school's expenditures on them.
13. Letter from President William Durden to the Dickinson College community, September 7, 2001 [www.dickinson.edu/news/usnews2001.html]. December 3, 2003.
14. Bollinger, L. "Debate over the SAT Masks Trends in College Admissions." *Chronicle of Higher Education,* July 12, 2002, p. B11.
15. Toor, R. *College Confidential: An Insider's Account of the Elite College Selection Process.* New York: St. Martin's Press, 2001, p. 2.
16. Goldsmith, G., cited in Golden, D. "Glass Floor: Colleges Reject Top Applicants Accepting Only Students Likely to Enroll." [*www.wsj.com*]. May 29, 2002.

17. Mamlet, R., cited in Herbert, D. "Admissions Office Says Demonstrated Interest Not a Factor." *Stanford Daily,* February 4, 2004, p. 1.
18. Confessore, N. "What Makes a College Good?" *The Atlantic Monthly,* 2003, *292*(4), pp. 118–126.
19. Dale, S., and Krueger, A. "Estimating the Payoff to Attending a More Selective College. An Application of Selection on Observables and Unobservables." National Bureau of Economic Research, Working Paper 7322, August 1999.
20. ibid.
21. Stacy Dale, personal communication.
22. Davenport, D. "How Not to Judge a College." Scripps Howard News Service, September 9, 2003.
23. Lewis, S., cited in Kucsynski, A. "Best List for Colleges by U.S. News Is Under Fire." *New York Times,* August 20, 2001, p. C1.

Chapter Two

1. Pierson, G. W. *Historical Statistics of the College and University, 1701–1976* [www.yale.edu/oir/pierson_original.htm].
2. Duffy, E., and Goldberg, I. *Crafting a Class.* Princeton: Princeton University Press, 1998, p. 35.
3. David Erdmann, personal communication.
4. *College Bound Seniors 2003,* The College Board [www.collegeboard.com], January 12, 2005.
5. Gould, D., cited in Shea, R., and Marcus, D., "Make Yourself a Winner." In *America's Best Colleges.* Washington, D.C.: U.S. News and World Report, 2001.
6. McMillen, S. "In Admission, How Do You Separate the Wheat from the Wheat?" *Chronicle of Higher Education,* June 27, 2003, p. B13.
7. McGinty, S. "The College Application and Issues of Access." [www.nacac.com/miatpa.sarahmcginty.pdf]. January 12, 2005.
8. Hargadon, F. "Advice from the Inside." In Georges, G., and Georges, C. *100 Successful College Application Essays.* New York: New American Library, 2002, p. 6.
9. Marthers, P. "Admissions Messages vs. Admissions Realities." In L. Thacker (ed.), *College Unranked: Affirming Educational Values in College Admissions.* Portland, OR: The Education Conservancy, 2004, p. 79.
10. Deacon, C., cited in Craig, E. "GU Defends Use of Legacy Admissions." *The Hoya,* April 16, 2004, p. 1.
11. Parker, T., cited in Klein, M. "Bill Aims to Increase All College Opportunities." *The Amherst Student,* November 12, 2003, p. 1.
12. Edwards, J. Education Policy Address delivered at the University of Maryland, November 21, 2002 [www.johnedwards2004.com]. July 25, 2004.
13. Karl Furstenberg, personal communication.
14. Bowen, W., and Levin, S. *Reclaiming the Game: College Sports and Educational Values.* Princeton: Princeton University Press, 2003.

15. Summers, L., address at the American Council on Education's 86th Annual Meeting, February 29, 2004 [www.president.harvard.edu/speeches/2004/ace.html]. January 12, 2005.

Chapter Three

1. The descriptions of the Wesleyan admissions review process are drawn from Steinberg, J. *The Gatekeepers: Inside the Admissions Process of an Elite College.* New York: Penguin, 2003.
2. Merrow, J., transcript of *Inside College Admissions,* broadcast on KVIE, November 15, 2000 [www.pbs.org/merrow/tmr_radio/transcr/]. January 12, 2005.
3. Shawn Abbott, personal communication.
4. E-mail from Duke President Nannerl Keohane to *Wall Street Journal* reporter Daniel Golden, February 13, 2003[www.dukenews.duke.edu/news/newsrelease4b4x.html ?p=all&id=1449&catid=2].
5. Cattau, D. "Parents Need Not Apply." [www.strongweb.com]. August 14, 2004.
6. Independent counselor cited in Worth, R. "For $28,000 You'll Get. . . ." *New York Times,* September 24, 2000, section 14WC, p. 8.
7. Jones, M. "Parents Get Too Aggressive on Admissions." *USA Today,* January 6, 2003, p. 13A.

Chapter Four

1. Information about the Carnegie Foundation and the classification system can be found at www.carnegiefoundation.org.
2. Michael Tamada, personal communication.
3. Boyer, E. L. *The Undergraduate Experience in America.* New York: Harper and Row, 1987; Boyer, E. L., and Boyer, P. *Smart Parents Guide to College.* Princeton, NJ: Peterson's, 1996.

Chapter Five

1. Fiske, E. *Fiske Guide to Colleges.* Naperville, IL: Sourcebooks, 2005.
2. Yale Daily News Staff. *Insider's Guide to the Colleges.* New York: St. Martin's Griffin, 2005.
3. Mitchell, J. *Winning the Heart of the College Admissions Dean.* Berkeley: Ten Speed Press, 2001.

Chapter Six

1. Bollinger, L. "Debate Over the SAT Masks Perilous Trends in College Admissions." *Chronicle of Higher Education,* July 12, 2002, p. B11.
2. Zwick, R. *Fair Game? The Use of Standardized Tests in Higher Education.* New York: RoutledgeFalmer, 2002, p. viii.

3. Atkinson, R. "Achievement Versus Aptitude in College Admissions." Paper based on keynote address delivered at a conference, "Rethinking the SAT: The Future of Standardized Testing in University Admissions," in Santa Barbara, California, November 16, 2001. Published in *Issues in Science and Technology,* Winter 2001–02, December 2001.
4. Jencks, C., and Reisman, D. "Admissions Requirements in the Public and Private Sectors." In *The Academic Revolution.* Garden City, NY: Doubleday, 1968, p. 281.
5. Shaw, R., quoted in Marklein, M. B. "The Answer to Multiple Tests." *USA Today,* August 17, 2004, p. 8B.
6. Bailey, D. "What's Wrong with College Admissions." *APA Monitor,* October 2003, *34*(9), p. 54.
7. Camera, W., quoted in Simon, C. "The SAT III?" *New York Times,* January 18, 2004, section 4A, p. 15.

Chapter Seven

1. Fallows, J. "The Early Decision Racket." *The Atlantic Monthly,* 2001, *288*(2), p. 372.
2. Avery, C., Fairbanks, A., and Zeckhauser, R. *The Early Admissions Game.* Cambridge: Harvard University Press, 2003.
3. Avery, C., quoted in Young, J. "Early Applicants Have Strong Advantage at Elite Colleges, Book Argues." *Chronicle of Higher Education,* March 7, 2003, p. 38.
4. Levin, R., cited in Arenson, K. "Yale President Wants to End Early Decisions for Admissions." *New York Times,* December 13, 2001, p. D1.
5. Parker, T., cited in Arenson, K., ibid.
6. Anthony Marx, personal communication.
7. Fitzsimmons, W., cited in Fallows, J. "The Early Decision Racket." op. cit., p. 42.
8. Avery, Fairbanks, and Zeckhauser, op. cit., p. 241.
9. Parker, T., cited in Chen, D., "Admissions at Amherst: A Grueling Journey." *The Amherst Student,* October 9, 2003, p. 1.

Chapter Eight

1. Susan Hallenbeck, dean of admission at Hood College, personal communication. She reported that the student was admitted after giving everyone a good chuckle.
2. Phillips, D. "The Question of the Essay." In Georges, G., and Georges, C. *100 Successful College Application Essays.* New York: New American Library, 2002, p. 12.
3. Bauld, H. *On Writing the College Application Essay.* New York: Quill, 1987, p. xvi.
4. McGinty, S. *The College Application Essay, Revised Edition.* New York: College Board, 2004.
5. Hughes, C. *What it Really Takes to Get into the Ivy League and Other Highly Selective Colleges.* New York: McGraw Hill, 2003.

Chapter Nine

1. The members of the Overlap Group were Amherst College, Barnard College, Bowdoin College, Brown University, Bryn Mawr College, Colby College, Columbia University, Cornell University, Dartmouth College, Harvard University, Massachusetts Institute of Technology, Middlebury College, Mount Holyoke College, Princeton University, Smith College, Trinity College (CT), Tufts University, University of Pennsylvania, Vassar College, Wellesley College, Wesleyan University, Williams College, and Yale University.
2. Rawlings, H., cited in "Rawlings-led Group Affirms Commitment to Need-Based Financial Aid." *Cornell Chronicle,* July 12, 2001, p. 1.
3. Report of the Common Standards Subcommittee to the 568 Presidents' Working Group, June 2001 [www.news.cornell.edu/releases/July01/568.presidents.report.html], March 23, 2005.
4. Leider, A., and Leider, R. *Don't Miss Out: The Ambitious Student's Guide to Financial Aid.* Alexandria, VA: Octameron, 2000, p. 42.
5. Carleton College Application for Class of 2008.
6. Trachenberg, S., cited in Bombardieri, M. "Needy Students Miss Out." *Boston Globe,* April 25, 2004, A1.
7. Martin, D., cited in Teicher, S. "Not Enough Financial Aid? Seek Counseling." *Christian Science Monitor,* April 26, 2004, p. 13.
8. Pemberton, S., cited in ibid.
9. Shapiro, M. O., cited in Russell, J. "Top Applicants Bargaining for More Aid from Colleges." *Boston Globe,* June 12, 2002, p. A1.

Chapter Ten

1. Student cited in Coomes, M. "Life After the Letter." *The (Louisville) Courier-Journal,* May 5, 2004, p. D2.
2. Lowenstein, M. "Admissions Had 506 Deposits, Will Fill Class from Waitlist." *Williams Record,* May 11, 2004, p. 1.

ABOUT THE AUTHORS

Sally P. Springer, Associate Chancellor at the University of California, Davis, is a psychologist with over thirty years of experience in higher education as a professor and university administrator. She is the coauthor of *Left Brain, Right Brain* (published by W. H. Freeman, 1998), which was honored by the American Psychological Foundation for contributing to the public's understanding of psychology. It has been translated into seven languages and appeared in five editions. Her second book, *How to Succeed in College* (Crisp Publications, 1992), is a guidebook for college freshmen. Dr. Springer received her bachelor's degree summa cum laude from Brooklyn College and her doctorate in psychology from Stanford University. She has served on the faculty of both SUNY Stony Brook and UC Davis. She volunteers as an admissions reader for the Davis campus and is a member of the National Association for College Admission Counseling.

Marion R. Franck writes about family life and local and national issues in a weekly column in the *Davis Enterprise*. She also pens the "parents page" of UC Davis's alumni magazine and feature articles for the campus's Web-based newsletter for parents. Previously, she worked at UC Davis as an advisor to new college teachers, as a lecturer in rhetoric and English, and as a counselor in the Office of Student Judicial Affairs. Ms. Franck is a magna cum laude graduate of Brown University and has served as an alumna interviewer for over ten years. She holds a master's degree in comparative literature from the University of Wisconsin.

Free Application for Federal Student Aid (FAFSA), 174–175, 176–177; compared with CSS PROFILE, 176, 180; methods of submitting, 175; verification of data, 178

Furstenberg, K., 39

G

General education requirements, 74

Geography: in college choice, 64, 70–71; role in admissions, 42–43

Georgetown University, 6, 37, 75

George Washington University, 6

Gettysburg College, 6

Gould, D., 31

Grade Point Average (GPA): inflation of, 26–27; role in admission, 23, 26, 27–28; weighting of, 26

Graduate school and college choice, 9–20

Grants: in financial aid packages, 181; sources of, 181

Gratz v. Bollinger, 40

Guidance counselors. *See* Counselors

Guidebooks, college, 83

H

Hamilton College, 6

Hampshire College, 128

Hargadon, F., 32, 35, 225

Harvard University, 6, 8, 41, 43, 148; admission rate for, 2; financial aid policy, 42, 183; and single choice action, 134–135; size of, 67

Harvey Mudd College, 6

Haverford College, 6, 65, 148

High school counselors. *See* Counselors

Historically Black colleges, 75

Honors classes, as admissions criterion, 25

Honors programs, in college, 67, 72

Hooks, as factors in admission, 36–43.

See also Legacies; Athletes; Underrepresented minorities; Diversity, as factor in admissions; Talent

HOPE scholarships, 186

Housing, 76

I

Illinois Wesleyan University, 6

Insider's Guide to Colleges (Yale Daily News Staff), 83

Institutional methodology, in financial aid, 176

Institutional mission, 11, 64

Intellectual atmosphere, of colleges, 77

International Baccalaureate (IB) courses and tests, 25

Internet: 4; in applications, 4; in college search, 84, 88–89

Interviews, 35–36, 160–163; by alumni, 160, 170; evaluative, 160; frequently asked questions, 161; at high schools, 86; informational, 160; role in admission, 35–36, 160; thank-you notes for, 162, 163; tips for, 160–163

Iowa State University, 185

Ivy League: and athletics, 41–42, 166, 168; and financial aid, 184; notification date, 195; origin and members of, 8

J

Jacksonville State University, 68

Johns Hopkins University, 6, 12, 37, 129

Jones, M., 58–59, 212

Julliard School, 69

K

Kaplan, S. H., 107

Kenyon College, 6

Keohane, N., 52

Krueger, A., 19, 20

Need aware colleges, 184
Need-based financial aid: 174–183; consensus approach to, 178; federal methodology, 175; institutional methodology, 176; packaging of, 180–183. *See also* Financial aid; Financing college
Need-blind admissions, 183–184
Nesbitt, D., 209
New England Conservatory of Music, 69
New SAT. *See* SAT
New York University, 6, 167
Newspapers, college, 89
Northeastern University, 6, 43
Northwestern University, 6, 199

O

Oberlin College, 6, 184
Occidental College, 6
Overlap Group, 178

P

Parent Loans to Undergraduate Students (PLUS), 182
Parental involvement, 215–220; in application process, 58–59; and college choice, 220; during college visits, 93; and receiving decisions, 197
Parker, T., 37, 133, 141
Pell Grants, 181
Pemberton, S., 192
Pennsylvania State University, 195
Pepperdine University, 6
Perkins Loans, 182
Personal qualities, role in admissions, 33–36, 48–49
Phillips, D., 150
PLAN exam, 118. *See also* ACT Assessment (ACT)

PLUS (Parent Loans to Undergraduate Students), 182
Pomona College, 6, 148, 166
Portfolio, to demonstrate special talent, 165–166
Preliminary SAT/National Merit Scholarship Qualifying Test (PSAT/NMSQT), 109–111. *See also* SAT
Prestige, of colleges, 63
Princeton University, 6, 8, 16, 148; admission rate for, 2; financial aid policy of, 183
Procrastination, 146–147, 222
Proofreading, 147–148, 155
PSAT. *See* Preliminary SAT
Purdue University, 195

Q

Quality, attempts to measure, 8, 12–13. *See also* Educational quality

R

Race, role in admissions, 40, 42; lawsuits regarding, 40
Rainbow Project, 123
Rankings, of colleges: alternatives to, 12; attempts to move up in, 14–15; criticisms of, 10, 12–13; *U.S. News and World Report* methodology for, 10–12, 15; popularity of, 14, 18; spoof of, 17
Rawlings, H., 179
Reclaiming the Game (Bowen and Levin), 41
Recommendations, 33–34, 156–159; from counselors, 28, 33–34, 159; number of, 158–159; from peers, 158; requesting, 156–157; role in admissions, 156; from teachers, 34, 157–158; waiver statement, 158

Index